Rethinking the New World Order

Georg Sørensen

First published 2016 by
PALGRAVE

Palgrave in the UK is an imprint of Macmillan Publishers Limited, registered in England, company number 785998, of 4 Crinan Street, London, N1 9XW.

Palgrave Macmillan in the US is a division of St Martin's Press LLC, 175 Fifth Avenue, New York, NY 10010.

Palgrave is a global imprint of the above companies and is represented throughout the world.

Palgrave® and Macmillan® are registered trademarks in the United States, the United Kingdom, Europe and other countries.

ISBN 978–1–137–48325–6 hardback
ISBN 978–1–137–48324–9 paperback

This book is printed on paper suitable for recycling and made from fully managed and sustained forest sources. Logging, pulping and manufacturing processes are expected to conform to the environmental regulations of the country of origin.

A catalogue record for this book is available from the British Library.

A catalog record for this book is available from the Library of Congress.

Printed in China

For Sebastian

Contents

Foreword by Michael Cox

One of the most prolific scholars and steadiest voices in IR over the past – very turbulent - twenty five years has been the Danish academic, Georg Sørensen. Always measured and never quick to rush to judgment in a profession where putting pen to paper on headline-grabbing subjects has become something of a habit of late, Sørensen is in many ways a model academic who many in the field today would be well advised to emulate. Never flashy, invariably wise, and more often than not closer to getting it right than many of the shriller voices in the field, Sørensen remains a writer to whom we can return time and again to get a clear fix on the world out there.

In this wide-ranging book Sørensen manages to say a great deal about a great many things in a relatively limited number of words. He begins where nearly all students quite reasonably are asked to begin in IR: by evaluating the claims made by liberal optimists and sceptical realists about the international system as it unfolded after the end of the Cold War – by far and away the most significant global event of the past quarter century. Others might dispute his claim that 'liberal and realist positions define the overarching theme in the discussion' of the emerging 'world order', and they are certainly free to do so. However, for those of us teaching IR it is still the case that these two approaches still appear to make most sense to more students than any others on the bloc - try though some of us have to suggest otherwise!

Sørensen though is not uncritical of either realism or liberalism. Nor is he unaware of the dark underside of liberalism in the economic shape of the modern capitalist economy. Nor to be blunt is he so wedded to 'old ways' of thinking about the world that he chooses to ignore other modes of thinking about international security. Indeed, he makes it abundantly clear that we need new ways of reflecting on the world which take into consideration the 'human' and the need to protect the individual from hazards that directly impact on their lives including, amongst other things, poverty, social injustice, environmental degradation and political regimes that do not recognize the rights of the human. But Sørensen also reminds us that states still remain the crucial players in international politics; and perhaps the easiest way of seeing how important it is to look at what happens when states fail or become 'fragile'. Yet as he goes on to point out, even if states are the building blocks of international society—even today—the chances of war between them is now fairly remote. So we thus live in a world, he implies, which has never been more 'war free' but in which all manner of dangers arising from state failure from Syria to Libya have never been so acute. And the situation could be getting worse as atrocities in London, Paris and Brussels—not to mention Ankara, Baghdad and Lahore—have shown only too clearly. Moreover, all this appears to be happening in a world where, according to Sørensen, 'the advanced liberal states are less willing and able to take the lead' and where our traditional institutions appear to be failing badly.

The kind of intelligent liberalism championed by Sørensen is therefore on the back foot: its theoretical strengths self-evident, but its shortcomings more obvious still in an increasingly unequal world where social changes in the advanced countries alone are undermining the established contract between the political class and those over whom they purport to rule. Donald Trump to this extent may be less the buffoon some think he is and more a harbinger of things to come. Progress is thus by no means inevitable as the once great liberal optimist Francis Fukuyama has recently suggested: and Sørensen, reluctantly, would seem to agree. Difficult and possibly dangerous times lie ahead therefore. The challenges facing the liberal project have never been more serious. It is one of the many virtues of Sørensens's volume that he does not shy away from confronting them.

PROFESSOR MICHAEL COX
Director. LSE IDEAS

Acknowledgements

I was hesitant about this project at first; I knew it would be complicated and frustrating. Fortunately, it has also been most enjoyable. The book would probably have come to nothing if not for the relentless insistence of my publisher, Steven Kennedy; he kept pulling me back to it every time I thought I had successfully run away. I am really grateful for his persistent support, which was followed through by his successor, Stephen Wenham. Mick Cox generously accepted the book for his *Rethinking World Politics* series where I believe it fits very well.

Aarhus Institute of Advanced Studies (AIAS) provided a perfect one-year retreat where I could focus on the project. Thanks to director Morten Kyndrup for taking me in and to AIAS fellows and staff for providing a stimulating and very pleasant working environment. Colleagues at the Department of Political Science in Aarhus were supportive as always. Impeccable secretarial assistance from Annette Bruun Andersen has, once again, been a vital part of the project. Hosey Nezam effectively helped out with all the technical details. I am indebted to the commentators who carefully read the manuscript and offered suggestions for improvement; they helped me sharpen the argument and make it a better book. Thanks to Mick Cox, Elias Götz, Steven Kennedy, Jørgen Dige Pedersen, Stephen Wenham and the anonymous reader appointed by Palgrave Macmillan. Chloe Osborne and Alex Antidius Arpoudam effectively steered the book through production. Kristine Kristiansen was a great help in compiling the index.

The book is dedicated to my son, Sebastian. He specializes in subjects I know little about: music and mathematics. But the enthusiasm and energy with which he devotes himself to these topics is a great inspiration to people around him, including myself.

AARHUS, February 2016

List of Abbreviations

AIIB	Asian Infrastructure Investment Bank
AMISOM	African Union Mission in Somalia
ASEAN	Association of Southeast Asian Nations
AU	African Union
BIC	Brazil, India, China
BRICS	Brazil, Russia, India, China and South Africa
CAR	Central African Republic
CCP	Chinese Communist Party
CFR	Council on Foreign Relations
COP	Conference of the Parties
DFS	Department of Field Support
DPA	Department of Political Affairs
DPKO	Department of Peacekeeping Operations
EU	European Union
FDI	foreign direct investment
FPÖ	Freiheitliche Partei Österreichs
FSB	Financial Stability Board
GATS	General Agreement on Trade in Services
GAVI	Global Alliance for Vaccines and Immunization
GCI	global connectedness index
GDP	gross domestic product
GEF	Global Environment Facility
IEA	International Energy Agency
IGO	intergovernmental organization
IIPE	illicit international political economy
IMF	International Monetary Fund
INGO	international non-governmental organization
IPE	international political economy
IR	international relations
ISIL	Islamic State of Iraq and the Levant
LDC	Least Developed Country
MAD	mutually assured destruction
MEF	Major Economies Forum

NAFTA	North American Free Trade Agreement
NATO	North Atlantic Treaty Organization
NCSES	National Center for Science and Engineering Statistics
NGO	non-governmental organization
NPT	treaty on the non-proliferation of nuclear weapons
NZEC	near-zero emissions coal
OAS	Organization of American States
OCHA	Office for the Coordination of Humanitarian Affairs
OECD	Organisation for Economic Co-operation and Development
OSCE	Organization for Security and Co-operation in Europe
PPP	purchasing power parity
R&D	research and development
R2P	responsibility to protect
TOC	transnational organized crime
TRIMS	trade-related investment measures
UIA	Union of International Associations
UN	United Nations
UNCED	United Nations Conference on Environment and Development
UNDP	United Nations Development Programme
UNEP	United Nations Environment Programme
UNESCO	United Nations Educational, Scientific and Cultural Organization
UNFCC	UN Framework Convention on Climate Change
UNSC	United Nations Security Council
US	United States
WEO	World Environmental Organization
WHO	World Health Organization
WMD	weapons of mass destruction
WTO	World Trade Organization

Introduction:
The Argument

The end of the Cold War was also the end of global or world order as we knew it: a bipolar standoff between two superpowers and their respective allies. The dissolution of the Soviet Union effectively terminated that order and gave way to—what exactly? It was certainly not clear at the time; surprisingly, it is not clear today, more than a quarter of a century later. The first reaction, understandably, was one of liberal optimism; if anything, the events marked the unabashed victory of political and economic liberalism. Liberal democracy and the liberal market economy would now encompass the whole world and peace, cooperation, security, order, common values, welfare and even the good life for all would eventually follow (Fukuyama 1989, 1992).

The next reaction was much more pessimistic and sceptical; it came early in the 1990s even though that decade was a liberal honeymoon period of high hopes. Realist scholars predicted that old friends would get at each other's throats now that the common enemy was gone (Mearsheimer 1991). At the same time, liberal hubris would produce an arrogant form of liberal universalism which amounted to imperialism. Such behaviour would help produce a clash of civilizations and, increasingly, future conflicts would appear at the fault lines of civilizations (Huntington 1993, 1996). The central division would be between the Western states, on one hand, and the Islamic and Confucian states-cum-civilizations, on the other.

Liberal optimism was not to be frustrated; an analysis from the late 1990s argued that ever more sophisticated economies would need to enter into ever closer networks of cooperation. Nation states would remain major units in international politics but would be compelled to cooperate in order to provide a protective umbrella for a globalized economy (Rosecrance 1999).

1

Then September 11, 2001, transformed the international agenda. The leading country, the United States, embarked on a global war on terror which led to the interventions in Afghanistan and Iraq. International terrorism became a major security issue. Later in that decade, it emerged that the globalized market economy was not the rock-solid foundation for a cooperating world which some liberals had made it out to be. The financial crisis that broke in 2008 disturbed the entire economic system, even though it was the established capitalist economies in North America and Western Europe that were hit the worst. The world economy did not break down completely, but maybe the crisis is not over. It was sufficiently serious so as to provoke a debate about the appropriate capitalist model for the system, especially about the proper relationship between free market forces and political regulation.

At the end of the first decade of the twenty-first century, *Time Magazine* pronounced the 2000s a 'decade from hell'; the 'most dispiriting' years Americans had lived through since World War II (Serwer 2009). Sceptics repeated their message: the end of history had been replaced by the return of history. Aggressive rivalry among great powers had not gone away but had instead intensified, especially between liberal and autocratic states, in the context of the re-emergence of a struggle among radical Islamists and modern secular cultures and powers (Kagan 2007).

Liberal optimists continued to disagree. One liberal observer introduced a theory of convergence which argued that significant forces were driving humanity closer together, towards creating one world of global citizens. Economic globalization, technological change, common material aspirations and the environmental hazards that threaten us all are the major factors in this process of global convergence (Mahbubani 2013).

Several other observers, with a variety of theoretical orientations, have made contributions to the debate about world order. I introduce them in due course. In spite of the divergence of views, I shall argue that the division between liberal optimists and sceptical realists is the major fault line in the world order debate. Liberal optimists look to processes of cooperation, convergence and shared values in an increasingly liberal world; sceptical realists emphasize conflict, divergence and the lack of shared values in a context of rivalry and competition. Additional contributions can be considered in relation to this primary disagreement.

The debate between liberal optimists and sceptical realists will surely continue. Real-world developments keep throwing up new events that point in one or the other direction. But it is a relevant time for stocktaking: a dozen years of liberal hopefulness after the end of the Cold War have been followed by a dozen years of new security threats, an abundance of violent conflict and a severe economic crisis. So where exactly are we today as regards world order? That is the question pursued in this book. I shall argue that both liberal optimists and sceptical realists make valid points but both also have significant shortcomings.

World order is a contested concept; I introduce it in detail in due course, a brief definition will suffice here. On one hand, world order is a governing arrangement among states, with the participation of other actors. That is the international dimension. On the other hand, world order also has a domestic dimension, which is about major aspects of socio-political conditions within states. Many sceptics share a view of world order as a 'thin' order where competition and rivalry among or within states always threaten violent conflict. Many optimists share a view of world order as a 'thick' order where the 'good life' is increasingly available to all people.

I begin with a presentation of the major contributions to the debate about world order (Chapter 1); that sets the context for my own analysis. The following chapters (2, 3 and 4) set forth the framework conditions that make up the context for the current world order. Chapter 2 is about domestic conditions within major types of state in the present system. I make the claim that we live in a world where all states are increasingly fragile. The term 'fragile states' has been used to signify the weak, post-colonial states in the Global South with frail economies, corrupt and ineffective political systems and a lack of national community. But both modernizing states, such as Brazil, India and China, and the so-called advanced states in Western Europe, North America and East Asia are increasingly characterized by fragility as well. Their political systems are less effective and sometimes corrupt; state capacity is also threatened because these states are less socially embedded and intense participation in economic globalization undercuts their room for manoeuver. National community is weakening also, under pressure from socio-economic inequality and patterns of migration. All this has consequences for world order because it affects the international roles that states and societies can play.

The fragility of states is bad for citizens, of course. It reduces the possibilities of living the 'good life' where security, order, justice, welfare and freedom are values that most people can enjoy. The situation is most serious in the very fragile states in the Global South because they must permanently live with insecurity and violent conflict. But there are also problems in many other states. They concern, among other things, the environment, health, economic inequality and personal security. That is a destabilizing element in the present world order.

Chapter 3 turns to international conditions with a focus on relations between states. I demonstrate that the traditional security dilemma of imminent war among sovereign states is much less pertinent in today's order. Liberals have a point: there is a 'democratic peace' among consolidated democracies; furthermore, even non-democratic states want to participate in economic globalization and in international institutions. Together with other developments, this means that traditional interstate war is in sharp decline. That important point is often overlooked because there is still a large amount of violent conflict in the world.

The decline of interstate war and the fragility of states are two major framework conditions in relation to world order. A third framework condition is discussed in Chapter 4; it concerns the power structure of the present system. It is argued that in terms of material power, the United States remains the most powerful country in the present order. But there is also a social side to power which concerns the ability to create and sustain a legitimate order; in this area the United States faces significant problems. Its dominant material power is not sufficient on its own to establish a stable and effective order and no other great power, or coalition of powers, is capable or ready to take on that task.

So the framework conditions point in different directions. On one hand, increasingly fragile states are less able and willing to create and sustain an effective and legitimate order. On the other hand, the decreasing importance of interstate war should improve the prospects for a robust world order. In material power terms, the United States and Western countries remain strong; the question is whether they are capable and willing to take the lead in establishing an effective and legitimate world order.

Given these three framework conditions, Chapters 5 through 8 examine patterns of world order in major areas of concern. Four sectors are analysed in detail: security, economics, institutions and values. Chapter 5 discusses the three dominant items on the security agenda: fragile states, great power rivalry and competition in different regions, and human security. The chapter concludes that we are headed towards increasing crisis and instability.

Chapter 6 is about economics and the shifting dynamics of globalization. The liberal expectation of convergence and cooperation in the economic field has to some extent been proven correct, but economic globalization is also highly uneven and there are strong limits to convergence. That creates backlashes against globalization and intensified cooperation.

Chapter 7 investigates international institutions and the current status of global governance. Is it 'good-enough governance' or is it a case of gridlock? The chapter argues that it is piecemeal governance in the sense that a great amount of governance is supplied but it does not provide solutions that go beyond short-term crisis management.

Finally, Chapter 8 is about the standing of liberal values in the present order. The chapter posits a tension between two basic liberal values: the value of *in*dependence versus the value of *inter*dependence. A move towards intensified interdependence has characterized the period since the end of the Cold War, but presently, the pendulum swings the other way: towards more emphasis on independence. That does not improve the conditions for establishing an effective world order.

In overall conclusion, liberals have a point in diagnosing substantial liberal progress after the end of the Cold War. But they seriously underestimate the tensions and contradictions built into the process. On one hand, the transformations inside and among countries throw up a host of problems that liberals tend to assume away; on the other hand, serious tensions between liberal values, such as the tension between independence and interdependence, are built into the current world order. As a result, destructive dynamics may prevail over constructive dynamics, not because realists are right about the omnipresence of conflict and rivalry in any world order, but because current domestic and international conditions impede the kind of progress that liberals tend to take for granted.

At the very moment when world order is more liberal than it ever was, both the economic and the political dimension of liberal order are in crisis. The liberal market economy is increasingly unequal and its financial infrastructure remains fragile and crisis-prone. There is a comprehensive set of international institutions but they are rather weak and in need of reform. Liberal values are nominally endorsed by most states but they are in internal conflict and make up no firm basis for a stable world order. We live in a liberal world order, but it is not nearly as peaceful, cooperative and converging as liberals have predicted it would be.

1

Debating the Post-Cold War World Order

Introduction

The debate about world order has been dominated by events: the fall of the Berlin Wall; the dissolution of the Soviet Union; the break-up of Yugoslavia; the terrorist attacks of September 11, 2001; the wars in Afghanistan and Iraq; the financial and economic crisis; the severe violence inside and around fragile states, including Syria, Libya and the Congo. But events do not speak for themselves; in order to evaluate their real significance, and their relative importance in relation to a myriad of other events, we need theory. Theories, however, disagree both about which events are important and about how certain events must be understood. And theories alone cannot tell us which theory to prefer among competing theories. Since there is no objective way of choosing the best theory, our choice will be influenced by our personal values and political priorities. That is why the debate about a subject such as world order is never-ending: analysing the world from the perspectives of different theoretical traditions can be broken down into three interrelated components: what goes on out there in the real world, the theoretical insights we employ in our study, and the values and priorities upon which these tools are based.

This chapter briefly goes through previous major analyses of the post-Cold War world order. The early years were dominated by the liberal optimists (and there is still solid support for their view); they were certain that the end of history was in sight because the last serious rival to a world of liberal democracies had been defeated. Realists, by contrast, envisioned a world of new and more intense rivalry between states leading towards a situation where we would soon miss the relative stability of the Cold War. Additional theories provide important elements to the central debate between liberals and realists. English School theory recognizes the importance of power but equally emphasizes the existence of common rules. That leads to a more nuanced, but also somewhat complex, analysis of world order. Marxist international political economy (IPE) underlines the continued importance of the capitalist world economy for world order. In sketching the views of these major theories, I focus on the big picture; discussions among more or less pessimistic realists, for example, or debates among Marxist IPE theorists on a range of topics, are not included. At the same time, I clarify the ways in which these theories help inform the present analysis.

I also address three further debates about world order; they are not theories in the wider sense but they cover developments that are of special importance for world order. First, there is the 'empires versus regions' debate; we are neither in a world of US empire, nor are we in a world of pure regions, but these analyses are relevant to an account of world order. Second, non-state actors, both malign ones such as international terrorists and benign ones such as transnational civil society networks, are of increasing importance but they are not trumping states as the most important units of world order. Finally, environmental concerns are by now a permanent feature of the current world order but the issue, in terms of world order, is rather a matter of bargaining between diverging interests than it is one of supreme concern for the future of the planet, as such.

The chapter ends with a brief presentation of the framework for analysis and a discussion of the core concept of world order.

The liberal view

The first influential view of post-Cold War order was liberal; that was not coincidental. More than four decades of bipolar confrontation between a liberal–democratic superpower and its communist–autocratic rival had ended with the outright victory of political and economic liberalism. This played directly into the optimistic liberal view of progress. Liberal philosophers, beginning with John Locke in the seventeenth century, had great faith in the potential for human progress in the modern civil society and the capitalist economy which could flourish in a state that guaranteed individual liberty. It was exactly this liberal economic and political system which had prevailed in the Cold War and the gate was now open for the expansion of the liberal system to the rest of the globe. That is what the end of history is about: the 'universalization of Western liberal democracy as the final form of government' (Fukuyama 1989: 3, 4; 1992). The new world order would soon be liberal and democratic, and because democracies collaborate and do not use violence against each other, it would also be peaceful and cooperative. Note that liberals take domestic developments seriously; for them, democratization within states is the fundamental basis for a new world order.

Fukuyama's argument is about the great prospects for liberal democracy in the world but it also connects to other major elements in liberal international theory. Interdependence liberalism foresees a high level of economic and other interdependence among countries that are modernizing and democratizing. Focus will then be on cooperation instead of military security. Sociological liberalism emphasizes the importance of transnational, non-state actors. The networks they create across borders reduce the relative importance of governments and add to the patterns of cooperation. Finally, institutional liberalism underlines how international institutions facilitate cooperation among states by creating arenas for negotiation and exchange of information (see Jackson and Sørensen 2016 for an overview of liberal international theory). Some of today's liberal international theory is more cautious about the prospects for solid liberal progress (e.g. Milner and Moravcsik (eds) 2009); others remain optimistic (e.g. Deudney and Ikenberry 2009; Mahbubani 2013). Yet all liberals share a vision of the possibility of progress.

The question is, of course, to what extent is liberal optimism warranted? It looked good in the beginning. The demise of the Soviet Union marked the victory of the liberal idea. What remained was the practical problem of setting up of liberal political and economic systems across the world. That went rather well at first. Most countries accepted the free market principles of a capitalist economy. The number of democracies in the world doubled, from 43 in the early 1970s to 88 by the late 1990s (Sørensen 2008). Most countries wanted to participate in transnational cooperation through international institutions. The Millennium Declaration, adopted by UN member states in 2000, confirmed universal allegiance to liberal principles.

In the new century, things have gone the other way. In many places, the transition to democracy turned out to be a frail political opening rather than a real change of the political system; many countries remained semi-democratic or semi-authoritarian. The financial crisis was the most serious economic slump since the 1930s. The commitment to liberal values was frequently only skin-deep, a set of rhetorical gestures with no real substance behind them. At the same time, September 11 conjured a different set of security threats.

For these reasons, we cannot have faith in a liberal idea about unimpeded progress. Society does not always move forward. History does not contain an inbuilt law of progress. Standstill, or regression, is possible too. More sceptical liberals were clear on this point early on. 'History', said Isaiah Berlin (1988) in a phrase he borrowed from Alexander Herzen, 'has no libretto'. But how pessimistic should we then be, given the fact that some substantial liberal progress has actually taken place? Are the present setbacks really that important in the larger scheme of things or can they be considered a mere bump in the road, a temporary obstruction in a larger process of uninhibited liberal progress?

As indicated, liberal optimism remains strong in some quarters. A recent contribution by Kishore Mahbubani argues that we are seeing the 'steady disappearance of absolute poverty' (2013: 18), in particular due to rapid growth in China and India. His general outlook is also very optimistic. The people of the world now share a common set of material and educational aspirations. These forces have created common values. Even while 'we retain our different cultural and religious identities, we will converge on some important and fundamental values' (2013: 84); these common values are clearly liberal in character: they include a global market economy that can foster economic growth and development, and basic liberal political values, including the rule of law.

In sum, there has been liberal economic and political progress after the end of the Cold War and this fact must enter our analysis of the present world order; but it does not mean we must fully endorse an optimistic liberal vision about a harmonious and peaceful liberal world order. History is not predetermined to move forward and upward and liberal principles are dynamic entities that may or may not be able to confront the major challenges of a globalized world. That calls for a more careful assessment of the current standing of liberal values in the current world order. Liberal progress is possible, but the optimistic liberal view of certain and secure progress after the end of the Cold War is not a valid guide to the assessment of the present world order. Both in the domestic heartland of liberal democracies and market economies and in the global realm of liberal world order there are difficulties which liberal theory and practice have not sufficiently confronted.

The realist view

For most realists, individuals are self-seeking and competitive in ways which may easily lead to conflict. And the international system of sovereign states is anarchic; it lacks an overarching authority, there is no world government. In a system of that kind, states have to provide for their own security and they are always in potential danger because other states may have malign intentions.

During the Cold War, the international system was relatively stable for most periods because there was a stable balance of power, according to realist analysis. Bipolarity is a clear and transparent structure because it comprises two superpowers, each with a large number of allied countries. In addition, both superpowers could rely on a large arsenal of nuclear weapons. An all-out nuclear war would be enormously destructive on both sides. In a situation of *MAD* (mutually assured destruction), nobody is really interested in a full-scale nuclear confrontation.

One influential realist, John Mearsheimer, argued in 1991 that the post-Cold War situation was potentially more unbalanced and therefore conceivably much more dangerous and conflict-prone than the earlier period. With the common enemy gone, rivalry and competition would re-emerge both inside Europe and across the Atlantic. That situation increases the risk of war in a 'Back to the Future' scenario (Mearsheimer 1991).

However, none of this happened. Instead of intensified rivalry, the Western European countries intensified cooperation, especially in the context of the European Union (EU). This led realist scholarship in new directions. On one hand, there is a new discussion about the content of the balance of power concept, including the idea that there can be different forms of 'hard' and 'soft' balancing (Pape 2005:

Paul 2005; Brooks and Wohlforth 2008). On the other hand, analysis of the balance of power was put in a larger context that included the personality of leaders, domestic politics, ideas and contingency (Wohlforth 2011: 456; Lobell, Ripsman and Taliaferro (eds) 2009).

Many realists will now grant that power competition or even violent conflict between Western allies is not a likely development. But they maintain that there remain dangers of violent confrontation in other parts of the international system. One prominent early analysis to that effect was put forward by Samuel Huntington (1993; 1996). He emphasized that sovereign states remain the most important actors in world politics, but future conflicts between them will follow the fault lines between civilizations. That is linked to the fact that most of the great powers in the post-Cold War world come from different civilizations. In that sense, the 'clash of civilizations' will dominate global politics. The clash would especially involve the Western states versus the Islamic and Confucian states (for a critique, see Katzenstein 2009).

Empirical analyses of violent conflicts between states in the second half of the twentieth century have not been able to confirm Huntington's thesis about the importance of disputes across civilizational boundaries (Russett et al. 2000). To the extent that conflicts involve different identities, they are frequently intra-civilizational, as between Sunni and Shia Muslims, or between Catholic and Protestant Christians. One set of post-Cold War conflicts, between Orthodox and Muslim peoples in the Balkans, would appear to confirm Huntington's idea. But even in this case it can be argued that the self-seeking interest of dominant political leaders was the central factor involved (Kaldor 1999).

Instead of a 'clash of civilizations', realists now focus on the rivalry and competition between the West and the emerging, non-liberal great powers, in particular Russia and China. The argument is that this represents a 'return of geopolitics' after a period where many observers thought that peace and cooperation would prevail (Russell Mead 2014; see also Kissinger 2014).

In sum, even if there is not a 'back to the future' reality where European great powers are in aggressive competition, there is a great deal of rivalry and competition out there. The processes of conflict and divergence emphasized by realists can be found in relation to several aspects of world order, as will be made clear in the chapters that follow.

The English School and world order

The English School is often seen as a via media between liberal and realist views of international relations (IR). English School theorists accept the realist starting point of anarchy, potentially aggressive power balancing and imminent risk of war among sovereign states. But they also acknowledge the existence of an international society among states who recognize each other and agree to be bound by a common set of rules; so there is emphasis on cooperation as well as on conflict (for an introduction, see Jackson and Sørensen 2016).

Several English School theorists have analysed world order; I rely here on two comprehensive contributions by Andrew Hurrell (2007) and by Barry Buzan (2004). Hurrell discusses three frameworks for approaching order: first, a 'thin' order focused on sovereign states with the question of war or peace among states as the central problem of order; second, a 'thick' order with international rules, including rights and duties for individuals and groups. The third framework further develops the 'thick' order by focusing on governance beyond the state including civil society groups and the role of market actors.

From this departure, the analysis examines five areas of global political order: war and insecurity; human rights and democratization; nationalism and the politics of identity; economic globalization; and the ecological challenge. For each of these areas the study provides an historical account and identifies current major dilemmas and limits to change. Hurrell also discusses the role of regions and the role of empire in relation to global order.

While Hurrell's conclusion is focused on morally desirable change, Buzan's analysis is preoccupied with creating a conceptual framework on the basis of which we can more accurately assess the development of international society over time. For that purpose he identifies three types of international social systems: interstate (between states); transnational (between transnational actors) and interhuman (between individuals). A full analysis needs to cover all three domains and the interactions among them. Particular attention is given to the interstate society. Buzan finds that we live in a 'modestly cooperative and ideologically liberal global international society' (2004: 233).

The downside of these rich and nuanced accounts is that the distinction between more important and less important elements of the current world order becomes blurred. We are instead provided with a grand survey of trends, patterns, structures and key debates related to global order. This is in no small measure due to the English School framework of analysis. The school does not offer a conventional theory of IR; it is rather an approach for combining different theoretical concerns—including the realist concern for power balancing, the liberal concern for institutions and cooperation, and the constructivist concern for common rules and norms—that all have a place in a comprehensive analysis of world order.

English School authors offer a nuanced and complex analysis of world order; the analysis in this book agrees with the English School's ambition of constructing a via media between the realist emphasis on conflict and the liberal emphasis on cooperation. But the grand surveys undertaken by Hurrell and Buzan make any clear identification of the most important changes a difficult undertaking. Hurrell combines three frameworks in analysing five areas and two alternatives; Buzan highlights eight master institutions and more than double that number of derivative institutions. Tying so many trends together is a formidable task; the present study will argue in favour of including several dimensions in the analysis of world order, but it will not go that far. Surprisingly, domestic developments are neglected in these otherwise far-ranging analyses. I shall argue that this is an important oversight.

Marxist IPE and world order

IPE focuses on the relationship between states and markets, between politics and economics. It comes in different theoretical versions (Cohen 2014); prominent among them are liberal, realist and Marxist IPE. Having presented liberal and realist takes on world order already, it is relevant to focus on the Marxist version here. There is by now a large number of these analyses that address the capitalist world economy and the recent financial crisis (for an overview see Frandsen 2011). They present many different varieties of Marxism; what unites them is a rejection of the notion of human frailty or a particular institutional failure as the root of the problem. The core predicament is seen as being connected to the nature of the capitalist system itself.

One view, adopted by Immanuel Wallerstein (2010) and David Harvey (2010), is that capitalism contains an inbuilt, systemic logic which means that crisis is a persistent feature of the system that will not go away; crises recur in a variety of ways and they accumulate in the sense that the next crisis always tends to be more serious than the previous one. David Harvey argues that 'the capital surplus absorption problem' (2010: 26) is the key problem for the system. For constant accumulation to go forward, capital needs outlets for an ever expanding surplus. In 1970, there was a need to find new investment outlets for $0.4 trillion each year; today it is $1.6 trillion and by 2030 it will be $3 trillion per year. Finding profitable outlets for this magnitude of surplus is 'a very tall order' (2010: 27) and we may be approaching a point where it is simply no longer possible; hence the depth of the current crisis.

For Wallerstein, sufficient profits for capital cannot be obtained in a situation of perfect competition; at least a 'quasi-monopoly of world-economic power is needed' (2010: 133). But monopolies are self-liquidating over time because new producers enter the world market. With the decline of profits for the leading products, the world economy ceases to expand and enters a period of stagnation. Two further elements add to the crisis: on one hand, rising costs of production (personnel, input and taxation) and, on the other hand, the extra pressure on the system generated by Chinese and Asian growth due to its 'overextending the distribution of surplus-values' (2010: 137). Overall, we have entered a period of structural crisis where the capitalist system is no longer able to mend itself; the major question is rather 'what will replace this system?' (2010: 139).

Even if both authors emphasize that the outcomes of capitalism's structural crisis are not given beforehand because political struggles play a fundamentally important role, there is a tendency towards determinism in their analysis. The systemic tensions built into capitalism make up the decisive driving force of the system towards structural crisis and transformation. In the present study it is recognized that the economic basis of world order and the tensions connected with it make up important elements for the analysis, but they must be seen in their interplay with other important material elements, such as politico-military power, and non-material elements, such as ideas and values.

Robert Cox (1996; 2002; Schouten 2009) represents this broader approach, inspired by Giambattista Vico and Antonio Gramsci. The key message from Cox as regards the 'world order' dimension of analysis is that the balance of world power is shifting (Schouten

2009); the global dominance by the United States will be replaced by something else. What will emerge instead is not yet fully clear; it might be a cooperative post-hegemonic order where states agree on peaceful cooperation for mutual benefit; or it might be a world marked by the open rivalry of conflicting power centres.

As indicated, my analysis agrees with Cox in that a study of world order must include the economic dimension and its relationship to politico-military, institutional and value dimensions. Cox also points to the need to study international relations as well as domestic developments in major groups of states, a view I have supported here. Yet it will also become clear that the present study gives more emphasis to issues of violent conflict, of war and peace, in the consideration of international and domestic dimensions.

As regards world order in the narrow sense, Cox's analysis, as many others, foresees a decline of the United States and the emergence of some form of post-hegemonic order. *The Making of Global Capitalism* by Leo Panitch and Sam Gindin (2013), another significant Marxist contribution, disputes that point. They argue that the making of global capitalism cannot be taken on by market forces on their own. It requires a state which has the strength, will and capability to create and supervise the necessary framework for capitalist market forces in terms of rules, regulations and respect for private property.

The United States began to undertake this role already in 1939 when a group of prominent businessmen foresaw the need to replace an outdated system based on imperialism with a system of universal free trade under the leadership and supervision of the United States. The first task of these ambitions was the restoration of Western European and Japanese capitalism after World War II, set in motion by the Marshall Plan and the establishment of the Bretton Woods system (the IMF and what is today the World Bank); that led to the 'golden age' of capitalist growth and expansion between 1950 and 1967. This was followed by a period of crisis (1968–82), replaced by Reaganite neoliberalism in the 1980s and 1990s.

Thus far, the account by Panitch and Gindin is rather uncontroversial but that is not the case from here on. The crisis period is not seen as the beginning of a long-term decline of the US economy. It was a phase of restructuring in order to contain and limit the demands from organized labour; that was a complete success. US real wages in the private sector in 1999 were below the level of 1968. Neoliberalism opened up to economic globalization spearheaded by the United States as facilitator and 'consumer of last resort'. Globalization further weakened organized labour, but also reinforced American leadership in core industries of computers, software, pharmaceuticals and aerospace.

Instead of being mired into crisis, then, the United States assumed concrete leadership in the globalization of capitalism. The United States oversaw the integration of China in the global economy. China remains dependent on the United States as the market for a major part of its output and is heavily penetrated by Western direct foreign investment. The basic framework for a global capitalist economy originates in the United States, which also continues to dominate international institutions when it comes to rules and regulations and response to crises. At the same time, increasing inequality and exploitation in the United States and elsewhere, and resulting tensions, are easily diffused into a densely globalized system.

In sum, the economic dimension is important in its own right, but the interplay between states and international institutions is equally important; a further inquiry into the distribution of power is a way of clarifying this relationship. World order cannot be reduced to inherent tensions in the structure of the capitalist economy.

Empire versus regions

What kind of power shift was it that marked the end of the Cold War? The Soviet Union fell apart; one superpower checked out of the game and left a Russia still strong in terms of nuclear arsenals but also plagued by a series of economic, political and social problems in relation to the transition away from planned economy and communist party rule towards something else which is still in the making. One superpower was left on the scene.

In military terms, the United States was and is way ahead of everybody else, claiming a staggering 41% of the global military expenditures (SIPRI 2012). To this should be added a capacity for military power projection and an unparalleled fighting competence. Concerning the economy, the United States retains a substantial lead over China as regards per capita GDP; in terms of innovation and enterprise the lead is even more dramatic. It is against this background that a debate about empire has emerged (Cox 2003; see Tønnesson 2004 for an overview of the literature); the dominance of the United States is so strong that it can be equated with, or even exceeds that of, the Roman or the British Empire.

But the notion of an American empire is misleading because empire is a situation of formal dominion. Empire means acquisition of territory, of outsiders taking formal control. That is not the case with the United States today. Therefore, those who speak of an American empire employ various prefixes or suffixes: it is an 'empire lite', an 'informal empire' or even a 'post-imperial empire', and so on. In other words, countries that may be dominated by the United States today still retain formal sovereignty. That is hugely important because formal sovereignty is a source of power. Outsiders cannot come in and do what they want; they have to negotiate with insiders about the concrete terms of their presence; and outsiders have to go home again, they will not stay forever. Fundamental political, economic or social change, then, depends on the willingness of insiders to cooperate.

'Empire' is not an appropriate label for this situation. Christopher Layne and Bradley Thayer, for example, misleadingly equate empire with preponderant power; several other observers follow a similar course. America is an empire because 'it surpasses all others in capabilities' (2006: 3). But that says little about how those capabilities can be put to use and with what effect. The authors do admit that empire is no longer about colonies, but, goes the argument, there is no real difference between colonies, on one hand, and an informal empire with 'ruling indirectly through local elites' (2006: 59), on the other.

Wrong; there is a huge difference between direct and indirect rule. Colonialism is out of the question today; nobody wants to bring it back. Informal domination, insofar as it can be established at all, takes place under entirely different conditions. Indeed, a number of utterly fragile states in Africa, in the Caribbean and in Central Asia would not have survived at all in the absence of formal sovereignty (Jackson 1990). They would have been carved up and taken over by stronger outsiders.

If it is not empire, what is it? The Chinese speak of a current world order of 'one superpower, many great powers' (Noesselt 2012); they have a point, especially when focus is on military power. When it comes to the economy, to the situation in international institutions, or even to the standing of liberal values, the status of the United States as a superpower is more ambiguous. The question for further analysis, then, concerns the actual strength and character of American power in various domains and in relation to various groups of states.

There is another powerful trend in the present world order which makes the examination of these issues even more pertinent. It concerns the diffusion of power and influence, including economic capabilities, to many different parts of the world. That trend has led towards the idea of a world of regions (Söderbaum 2015; Weber and Jentleson 2010; Kupchan 2012).

It is certainly true that a number of regions in the world have received much greater attention in recent years, not least because they contain successful modernizing countries such as the BRICS. But the concept of region is complex and it is not entirely clear that regions are significant elements of the current world order. There are at least three ways of approaching the entity of region. First, the geographical approach is the designation of specific regions in territorial terms. Second, 'regional ties' is the assessment and analysis of economic, political, social, cultural, security or any other type of link in a region. The issue of regional security complexes bound together by common security concerns and the issue of economic interdependence has been particularly important in this respect. The analysis of ties opens to an evaluation of the level of 'regionness' of various areas. Finally, 'regionalism' concerns political initiatives supporting regional cooperation and integration (Hettne 2005). Tying this together, regions can be defined as 'a cluster of states that are proximate to each other and are interconnected in ... a significant and distinguishable manner' (Paul 2012: 4). Western Europe, the Middle East, Latin America and South, East and Southeast Asia are some of the most important regions.

Regions are not yet major players in world politics, with the possible exception of the European Union in relation to trade and a few other areas. Regional cooperation is mostly inward focused, in particular on economic cooperation, such as the ASEAN in Southeast Asia or the Mercosur in Latin America. Other regions, such as the Middle East, are better known for their problems than for their solutions; they are plagued by patterns of enmity that put security on top of the agenda.

Still, we must not downplay the relative importance of regions. The Cold War was an overlay in the sense that regional and local affairs were heavily influenced by the confrontation between the superpowers and the patterns of hostility and cooperation which they generated. Liberals, as we saw earlier, were confident that universal liberal values of democracy and market economy would be the new global overlay, compelling all countries towards global integration. But since successful modernization will not always lead in a distinctly liberal direction, regions are bound to increase in importance almost by default. It will not be a 'world of regions' because globalization, global institutions and common global problems tie us all together, but it will be a more decentred world.

In sum, the debate about 'empire versus regions' raises the question about the distribution of power in the present world order. We are not in a world of American empire, but the United States is still the leading country in terms of material power. We are not in a world of regions, but we are approaching a world where power is more dispersed than earlier. That points towards a power analysis which strikes a balance between 'empire', on one hand, and 'regions', on the other (for a version of that view, see Acharya 2014; see also Chapter 4).

Non-state actors: Good ones and bad ones

Realists consider sovereign states the major building blocks of world order: they make up the rules that others play by; they control the means of violence; they are the members of the UN system that negotiate and regulate international affairs. Essentially, world order is a governing arrangement among states. Liberals point to the increasing importance of non-state actors. Liberals have a point; in recent years, it has become clear that a variety of non-state actors influence world order in more significant ways than earlier. But liberals tend to focus single-mindedly on non-state actors that provide transnational goods, such as networks and cooperation. Non-state actors can also provide transnational *bads*, such as international terrorism, transnational crime and drug trade.

Among the latter, terrorism is arguably the most important threat. Terrorism has existed for a long time, but the 9/11 mass-murder terrorism connected to al-Qaeda was a novel phenomenon. It made George W. Bush declare a 'global war on terror'; the Bush administration explicitly defined this undertaking as a 'long war' indicating that it replaced the Cold War as the new global threat to the free world (Buzan 2006: 1101).

Western societies are increasingly complex and therefore vulnerable to external shocks such as terrorism. Some scholars think that terrorists could soon achieve access to weapons of mass destruction (WMD) and that opens to nuclear terrorism (Allison 2004). Even if international terrorists are primarily radicalized Muslims, a minor proportion of the Muslim populations both in the Western world and elsewhere are possible recruits for radical activities. Western interventions in Iraq and Afghanistan create blowback effects in the sense of radicalizing people towards terrorist activity (Mann 2003).

At the same time, it is no simple matter for terrorists to obtain WMDs, in particular nuclear weapons (Bowman 2002); Western societies may be complex but they are also capable of taking countermeasures against international terrorism; by the early 2010s, many politicians thought that we had put 'the decade of fear' behind us and were looking forward to less terrorist activity. Western interventions in Iraq and Afghanistan have not been very successful operations in terms of state-building and democratization, but they have been successful in terms of helping neutralize international terrorism. Al-Qaeda has not been a significant force in Afghanistan for some time; parts of the Taliban forces may be terrorists, but they are not international terrorists because their ambitions of influence and control and their scope of operations do not go beyond Afghanistan. In general, most terrorists are national, rather than international; they want to succeed in a specific country, such as Afghanistan, Iraq, Sri Lanka, India, Sudan or Nigeria.

But then came the attacks in Paris in 2015, as well as the San Bernardino attack in the United States in December of that year. All were, directly or indirectly, related to the Islamic State of Iraq and the Levant (ISIL). It is a further cause for concern that the latter attack was undertaken by an apparently well-integrated and successful middle-class couple with no direct connections to radical Muslim circles (Hautkapp 2015). Fear has to some extent re-emerged in the general population (Burger 2015); it is clear that the threat from international terrorism is important and needs to be taken seriously.

Still, this kind of terrorism is not an existential threat to mankind in any way comparable to the MAD scenario of the Cold War. I shall argue that it is part of a shifting pattern of threats. The major security problem in the old world order was nuclear war among the great powers; the major security problem in the present order is violent conflict inside fragile states. Some of that conflict acts as an incentive to terrorist attacks within Western countries, often targeting those countries that are involved in the conflicts within fragile states.

A side effect of international terrorism is the enormous growth of security and surveillance institutions in the Western world in general and in the United States in particular. The *Washington Post* spent two years attempting to uncover 'a hidden world, growing beyond control' (Priest and Arkin 2010). It counted 1,271 government organizations and 1,931 private companies working on programmes related to counterterrorism, homeland security and intelligence in some 10,000 locations in the United States; 854,000 people hold top-secret security clearances. It is secretive, non-transparent and it is coordinated and controlled by no-one. In that sense the 'homeland security' state has negative consequences for liberal democracy.

ISIL and al-Qaeda are examples of terrorist networks that can be considered a transnational bad. There are other networks in this category, related to additional transnational bads such as crime, drugs, pollution and economic fraud. But there are also many networks involved in providing transnational goods. According to one early liberal analysis by James Rosenau (1993), we are on the move away from a state-centric international system towards a multi-centric system made up by individuals who are much less tied in with the states of which they are citizens than they used to be. Individuals are well educated, mobile, have great access to information and are increasingly aware of the ways in which global dynamics affect their lives. They are becoming increasingly involved in all kinds of organizations and networks that create and influence the global agenda. In other words, a great diffusion of power is taking place.

For Rosenau, these developments indicate a profound transformation of the international system. The old 'state-centric' world persists, but it is increasingly competing with a vast array of individuals who organize across borders and stake out their own claims about the future world order. A famous example is 'the Battle in Seattle' in 1999, where thousands of activists protested against the WTO Ministerial Conference and demanded a stopping of the WTO talks in favour of a more radical agenda of decreasing world hunger and disease.

A recent book by Moisés Naím (2013a) presents a more generalized analysis of what is seen as a diffusion of power. His argument is that the conventional holders of power in political, military, corporate 'macro-structures' of power are being increasingly undermined and challenged by 'micropowers'–'insurgents, fringe political parties, innovative start-ups, hackers, loosely organized activists, upstart citizen media outlets, leaderless young people in city squares, and charismatic individuals who seem to have "come from nowhere" are shaking up the old order' (2013b: 1). The rise of micropowers is due to three 'revolutions'; the 'More revolution' means that many more people are living longer and healthier lives and that makes them more difficult to 'regiment and control' (2013a: 58). The 'Mobility revolution' implies that people are able to move around a lot more than earlier; they cross borders, they communicate globally, they easily switch loyalties of any kind. Finally, the 'Mentality revolution' concerns the aspirations of the rapidly growing middle classes all around the world. They shake off traditional values, take nothing for granted and do not easily defer to authorities; they are ready to 'take to the streets and fight' (2013a: 64) for their gains.

However, these analyses place too much emphasis on the autonomy of individuals and groups in relation to states and other macropowers. It is certainly true that individuals and groups are much more active across borders than earlier; in that sense a global civil society has emerged, made up of thousands of non-governmental organizations (NGOs), professional associations, religious groups and so on. But it typically does not compete with or replace the system of sovereign states. On the contrary, these organizations are closely related to, and work together with, both their home states and the international organizations of states, including the UN (Friedman et al. 2005). They are increasingly involved in the making of global governance, that is, the regulation of an intensely globalized world.

Both Rosenau and Naím paint an overly homogenous picture of both micropowers and macropowers in order to pitch them against each other. But the battle lines cut across these distinctions: micropowers spend most of their time trying to engage the macropowers of their choice; and macropowers attempt to reach out to old and new supporters in order to mobilize them towards their own efforts.

While states remain the major players in global governance, they have changed as well. There has been an expansion of transgovernmental networks. In earlier days, foreign connections went through foreign ministries; today, thousands of transgovernmental committees meet to regulate specific issue-areas, such as health, immigration, police, environment, agriculture, education and so on. These transnational webs of politics and governance (Cerny 2010: 22) are major players in the making of the specific rules of operation in the various sectors of the current world order.

Some scholars find that the networks are important enough to amount to a 'new world order' (Slaughter 2004) of cooperation and regulation for the common good. There is an element of truth in that; in the absence of a world government, which we will most probably never have, the regulatory networks fill important functions in providing a form of 'polycentric' governance (Scholte 2010). But they have not developed to an extent where they amount to a new world order. At the present time, the networks are thoroughly dominated by individuals and groups from the West, what we might call the OECD-world (Slaughter 2004: 228–9); that is, polycentric governance is not really a global institution. Further, the networks are not very powerful when it comes to major issues of taking action against a financial crisis, paving the way for reform of the UN system or providing security to fragile states. This remains the prerogative of sovereign states and most of the work in these larger issues continues to go through foreign ministries.

In sum, non-state actors are an increasingly important feature of the present world order. They are involved in supplying transnational bads as well as transnational goods. International terrorism is a transnational bad of considerable importance, but to characterize the present order as being overwhelmingly occupied by a 'global war on terror' would be misleading. A global civil society of organizations and networks provide transnational goods in the sense that they help provide global governance. But they are tied in with states, and their efforts do not amount to a new world order. They rather signify a transformation of modern states away from national government, towards multilevel governance in a more globalized world.

Overall, the analysis of non-state actors should not be artificially separated from the analysis of states. Non-state actors make up significant parts of the civil societies which animate the development and transformation of states. Both when such actors are problematic and may lead towards a 'national security' state, and when they are benign and help foster a 'multilevel governance state', they are influential and need to be taken into account. But they are not separate or isolated phenomena bringing a 'new world order' to life where states are marginalized or even irrelevant. The discussion of the power structure in Chapter 4 will return to the debate about concentration versus diffusion of power.

The environmental challenge

Concerns about the environment have been around since the Industrial Revolution, but for a long time environmental problems were regarded as minor issues of national concern; they were not present on the international agenda. That changed in the 1970s and 1980s; the first worldwide environmental conference took place in Stockholm in 1972, attended by 114 countries. The *Club of Rome* think tank published *Limits to Growth* that same year; it spoke about the depletion of natural resources and the limited carrying capacity of the Earth. That is to say, there are limits as to how much the global environment can support in terms of population growth if serious problems of degradation should be avoided.

That led to ideas about sustainable development, meaning that human needs must be met in ways which ensure the sustainability of the environment and natural systems. The United Nations Conference on Environment and Development (UNCED) in Rio de Janeiro in 1992 marked the beginning of a process where most countries started to think about ways of integrating sustainable development goals in their policies of economic development.

These concerns were spurred by disturbing global macrotrends. It took 123 years for the world population to double from one billion to two billion (by 1927); it took a mere 50 years to go from four billion to seven billion (by 2013). Rapid population growth combined with global demand for increased living standards has vastly increased global economic activity. That means rapidly increasing energy consumption and global warming. Land degradation, depletion of forests, loss of biodiversity and pressure on freshwater and marine resources are additional consequences (Chasek, Downie and Brown 2010).

There is of course a long-standing debate about the gravity of the environmental problems. It is a complex issue because the evaluation of current conditions as well as the scenarios for future developments must rest on uncertain estimates and disputable assumptions. The extreme positions on either side of the debate are 'modernists' and 'ecoradicals'. The former argue that the growing environmental problems will be matched by an even faster growth of technological competence and scientific knowledge which will strongly improve our capacity to protect the environment. Take global warming due to fossil fuel combustion; that problem stands to be dramatically reduced due to more effective ways of providing energy from the sun. According to modernists, solar energy technology will solve the global warming problem long before it becomes overly serious.

'Ecoradicals', on the other hand, are convinced that the Earth's ecosystem has a limited carrying capacity and that population growth is bringing us dangerously close to that limit. Technological remedies are not likely to take care of the problem. Instead, dramatic changes in modern lifestyles in an environment-friendly direction combined with strict population control are necessary. At the same time, ecoradicals are a very mixed group and their proposals move in several different directions (Best and Nocell 2006).

The currently dominant views of the environmental problems in the Western world are certainly not ecoradical but nor are they traditionally modernist. A 'green' agenda has emerged on the policy priorities of most Western countries. There is also wide acknowledgement of the need to supplement the traditional notion of national security (against external armed threat) with a notion of human security which focuses on threats to individuals, including environmental degradation and climate change. A UNESCO report from 2008 even contains an elaborate set of regional and subregional recommendations for the promotion of human security around the world (UNESCO 2008).

Even so, human security was probably higher on the agenda in the 1990s because the end of the Cold War reduced the urgency of traditional security concerns and Mikhail Gorbachev explicitly endorsed a human security agenda. In the new millennium, however, human security concerns were somewhat overshadowed by the threat from international terrorism, massive violent conflict in fragile states and the financial crisis. Still, as far as the environment is concerned, the United Nations continues to hold annual climate conferences, the so-called COP (Conference of the Parties) meetings, with COP 21 in Paris in December 2015 as the most recent. A host of climate issues are discussed, including the Kyoto Protocol, technology transfer, emissions reporting, financing for environment measures and so on.

The meetings demonstrate that the global environment is now a major issue in world politics. At the same time, it is not a virulent issue on the top of the global agenda. If it were, the hesitance of the world's leading power, the United States, to get seriously involved and make commitments in this area would be the cause of much greater global concern. The United States never ratified the

Kyoto Protocol and has not made commitments to the provision of climate finance in the developing world. It was only in June of 2013 that President Obama put forward the first US plan ever for the reduction of carbon pollution.

After a period of rapidly increasing prominence on the international agenda in the 1980s and 1990s, environmental problems have achieved a place on the political itineraries of most countries. Environmental concerns have not replaced or outcompeted traditional economic and security issues. There is by now an international environmental constituency around the UNESCO, the UNDP and the COP conferences. Rather than an urgent issue, it is residual, coming forward in the absence of pressing security or economic concerns. It often comes up in the form of a blame game about who should do how much and who should pay the bill. It is an 'everyday politics' issue, not yet a matter of planetary survival. In sum, environmental problems are serious and they have an established place on the current international agenda, but not in a way to make them a defining feature of the current world order.

Liberals generally believe that problems related to the environment present a common, global challenge to mankind that compels states to cooperate in finding the best ways to confront it. Realists are convinced that the environment issue is another source of conflict that can be added to an already long list. The mix of 'common fate' and opposing interests in relation to the environment is discussed in Chapter 6.

A framework for analysis

Optimistic liberals emphasize the ideological victory of liberalism and the spread of liberal economic and political values in a world of increasing cooperation; realists look to the recurrent power rivalry and conflict between sovereign states; both make valid points. But they tend to be 'hedgehog analyses' (Berlin 1953) in the sense that each of them points to 'one big thing' as the central feature of the current world order.

In this, they are joined by other contributions discussed above. Marxists focus on the inbuilt tensions in the capitalist system; the 'empire versus regions' debate presents different views of where power is situated today. Some think that non-state actors, either 'bad'

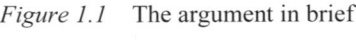

Figure 1.1   The argument in brief

Framework conditions

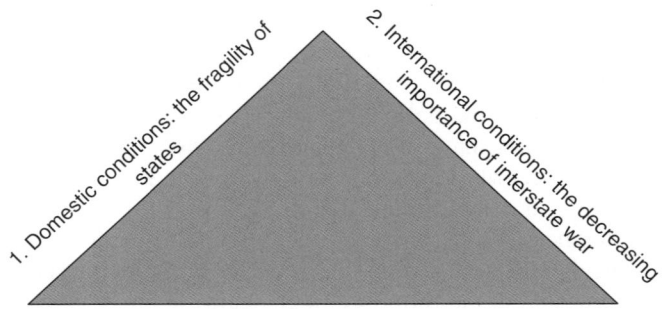

3. The distribution of power

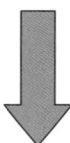

Patterns of world order in major areas

- Security: Intervention, order and legitimacy
- Economics: The dynamics of globalization
- Institutions: Governance or gridlock?
- Values: A victory or crisis of liberalism?

ones or 'good' ones, are the new defining feature of world order. And finally, others find that the environmental challenges now overshadow everything else.

The problem is that overemphasis of only one dimension leads to a biased general picture; a 'hedgehog analysis' must always be insufficient because world order cannot be reduced to one single, supreme aspect; it must encompass several major dimensions. It needs to be a 'fox analysis' because the fox knows many important things rather than one big thing. How many things exactly is without doubt the pertinent question; if we go to the other extreme, world order would be an endlessly complex collection of structures, actors and processes. The 'fox analysis' in the above is of course primarily the English School contributions by Hurrell and Buzan. I have acknowledged their richness and criticized their tendency to be overly complex.

That raises the question about how to proceed, given the ambition to avoid an overly reductionist 'hedgehog' analysis as well as an overly complex 'fox analysis'. My answer is set forth in the chapters that follow. I suggest a compromise in that my analysis contains a 'hedgehog' element as well as a 'fox' element. The former is of course the overarching debate among liberal optimists and sceptical realists; the latter is the explication of various structures, actors and processes that are all parts of the big picture of world order.

Chapters 2–4 are about the general framework conditions that define the context for the present world order. Having established these framework conditions, Chapters 5–8 focus on the specific patterns of world order in four major areas. The argument can be summarized as (see figure 1.1).

Conclusion: Rethinking the new world order

The 'major areas' singled out are inspired by the major theoretical traditions of the IR discipline. Realists focus on security; many liberals single out governance networks, in particular international institutions; English School theory arguably combines realist and liberal concerns and adds its own twist. IPE is a diverse field, but the general focus when it comes to world order is on the global capitalist economic system. Finally, some liberals, as well as social constructivists, take ideas as the basis for their analysis. In the present context of world order investigation it is relevant to focus on the issue of common liberal values in the world (for an overview of theoretical traditions, see Jackson and Sørensen 2016).

Before embarking on all this, however, it is necessary to say a bit more about the core concept of this study: world order.

World order: The concept

The concept of world order is what Gallie (1956) called 'essentially contested'; that is, there is no agreement at all about what it actually means and how it should be defined. Yet definitions are important because they help give substance to the arguments made; in a sense they are in themselves small theories. The confusion surrounding 'world order' comes from several sources; I will name two. On one hand, politicians use 'world order' as a description of or justification for specific policies. In 1991, George Bush saw a 'New World Order' emerging after the First Gulf War, an order 'where the rule of law … governs the conduct of nations'. Both Bush and Gorbachev used the term to signal a more intense cooperation after the Cold War. On the other hand, pundits use the term for every conceivable change in the world that they consider important; it may concern some aspects of the environment, of economics, of governance, of civil society and so on (e.g. *The Guardian* 2015).

Neither the politician version of world order nor the pundit version of it is sufficient for present purposes, which require a more general definition. The classic discussion of order in this sense is by Hedley Bull. His point of departure is the international society of sovereign states. International order, according to Bull, is here when sovereign states are able to live in relative peace among each other and to uphold their security and independence (Bull 1995: 16–19). This can be called a 'thin' version of world order; it is founded on a realist view of the world: the international system is anarchic; political authority is vested in sovereign states; there is no world government. Under these conditions violent conflict can always break out between states that are armed and live in fear of each other. In such a fragile system, a 'thin' order of peace, security and independence is as much order as can be hoped for. The gravest challenge to such an order is the rise of new great powers such as China and India, because they shake up the balance of power.

Hedley Bull focused on this 'thin' version of order, but he also defined a wider, 'thick' concept of world order which is not merely about relations between states; it concerns 'the elementary goals of social life among mankind as a whole' (Bull 1995: 19). World order in this wider sense concerns the good life of all human beings; it involves not merely order and security but welfare, freedom and justice for all people on the planet. Such a conception of world order must involve more than relationships between states; it must also involve the activities of civil societies and markets. Further, world order in the 'thick' sense is clearly not just concerned with cross-border relationships. It must look inside states as well in order to discover whether citizens are or are not living the good life.

Hedley Bull's preoccupation with the 'thin' version of world order was perhaps justified because his study took place in the mid-1970s where the bipolar confrontation between superpowers heavily armed with nuclear weapons was at the top of the world order agenda. But this has changed dramatically in the second half of the twentieth century, especially after the end of the Cold War. During this period, aspirations for world order have grown in both scope and ambition. The Millennium Declaration, endorsed by more than 150 states at the UN General Assembly in 2000, identified several fundamental values considered to be 'essential to international relations in the twenty-first century'. They include democracy, equal rights, social justice, respect for diversity, sustainable development and shared responsibility for managing economic and social development and threats to peace and security (UN 2000).

The 'thin' and the 'thick' versions of world order may be thought of as opposite ends of a continuum. The 'thin' order is a limited and fragile one, always crisis-prone because changes in power relations may lead to new conflicts which constantly have a possibility of becoming violent. The 'thick' order is extremely ambitious because its full implementation means that the 'good life' with welfare, rights, security, justice and order is made available to all people. In between are of course a large number of different possibilities for world orders that are less pessimistic than the 'thin' order and less optimistic than the 'thick' order. It is the aim of this book to come up with a diagnosis that is as precise as possible of where we are in terms of world order at the present time.

World order is not merely about relations between sovereign states. It is also about order within states; millions of people live in mortal danger today because they must survive inside states that cannot and will not provide for their security, not to mention their welfare and their rights. Domestic conditions have an impact not merely at home but also on international relations. If there is profound economic and social crisis, if social compacts are breaking up, if domestic politics is moving in new directions, all this will have consequences for what states can do externally. In other words, international order is closely connected to domestic order.

In sum, world order is defined as a governing arrangement inside and among states, with the participation of other actors. There are systemic constraints in relation to a stable and well-functioning world order but there are also domestic constraints; both dimensions, and their interplay, must be addressed in a proper examination of world order.

2
The Fragility of States

Introduction

This chapter turns to domestic developments within states. The ambition of world order today is to provide the good life for all people, as emphasized in the Millennium Declaration. In order to assess whether those conditions are present or not, international relations are important but we cannot merely look at international relations; we must also focus on domestic developments because the prospects for ordinary people deeply depend on the conditions inside the states where they live their lives. It is the interplay between international and domestic developments which determines what kind of world order we have at any given time. In relation to the overall debate between liberals and realists, this chapter is a warning against an overemphasis on liberal optimism.

Many students of world order disregard domestic developments and focus only on international relations. But what states can do in international relations depends heavily on domestic conditions. If the home front is in order, with an effective and well-functioning political system, a contented and relatively well-to-do population and a sound national economy, states are free to focus on the international sphere. My argument is that problems in these areas are increasingly serious, not merely in the weak states in the Global South—the entities for which the term 'fragile states' was originally coined—but across all types of states, including the so-called advanced liberal states in the Global North.

So we have to look inside different types of state in order to assess domestic conditions for world order. We cannot study every aspect of all states, of course, nor is it necessary. The aim is to discover significant features of statehood that are relevant for the investigation of world order. I make two arguments in this chapter. On one hand, there are three major modalities of sovereign statehood in the present international system. First, the advanced capitalist states in the Global North, especially in Western Europe and the United States. Second, the modernizing states such as China, India, Russia and Brazil, where the main focus will be on China. And finally the weak post-colonial states in the Global South; they were always fragile and the argument is that current processes of economic growth in some of these states do not represent a significant move away from that situation.

On the other hand, I argue that problems in relation to socio-political cohesion (Buzan 1991) are a serious and rising concern across all states, even if the concrete manifestations vary among major types of state. That is what is meant by the claim that we live in a world of increasingly fragile states.

Types of state in the present international system

The standard picture of statehood in IR builds on the modern state that came out of the process of state formation in Europe (Sørensen 2001). That state is a resourceful entity; it possesses a capacity for self-government, an economic resource base and an ability to defend itself militarily. Modern economies are thus national economies in the basic sense that economic development took place in a national space, even if there was significant exchange with other economies. The state has a monopoly on the legitimate use of force; domestic law and order is based primarily on popular support for the system of government. Finally, there is a national community of citizens bound together by cultural and historical bonds.

It is clear that sovereign states in today's world do not correspond to that classic picture of modern statehood. Political, economic, normative and other developments transform states; they do not stand still. There are three major types of state in the present international system.

The type most different from the modern state is the weak post-colonial state in the Global South. Decolonization gave sovereignty to states with weak and underdeveloped state institutions. In Africa, for example, there was no pre-colonial tradition of statehood, and the institutions erected during the colonial period were not sufficiently viable after independence. State power thus became concentrated in individual political leaders. The 'national economy' is a highly heterogeneous space, with subsistence farming and a vast informal sector. Instead of a national community, people are divided along ethnic and communal lines.

The advanced liberal states that had emerged mainly in Western Europe and North America around the mid-twentieth century have changed. Instead of modern states, I have proposed elsewhere to call them postmodern states (Sørensen 2001, 2004). Whereas modern states were primarily national entities, with a national government, a national economy and a national community, postmodern states are more integrated with each other at all levels. At the political level, there is multilevel governance in the context of supranational, international, transgovernmental and transnational relations. In economic terms there is 'deep integration' in the sense that major parts of economic activity are embedded in cross-border networks. The national community persists, but collective loyalties have also increasingly been projected away from the state.

Modernizing states, such as the BRICS (Brazil, Russia, India, China and South Africa), finally, contain mixtures of modern, postmodern and weak statehood. The economic characteristics of weak states, for example, are appropriate for many parts of India, but the country also has major elements of a modern and postmodern structure. A similar amalgam can be found in China, but this country is a much more active participant in economic globalization. At the political level, the picture is also mixed. All five countries contain elements of weak statehood (ineffective institutions, corruption, less rule of law), but they also contain elements of effective statehood. In short, modernizing states are, by definition, in-betweens.

It is clear that the possibility for the good life varies enormously among different types of state; the situation is best in the advanced liberal states and worst in weak, post-colonial states. The transformation of modern, modernizing and even some weak post-colonial states has made them stronger in some respects; they are wealthier, better able to provide the good life for at least some parts of the population. But as I argue in the following sections, the transformations have also made them weaker in the sense that they are all plagued by decreasing socio-political cohesion. In political terms, less cohesion means that the state apparatus is less effective, has less capacity and enjoys less legitimacy. In economic terms, less cohesion means that national economies are de-nationalized in the context of globalization and that the basis for material welfare of the population deteriorates. In terms of national community, less cohesion means that states are less capable of providing for citizenship rights and that they lose popular support in return.

The argument is not that all states are developing in just one direction, towards increased fragility; states are in processes of transformation which make them weaker in some respects and stronger in others (Sørensen 2004). The weaknesses, however, are especially relevant when considering the abilities of states to contribute to building an effective and legitimate world order.

There has been a debate about the overarching concept of 'fragile states' as used in relation to the Global South. The argument is that the concept is a 'normative tool and a policy label' (Grimm et al. 2014: 205) of little analytical utility (Call 2008) because Southern nations are vastly different from each other. My view is that the concept can be clearly defined and that problems concerning state fragility can be found in any given state in the international system. Such problems are relevant for the study of world order.

Advanced liberal states

The idea that sovereign states are strong, robust, effective and adequate frameworks for the good life of their citizens is invariably connected with the advanced liberal democracies. The modern state emerged first in Europe; it was then exported to North America, and, in a later stage, copied in East Asia. Consolidated liberal democracy emerged late in Europe: several European nations, including Germany and Italy, were not democratic for most of the period between the world wars. At the same time, the roots of democracy run deep: the ancient Roman state involved representation and political rule based on law and rulers saw themselves as guardians of the public good.

So the development of statehood is an ongoing process which in Europe's case has lasted more than two millennia: modern states were not fully in place until the mid-twentieth century. The concrete model of the good life in advanced liberal democracies was first realized in the United States. It is built around a well-to-do and successful middle class, with good jobs, secure incomes, comfortable lifestyles and an ability to provide for the future of their children and for safe retirement. It was this model that was effectively adopted in Western Europe and Japan in the context of the post-war reconstruction.

The process took place under the Bretton Woods system of 'embedded liberalism' (Ruggie 1982). A major goal of this system was to nurture economic cooperation so as to avoid the protectionism of the interwar period. But it was not a system of excessive free market rule. Some sectors were not, or only marginally, liberalized; they included agriculture and most services. And manufacturing sectors under threat from low-cost exporters, including textile and clothing, were protected by special arrangements. It was this system of semi-liberalization that allowed countries to build 'customized versions of capitalism' with national approaches to welfare arrangements, tax regimes, labour markets and different styles of corporate governance (Rodrik 2011: 67–76).

The Bretton Woods system entered a period of crisis in the 1970s (Gilpin 1987). The first tendencies were a reversion towards protectionism, but by the late 1970s a new, neoliberal consensus emerged, spearheaded by Ronald Reagan and Margaret Thatcher. For a long period now, the main values of a neoliberal consensus have dominated policymaking in the advanced liberal democracies, irrespective of the color the government. There have been changes over time, of course, but two common principles stand out:

- An open world economy: reduce barriers to trade and capital flows, and promote the internationalization of production.
- A new financial orthodoxy: control inflation, provide tax reductions, seek balanced budgets and make state ministries and agencies more effective (modified from Cerny 2010: 140–56).

It was these neoliberal principles that led to a new phase of intensified economic globalization (Dicken 2011). Economic globalization, in turn, is a driving force behind the reduced socio-political cohesion in the advanced liberal states. Let me begin with economics; it is clear that economies today are much less nationally segregated than earlier. The process of 'deep integration' means that production chains of goods and services are increasingly organized across borders. Instead of the national corporation, the typical firm is the transnational corporation, that is, a firm operating in more than one country. The car industry was a forerunner in the process of combining inputs from many countries and then marketing the final product worldwide. Today, most other major industries have followed suit (Dicken 2011).

Another major sector has been thoroughly internationalized since the 1980s: finance. There is now a globally integrated financial market where the volume of transactions exceeded world trade by a ratio of 60:1 already in 1995; by 2013, three days of foreign exchange turnover was sufficient to cover world trade for a year (Chandler 2013).

The previous history of advanced liberal states has been one of creating national economic cohesion from the bottom up: states undertook infrastructural and market-building projects that tied together and integrated localized economic circuits centred on the towns. Railroads were a decisive element in this development (Zürn 1998: 41–63). Developments under the neoliberal globalization regime have gone the other way: towards disaggregation because national networks are now interlocked in transnational processes of production, distribution and consumption. The world of work was once set in the framework of the Fordist factory system. Today, it increasingly depends on complex transnational economic undertakings. 'Ordinary people in everyday life are growing more and more aware that their fates depend not so much on decisions taken at the national level but on wider developments and transformations at international, transnational, and translocal levels' (Cerny 2010: 78–9).

The social consequences of neoliberal globalization remain disputed for two reasons: on one hand, the neoliberal principles did help foster economic growth in several countries, combined with low inflation. On the other hand, welfare systems vary considerably, even among the advanced liberal states, and that accounts for some variation in the effects of economic globalization (Rodrik 2011; Cerny 2010). Even so, it is also clear that there are some general consequences that pertain across these differences and they point to less social cohesion as a major consequence of globalization.

First, the neoliberal globalization game creates winners and losers, both in the advanced liberal states and elsewhere. Winners are those able to capture the benefits of globalization. They tend to be the well-educated elites: the owners and managers of companies and the professional, technical and bureaucratic staff of public and private companies and institutions. The losers are those who suffer the downsides of globalization in terms of unemployment, more limited opportunities, reduced incomes and marginalization (Cerny 2010: 174).

Second, it is a coalition of 'winners' that dominates the political scene in the advanced liberal democracies. The globalization process itself has narrowed the room for alternatives when it comes to social and economic policies because the markets expect 'not just fiscal consolidation but also, and at the same time, a reasonable prospect of future economic growth' (Streek 2011: 12). These pressures are behind the policies of public bailout of financial institutions, general austerity measures and the downward pressures on the social wage. To the extent social policy comes into play, it is used to enhance the flexibility of labour markets and to limit the scope for wage increases (Jessop 2002: 168). At the same time, 'regulatory capture' is part of the story: the publicly appointed regulators of finance are recruited from the very companies whose interests they should keep at bay; Posner (2010: 173) calls this the 'revolving door' problem.

The result of this is an increased gulf between citizens and their governments. When governments aim to behave 'responsibly' as seen by international markets and institutions, there is less room for being responsive to their citizens (Mair 2009). Some commentators speak about a 'new crisis of democracy' (Zakaria 2013); one indicator comes from the polls on trust in government in the United States: in 1964, 76% of Americans agreed with the statement 'You can trust the government in Washington to do what is right just about always or most of the time'; by 2010, it had fallen to 19% (Zakaria 2013: 23).

Much increased political frustration is also the result of these developments. In the United States, there is a 'new politics of extremism'. Mann and Ornstein (2012) analyse the political deadlock connected to rising partisanship, especially on the Republican side. They quote Mike Lofgren, a veteran Republican congressional staffer, for saying that the Republicans are 'becoming less and less like a traditional political party in a representative democracy and becoming more and more like an apocalyptic cult … [where] virtually every bill … is now subject to a Republican filibuster' (quoted from Mann and Ornstein 2012: 54–5). The reasoning behind this behaviour is simple, as explained by a Republican executive: 'Should Republicans succeed in obstructing the Senate from doing its job, it would further lower Congress' generic favourability rating among the American people. By sabotaging the reputation of an institution of government, the party that is programmatically against government would come out the relative winner' (quoted from Mann and Ornstein 2012: 55). Neoliberal globalization as described here is not the only factor behind these developments. A recent analysis points to the role of interest groups in politics, gerrymandering, shifts in the racial mix of the US population, rising inequality and a gap between younger and older generations on social issues (McCarty et al. 2006).

In the European Union, there is also a process of increasing political polarization, emphasized by the financial crisis, which turned into a serious crisis for the most integrative economic project of all in the EU context: the common currency of the euro. This is a crisis both at the member state level and at the EU level. Some member states—Greece is probably the best example—are fragile, ineffective, have serious corruption problems, weak capacities for adopting and implementing rules and regulations and are excessively dominated by vested interests that have been successful in taking care of themselves while claiming to work for the common good.

At the EU level, focus has been and remains on short-term stabilization of debt-ridden countries via austerity measures. In the popular perception, not entirely inaccurate, the European Union appears very keen on bailing out banks but not very interested at all when it comes to bailing out ordinary people. The result is a swing towards EU-scepticism exacerbated by the pressures of migration, high unemployment and the closed 'Eurocratic' system in Brussels. On one hand, it is widely acknowledged that there is a need for closer cooperation, for 'more Europe', in order to face the many challenges raised by the crisis. On the other hand, European leaders face sceptical citizens, national parliaments and national courts. This is the European version of gridlock: the 'necessity and impossibility' of integration (Leonard 2011).

Behind these developments is a larger tension between democracy and globalization. Liberal democracy always developed within the context of sovereign states. The reason is simple; the basic requirement for democracy is the existence of a *demos*, the citizens that agree on forming a political community. Outside of the independent nation-state, there is no such community and for that reason 'genuine democracy' is not possible outside of national boundaries (Kymlicka 1999: 124).

The practical difficulties related to democracy across borders have to do with democratic accountability. International institutions cannot easily provide citizens with opportunities for participation, influence and control. They are far away, fenced in by large bureaucracies, and less able to open up to public debate across borders (Dahl 1999).

There is not a cross-border public domain in EU-Europe, for example, that can engage citizens in debates about the future of Europe. There is no common language, no political parties or media outlets that can captivate the attention and emotions of the public. The best thing that can be said about the European Union from a democratic point of view is perhaps that it helps provide output legitimacy (Scharpf 1997) because working together provides opportunities for regulation that are not possible within the confines of the nation-state. But given the way that the system currently works, that is not enough to secure massive public support and engagement.

I have argued that neoliberal globalization has led to less economic and less political cohesion in the advanced liberal states. Let me return to the issue of social cohesion. It was argued earlier that, more than anything, the well-situated middle class is the core expression of the good life in these countries. This middle class is now under severe attack both from above and from below. First, inequality is sharply rising. In the United States, the richest 1% took home about 9% of total income in the mid-1970s; today they take home more than 23%. Meanwhile, huge sections of the middle class have stood still, with no substantial progress over some three decades; median incomes in the United States have been stagnating in real terms since the 1970s.Technological change reduces the amount of low-skilled middle-class jobs; together with outsourcing in the context of economic globalization, the pressure on the middle class has increased (Fukuyama 2012).

Europe and Japan display similar problems even if they have less overall inequality. A recent OECD report documents that the rise in income inequality and relative poverty has affected almost all OECD countries over the past two decades (OECD 2011). The standard answer to these problems is usually to recommend more focus on education: lifelong learning and skills enhancement. That connects directly to the American dream: through hard work and diligence, you can move upward and be successful. But a recent comprehensive study seriously questions that view (Pikkety 2014).

Pikkety's analysis documents that in an economy where the rate of return on capital outstrips the rate of growth, inherited wealth will always grow faster than earned wealth, even by a wide margin. The incomes of the richest 1% mentioned earlier do not primarily stem from work; they derive from capital gains: the larger the income, the higher the share coming from financial assets. There was a longer period in the mid-twentieth century where high post-war growth rates combined with strong organized labour and high tax levels were able to stem the trend towards higher inequality, but that period was the exception, not the rule. Access to capital gains is much more lucrative than hard work. For quite some time we have been back in a 'Jane Austen world': marrying into wealth is a much better strategy for success than trying to work your way up.

It is going to be difficult, if not impossible, to reverse the dominant trend: advanced capitalism remains combined with high levels of inequality and low levels of social mobility. The recommendation by Pikkety is a 'confiscatory' global tax on inherited wealth and enforced transparency for all bank transactions. For the United States, he recommends an 80% tax on incomes above $500,000 a year. Such proposals are not at all likely to be successful; that means the current trend towards inequality will continue.

The squeezing of the middle class from above in advanced capitalist societies is combined with an influx of immigrants who often occupy the low-skilled jobs in the industry and service sectors. That pressures the social and economic conditions of the middle class from below. Germany, for example, boasts a high degree of employment compared to other EU members, but Germany also has 4.3 million full-time workers on low wages and a large number of part-time workers in the same category. They are the ranks of the 'working poor', people who are likely to experience poverty even when they are employed. Working poor and unemployed in Germany made up 10 million of a labour force of 43 million in 2013 (DW 2015). In the United States, there has been a very large influx of Hispanic immigrants who are also concentrated in the lower rungs of the labour market; they made up 12% of the total US population by 2000 (Huntington 2004).

Samuel Huntington has argued that what he calls the 'Hispanic Challenge' is a threat to US socio-cultural cohesion because it threatens to turn the United States into 'a country of two languages and two cultures' (Huntington 2004: 45), where Hispanic immigrants support values radically different from the Anglo-Protestant culture of the founding settlers. Even if this may be going too far, it demonstrates the challenges to socio-cultural cohesion brought about by large-scale immigration.

In Europe, nationalistic movements that stress a very exclusive definition of national identity have emerged. Examples are the *Front*

National in France, the *UK Independence Party*, and the *Danish People's Party*. Some of these movements are highly focused on the issue of immigration, but most of them are also very sceptical about more intensive cooperation across borders. The claims of 'outsiders' threaten the social and economic well-being of 'original' citizens; immigrants also threaten a historically specific, narrow conception of national identity which leaves no room for unadapted newcomers.

In sum, after more than three decades of neoliberal globalization there is less socio-political cohesion in the advanced liberal states. Globalized economies, including globalized financial markets, mean that there is now much less national economic cohesion than earlier. That puts pressure on governments because their ability to control and regulate is reduced at the national level and not easily recaptured at the international level (Rodrik 2011). At the same time, national governments are dominated by the winners in the globalization game and are losing credibility among ordinary people, who are often among the losers. States are less legitimate and less democratically accountable in the eyes of a squeezed middle class; various forms of political gridlock are the result of that situation and there are no simple ways of addressing the tension between democracy and globalization. The problems are exacerbated by the trends towards less cohesion in the community of people, the nation.

Under current conditions, world order is not able to provide for the good life for large sections of the populations of advanced liberal states. The problem is not a simple one of more redistribution because it is linked to problems concerning socio-political cohesion in several areas, including economics, politics and community. Dani Rodrik believes that we face hard choices because the current version of neoliberal globalization cannot go together with a strong, cohesive nation-state, and with democracy. If the current version of globalization continues, the only way to preserve democracy will be to create a much stronger, democratically based, form of global governance, even a world state.

For the time being, however, no such 'big solutions' are on the table. There is global governance, but it falls far short of what is required to control and regulate current globalization and its democratic foundation is rather thin. Primarily, neoliberal globalization continues unabated; there are no strong tendencies towards reining it in and bringing it under stronger democratic control. That is perhaps because it is not so easy to provide nationally adapted versions of such a modified globalization that would better address the downsides of the current model and avoid a problematic return to simple national protectionism. First and foremost, it is because dominant political coalitions in the advanced liberal states are not looking in that direction for their preferred solutions.

Modernizing states: China and the other BRICS

Modernizing states are countries that appear to be on the way towards economic development. The focus here is on China and the other BRICS, but there are several other countries in this category, of course, including Chile, Mexico and Argentina in Latin America, Indonesia, Thailand, Vietnam, Malaysia and the Philippines in Asia, and Nigeria and Kenya in Africa. That does not exhaust the list; it can be made more or less inclusive depending on how one defines 'successful economic development'.

That discussion is less relevant here, where focus is on the fragility of what are arguably the leading modernizing states: the BRICS, and especially China. There has been much talk about the decline of the West and the ways in which the rise of China and other BRICS will lead to a new global order; we return to this issue of relative power in Chapter 4. The argument here is that the BRICS in general—and the leading country of that group, China, in particular—are fragile states in several respects.

In order to discuss this state of affairs, it is necessary to begin with a critical view of liberal modernization theory. That outlook tends to apply a uniform development image to all countries: all countries were once traditional and backward and several Third World countries remain that way today. But they will eventually follow the same developmental path taken earlier by the developed countries in the West: a progressive journey from a traditional, pre-industrial, agrarian, non-democratic society towards a modern, industrial democratic mass-consumption society. It is this 'great convergence' which is now well under way in Asia and elsewhere (Mahbubani 2013).

But the evolutionary view is wrong in two ways: first, the starting points for most modernizing states are fundamentally different from the starting points of most advanced Western countries; all countries may at one point have been less industrialized than they are today, but that does not put them in the same category: 'traditional' or 'backward' means very different things in different countries and history matters. Second, a successful process of industrialization and economic development does not necessarily mean that countries converge. The paths to modernity followed by today's rising powers are not copies of the West; they are each following 'unique paths towards modernity based on their own political, demographic, topographic and socioeconomic conditions' (Kupchan 2012: 87). That also means that there is no inbuilt law of history ensuring that progress and modernity as we now understand them will eventually arrive in any country; in that sense the term 'modernizing' is potentially misleading.

Modernizing states, then, each contain uneven mixtures of very different characteristics. In India, for example, the economy is made up of a large sector of traditional agriculture and an informal petty urban sector but the country also has larger elements of a modern industrial structure. It even has advanced economic sectors that are now seeking active integration in cross-border networks via direct investment. A similar picture can be found in China, but this country is already a highly active participant in economic globalization. Russia may have modernized even more, but it is also deeply reliant on the export of energy and raw materials and imports of more sophisticated products.

This mixed picture also applies to the political level. Massive corruption and defective state structures remain a serious problem across the BRICS, but in some areas there is a higher degree of effective national government. China has several elements of a strong national government and it is the economic giant that has been hyped to rival Western dominance in the near future. Since China is the number one challenger to Western dominance from the ranks of modernizing states, it is relevant to focus on that country. What is it that points in the direction of fragility in China? Nothing much according to many observers who see China as an up-and-coming superpower with special emphasis on economic achievements: China was set to overtake the United States as the world's largest economy already by 2014 according to one of the most aggressive estimates (Schuman 2014). But this is in several ways a misleading indicator of Chinese power (Beckley 2011) and the challenges to China are serious.

Politics first: China is the only great power that is led by a communist party. The law is important to the Chinese Communist Party (CCP) as an instrument of governance but it does not directly constrain the leadership. The party considers itself above the law and legal authorities cannot investigate party members on their own; they need the consent of the party. In case of high-ranking officials, such as former Chongqing Party Secretary Bo Xilai, for example, the party conducted its own investigation before it handed over the case to the courts. Party organs oversee the work of courts, prosecutors and police and are empowered to intervene in order to obtain the desired outcomes (Lawrence and Martin 2013: 27).

This leaves unconstrained power in the hands of a small party leadership: the seven members of the CCP Politburo's Standing Committee currently headed by General Secretary Xi Jinping, and next the Politburo itself, consisting of 25 members. There is a ranking in the top, but not a supreme leader since the time of Deng Xiaoping. The intention is to guard against excesses either to the left (Chairman Mao) or to the right (a Chinese version of Mikhail Gorbachev).

Effective leadership of a country of 1.3 billion people is not accomplished by seven or 25 leaders alone, of course. Successful leaders must win consensus both at the top and further down in the hierarchy. Factionalism is common: top leaders will rely on and promote officials from their own networks known to be loyal supporters; much competition within party and state is built on bureaucratic constituencies. Factionalism is exacerbated by bureaucratic competition: because of many instances of unclear or overlapping jurisdiction, different official entities engage in 'unproductive competition' for control (Lawrence and Martin 2013: 14–7).

In the days of supreme leaders, or strongmen, the concentration of power allowed for sweeping reforms but also for horrible mistakes. For example, the so-called Great Leap Forward beginning in 1958 was supposed to boost industrialization, but it was a disaster that led to widespread famine and deprivation. Yet Mao Zedong held onto the strategy for a long while, even after it had proven catastrophically wrong (Riskin 1987: 276). The current system of leadership shields against such excesses; on one hand, there is less room for a strongman who can lead the country astray; on the other hand, there is a general consensus about three key priorities: (a) continued leadership by the CCP; (b) economic growth; and (c) stability. Within this framework there is plenty of room for disagreements about concrete policies of course; the core question, however, is whether any concrete policy is able to constrain and manage the tensions and weaknesses built into the current system.

First, there is the issue of corruption. Capitalism with Chinese characteristics integrates political and economic power. The political elite have access to state-owned and mixed enterprises and can create their own privately owned firms; in that sense it is a bureaucratic capitalist class open to involvement in the exploitation of public authority for personal gain, which is the standard definition of corruption (Wedeman 2004). Corruption exists at the lower levels as well, of course. According to a 2011 report from China's central bank, up to 18,000 corrupt officials fled the country between 1994 and 2008 taking with them $120 billion in stolen funds (Broadhurst 2013).

The ancient Chinese practice of social networking, *guanxi*, may help get things done but it is also a framework that supports corruption. *Guanxi* means 'drawing on connections in order to achieve favors in personal relations' (Luo 1997: 2). The factions around senior officials are formed around such interpersonal *guanxi* networks. Therefore, the fight against corruption contains a clear political dimension because it pitches competing networks against each other. Current General Secretary Xi Jinping identified corruption and graft as 'pressing problems' in 2012 and pledged to 'make sure the party supervises its own conduct and enforces strict discipline' (cited from Wedeman 2013). But his extended family has also accumulated massive funds in real estate, minerals and other sectors. So the justice conducted by the party itself always runs the risk of being selective: 'Officials who keep on the right side of their superiors and colleagues may engage in large-scale corruption, while other officials may be investigated for lesser infractions because they have fallen afoul of powerful officials' (Lawrence and Martin 2013: 19).

Corruption is endemic in the current Chinese version of bureaucratic capitalism. China ranks 80th in the 2014 Corruptions Perceptions Index, on a par with Senegal and Swaziland. A serious effort to eradicate corruption would require a substantial strengthening of the independence of the courts, a much more independent role for the media and a readiness by the party to accept supervision from the outside; nothing of that is on the cards.

This situation in turn threatens the goal of stability because it potentially undermines legitimacy, that is, the right of the party to rule as seen by the people. This is a difficult subject because there are several sources of legitimacy and exact levels of legitimacy are not easily assessed. Chinese analysts themselves found increasing evidence of a legitimacy deficit or even a crisis, as reported in a large number of party school journals, university journals and public policy journals between 2003 and 2007 (Holbig and Gilley 2010).

One observer recently argued that corruption 'is the biggest threat to social stability and to the Communist Party's durability in power' (Richburg 2014), but that is probably going too far. The legitimacy of the regime rests first and foremost on its ability to deliver economic growth and improved material well-being. As long as it succeeds in this regard, people are willing to accept some level of corruption (Feldman 2013). The problem is that economic growth creates its own set of problems, including inequality, environmental degradation and social instability. I return below to the problems facing the economy.

Another major source of legitimacy is nationalism but, again, this is a double-edged sword. Nationalist sentiment may be a powerful token of social mobilization and cohesion, but it can also grow out of control and become an aggressive and destructive force. This is true in the domestic realm because China is a multi-ethnic state which means that nationalism can be a threat to national unity. And it is true in the international realm, because policies based on nationalism can run astray and lead to unwanted confrontations (Holbig and Gilley 2010: 402).

I have argued that the Chinese leadership is very strong in the sense of enjoying unconstrained power, but this situation contains inbuilt weaknesses that threaten social cohesion. The question is whether undisputed power by the party can continue to be combined with the goals of economic growth and stability.

We turn to the challenges facing the economy; what are the major obstacles to continued economic growth and material betterment for the majority of people? It is clear that China can boast immense economic achievements since the introduction of reforms in the late 1970s. China has indeed grown faster and longer than any economy in history. Annual double-digit growth rates for almost three decades have lifted more than 600 million people out of poverty, a stunning accomplishment. There is also a general consensus that the present time marks the end of the 'hyper-growth' phase.

The early economic reforms emphasized agrarian reform combined with township and village enterprises. Since 1989, however, the accent has been on the big cities with investment in infrastructure, housing and finance combined with a massive influx of foreign direct investment (FDI). It is this strategy of growth which is now facing rising problems. Export growth cannot continue at previous levels; the extremely high investment rate at nearly 50% of GDP between 2007 and 2011 cannot continue (Wagstyl 2012) and the supply of cheap labour is declining.

One problem is unproductive overinvestment; to keep the economy on steam, state-owned enterprises have invested heavily in infrastructure and real estate; key manufactured foods have also been in serious oversupply. China now has a number of 'ghost cities', such as Ordos in innermost Mongolia with 20,000 inhabitants, built for more than a million people. Another problem is the challenge to the export sector. China wants to graduate into high-tech industries but these activities remain heavily dominated by foreign firms (accounting for some 85% of high-tech exports), and the demand from developed countries is slow. China also wants to boost domestic consumption; it has grown, in particular in luxury sectors, but consumption remains at 35% of GDP compared to 70% in the United States so 'rebalancing' is not a success and 'a nasty slump' may be on the cards (Krugman 2013; *The Economist* 2015).

In sum, the economy may look strong but it faces a number of challenges connected to a model of accumulation which is now close to exhausted and severe problems that require major reform. Two fundamental additional downsides of the Chinese model of development are environmental degradation and increasing inequality. China is in an environmental crisis with air pollution, water contamination and land deterioration being the most severe problems. The country accounts for nearly half of the world's consumption of coal; this, together with the rapid process of urbanization, has produced the urban smog problems dubbed the 'airpocalypse' by Beijing residents. In 2015 the city had a concentration of hazardous particles 40 times above the level deemed safe by the World Health Organization (WHO); the WHO air quality standards are met by less than 1% of China's 500 largest cities; according to one 2015 report, breathing Beijing air caused as much damage as smoking 40 cigarettes a day (Ferris 2015). More than 70% of China's rivers and lakes are polluted according to government reports; access to clean water is a major problem both in the cities and in the countryside where an estimated 300–500 million people lack access to piped water (Xu 2014). The water problems are compounded by desertification due to the overuse of chemical fertilizers, over-irrigation and the failure to rotate crops; more than 400 million people are affected. Recent initiatives have taken stronger moves against polluters (Bloomberg 2014) but the problems are huge and China will remain heavily reliant on coal at least until 2030.

Increasing social and income inequality must be expected in a process of rapid economic development but in China the rise in income inequality has been unusually sharp. The standard measure is the Gini coefficient where zero represents complete equality and one represents complete inequality (i.e. all income to one person). The Gini coefficient for China was 0.3 around 1980; by 2013 it had risen to 0.55 (the official statistic is 0.47), reflecting deep divides between rural and urban areas, and between more developed coastal regions and less developed inland regions (Swanbrow 2014). The present number puts China in the most unequal third of all countries.

The measurement of poverty is more complicated because the choice of poverty line is crucial for the result. All studies confirm that there has been a substantial poverty reduction in China. Rural poverty, for example, affected more that 30% of the rural population in 1987; the present figure (2011) is below 5%. The government introduced a new poverty line in 2011; based on this line, the number of rural poor was 122 million that year (Li and Sicular 2014). In total, some 170 million remain under the $1.25-a-day (purchasing power parity (PPP)) international poverty line; 30% of the population was under $2 per day in 2008 (World Bank 2012).

The achievements in poverty reduction are impressive but they are combined with a growing sense of relative deprivation in the countryside and among workers. In many areas, the minimum wage is barely enough for subsistence; even in the industrial zone of Shenzhen, the high cost of living makes it increasingly difficult to attract workers. These developments were behind the concerns expressed by Premier Wen Jiabao already in 2007 where the Chinese growth model was pronounced unstable (income inequality); unbalanced (urban/rural gap), uncoordinated (investment ahead of consumption) and unsustainable (environmental degradation); he repeated those concerns leaving office in 2013 (see Chan 2013).

What are the prospects for the regime to maintain legitimacy and stability in the face of these challenges? The rapid changes in relation to capitalist growth have supported a trend towards pluralism in Chinese society, comprising both old and new groupings. One analysis makes a distinction between 'the folk society' and 'civil society'; the former are groups from family churches, folk religions and so-called *Qigong* (meditation) groups, and a number of ethnic minorities. The latter are the community groups, non-governmental organizations (NGOs), unions, indigenous groups, professional associations, and so on, connected to the general process of modernization; they combine with a proliferation of international NGOs that have become active in China (Xia 2014).

The question is to what extent the regime is losing legitimacy (and stability) in the face of a stronger civil society which is quicker to point out the downsides of the Chinese development model. An evaluation of this question must take the specific Chinese cultural context into account. In the West, social protest is based on the liberties connected with individual rights. In China, social protest is more concerned with the duty of the state to provide for well-recognized rights to a decent livelihood for citizens. That is to say, to Westerners, '*liberty* rather than *livelihood* is the foundation of political morality' (Perry 2008: 44, emphasis in original). In China, it is typically the other way around. It follows that social protest in China is most often *not* transcending the established political system by demanding individual rights and liberties. Protests are sooner conformist in relation to the system; they require the state to live up to its obligations in terms of providing secure livelihood for its citizens (Perry 2008); the intention is not to change the system in a more democratic direction.

At the same time, the state is very active in controlling civil society in China. One observer calls the system 'consultative authoritarianism'; it combines some officially tolerated pluralism with control mechanisms used by the state in order to steer civil society activities in desired directions. In effect, 'this is *not* democratization but rather a sophisticated authoritarianism that uses more indirect tools of social control … [the system] balances the expansion of civil society with more sophisticated state control' (Teets 2013: 36).

So, on one hand, democracy is not on the cards; on the other hand, a balance between state and civil society which rests on control and coercion must be inherently unstable. This is reflected in the expansion of the repressive apparatus in China. In 2013, the domestic security budget of $124 billion exceeded the budget for external security (military spending) standing at $114 billion. The figures demonstrate the importance of domestic threats in the eyes of the regime (Chan 2013).

In sum, China is the leading country among the 'modernizers' because of its tremendous progress in terms of economic growth and social transformation. I have argued that China is not as strong as it seems and that there are political, economic and society elements which threaten social cohesion. The regime is both powerful and resourceful but it incorporates a version of bureaucratic capitalism in which corruption is pervasive and potentially includes the very top leaders in the hierarchy. The economy has been booming, but the current model of accumulation is fraught with tensions to some extent acknowledged by the regime but still awaiting major reform. There has been a 'controlled expansion' of civil society within a framework of 'consultative authoritarianism' but that unstable system has grown within the framework of an increasingly repressive state that is focused on the domestic scene rather than externally when it comes to serious security challenges. China will not fall apart; it remains a robust system in many ways. But the domestic scene will compel China to look inwards, towards its own problems, for a considerable period of time. It will surely look after its regional and global interests, but it will not be a leading player in the construction of world order.

On most fronts, the other modernizing giant, India, faces even more serious problems than does China. India has also had a period of strong economic growth since the liberalizing reforms of the early 1990s. Still, India's GDP is less than half of China's in per capita terms ($3,285 versus $7,945 in $2005 PPP) and poverty is rampant: almost 30% of India's population (300–400 million people) persists in 'severe poverty' (UNDP 2013) and close to half of India's children are undernourished.

India's political system is much more open and transparent than China's, of course. At the same time, India's democracy has traditionally been dominated by a ruling coalition made up of the industrialists, the upper echelons of the bureaucracy and the rich farmers; the power of business groups has grown over the last decades. Most of the time, politics transpires within the limits acceptable to the members of the coalition; major reform or redistribution is not possible against the coalition's interests (Kohli 2012). That preserves a sharp hierarchy in Indian society, exacerbated by the caste system. Corruption and poor governance are major problems; in spite of healthy growth, India has not been able to confront environmental challenges, access to clean water and infrastructural barriers in a way that opens to a more inclusive process of economic development. India's continued lack of socio-political cohesion will force it to focus on domestic issues. In terms of world order, India is a regional player, not a global player.

Russia is, on paper, the richest of the BRICS, with a GDP per capita of $14,461 in $2005 PPP (UNDP 2013). But Russia's wealth is comprehensively dependent on oil and gas, which provides 70% of export earnings and 50% of state revenues. Several years of high energy prices have provided little incentive for reforms to create a broader economic foundation. Vladimir Putin's rule is based on an alliance with the economic elite headed by the oligarchs. It is a patron–client system characterized by endemic corruption. A combination of repression and systematic weakening of public institutions has further undermined the state under Putin's reign (Mendras 2012). (For a discussion of the Ukrainian crisis, see Chapter 6.)

In sum, many modernizing states have made impressive progress when we focus narrowly on economic growth. But taking a closer look, they are also fragile states with severe weaknesses in terms of socio-political cohesion. I have focused on the leading modernizer, China; other major modernizers such as India and Russia have problems as well. To a significant extent, these countries are compelled to look inward, towards their domestic problems. They do play an increasing role internationally as well, but in an ambiguous way: they participate in the existing order, but they are also posing challenges to it, especially in the case of the illiberal states, China and Russia (see Chapters 6 and 7).

Fragile states in the Global South

We come to the states in the Global South for whom the term 'fragile states' was originally intended. These states were fragile at independence and have remained so to the present day. They have not stood still, of course; there has been some economic growth in several countries and also processes of state- and nation-building. Even so, the economic sectors in fragile states remain weak and externally dependent. Governance is poor in that public institutions are ineffective and corrupt; and there is not a strong national community because citizenship is undeveloped (the state has very little to offer) and loyalties are directed towards local ethnic communities rather than towards the state (Brock et al. 2011).

How could fragile states be so weak from the beginning? Most of them were colonies in earlier days; the colonial masters were looking for control and stability rather than for development and societal transformation. They often struck up alliances with some ethnic groups against others so that control could be sustained by local alliance-partners; that was a crucial factor in the shaping of ethnic tensions. Economic undertakings were linked to the needs of the motherland for raw materials and primary goods, not to local concerns. The most developed public institutions were those connected to repression and disciplining of locals; institutions involved in development of any kind were neglected.

At independence the biggest prize for local elites was control of the state apparatus. That gave access to resources, including aid, to presence in international institutions such as the UN system and to new profits from the regulation of transactions across borders. The new local rulers did not face a community of people, a nation, nor could they draw on any legitimacy based on national consent. The rulers were connected to specific ethnic groups: they were the clients for whom the leaders were the patrons and any legitimacy leaders could claim rested on these patron–client relationships (Jackson and Rosberg 1994).

During the Cold War, fragile state leaders could play on the East–West confrontation to secure favourable alliances with external sponsors, even if it was well-known that they were self-seeking autocrats with little concern for the welfare and safety of their populations. The game became more complex when the Cold War ended; at the same time, more domestic groups were mobilized in favour of political and social change.

But leaders were rarely willing to step down and relinquish power, even after several decades in office. Thus came a period of more intense intrastate conflict in fragile states, often combined with the participation of external forces, as it happened in Somalia, Afghanistan, Sudan, Rwanda, Haiti and Liberia. It is this situation which has pushed the international debate about humanitarian intervention and a 'responsibility to protect'; we will return to this issue in Chapter 5.

Most fragile states are in Sub-Saharan Africa, parts of South Asia, Central America and the Middle East. They are vastly different in many respects, of course. Some have broken into the ranks of middle-income countries (e.g. Pakistan, Yemen); some are in the aftermath of very comprehensive foreign intervention (e.g. Afghanistan, Iraq);

others have a very long history of violent domestic conflict (e.g. Democratic Republic of Congo, Central African Republic). Some states appear in the process of moving away from fragile statehood (e.g. Tanzania, Ghana) but there have also been recent, less expected breakdowns (e.g. Syria). Despite the substantial variation, they are all part of the larger group of states in the Global South who remain problematic for the construction of an effective world order.

Conclusion

The idea that all human beings have rights which entitle them to a good life is contained in the UN Charter of 1945. It has been repeated in several declarations since then, most recently in the Millennium Declaration adopted by almost all states in 2000. The ambition of the good life for all raises the bar for world order: a stable balance of power or interstate peace is not enough to make up an effective order; nor is it enough that some people in some states have access to the good life. This high ambition compels us to look inside states in order to ascertain the extent to which liberal optimism about progress is warranted.

The present chapter has surveyed domestic conditions in three major types of state: the advanced capitalist states in the Global North; the modernizing states with focus on China and other BRICS; and the weak states of the Global South. The claim was that all types of state are fragile in the sense that they have problems with sociopolitical cohesion. For that reason, the aspiration of the good life for all is increasingly difficult to meet in most countries.

The group of advanced capitalist states has been through more than three decades of neoliberal globalization. That has disaggregated national economies, uprooted political systems in the direction of political polarization and gridlock, weakened the ties between citizens and the state and paved the way for a vastly reduced social cohesion. The middle class is squeezed from above and from below, and the gulf between winners and losers in the process of globalization has grown much deeper. An alternative model of development is not currently on the cards.

Modernizing states have made great headway in terms of economic growth and, for some, the reduction of abject poverty. Now they face new problems, as exemplified by China. The accumulation model based on export growth is losing steam, environmental degradation and increasing inequality are severe problems and the autocratic political system is bent on preserving strict social control while it must also struggle to maintain legitimacy. China has its own version of winners and losers in the process of globalization and the existing model of development has less and less to offer those on the losing end.

Fragile states in the Global South have not stood still. Some states have had decent growth rates and moved a number of people out of poverty. But they have not got rid of defective political systems, vast socio-political cleavages, and a high degree of external dependence. A number of fragile states have very high levels of domestic violent conflict.

Domestic conditions in sovereign states must deeply affect the prospects for world order. I have argued that the good life for all is hindered by processes leading to more fragile states with less socio-political cohesion. The following chapters will demonstrate how these adverse conditions compel states to prioritize domestic problems and to be more self-interested and less constructive players when it comes to building a well-functioning world order.

3

The Decreasing Importance of Interstate War

Introduction

The world is full of violent conflict today. Civil war rages within a number of the most fragile states, including Syria, Sudan, the Central African Republic, the Congo and elsewhere. In relation to that, there has been a resurgence of international terrorism. But there is one hugely significant area where the level of violent conflict is historically low, namely when it comes to interstate war, that is, war between independent states. Sceptical realists are not impressed by this development; liberal optimists are much more encouraged. I argue that the liberals have the upper hand on this issue.

This chapter makes the claim that interstate war is of significantly decreasing importance in world politics. For realists, the history of world politics is the history of war; their argument is connected to the existence of anarchy among states. The international system is a system of independent political units, the sovereign states. There is no central authority above the states, no overarching government; in that sense, the system is anarchic. Because of anarchy, war is always a possibility and peace must always be momentary.

The Cold War was a temporary relief from this clear and present danger. During that time, there was a significant measure or order, that is, predictability and stability, in international affairs. Two superpowers confronted each other backed by their respective allies; armed with nuclear arsenals they were roughly equal in terms of military power and they were both concerned about MAD (mutually assured destruction) so they were careful not to rock the boat too much. For some realists, that bipolar stability is now in the process of being replaced by multipolar instability of the kind that led to two world wars in Europe; insecurity, disorder and potential war are back. 'We will all soon miss the Cold War', John Mearsheimer proclaimed already in 1990.

Some also claim that the problem is much larger than the change in the distribution of power among states. World politics in the new century is seen as an era of 'turmoil, threats, crisis, and question marks' (Booth and Wheeler 2008: 266). For Booth and Wheeler, this means that the risks and uncertainties wrought by anarchy are more acute and relevant than ever before (Booth and Wheeler 2008: 265, 267).

Against such views, this chapter will argue that important changes are taking place in world politics. Anarchy need not be a condition of imminent war between enemies; it can also be a condition of close cooperation among friends. The threat of imminent war is not something that can pop up everywhere: it is connected to specific conditions of enmity among sovereign states and these specific conditions are becoming much less frequent. It may be that sovereigns in earlier days thought of one thing only: kill or be killed (Hobbes 1946: 101). Today's persons of sovereign authority have a variety of other topics on their agenda; lethal external threat is not even among their primary concerns.

The concrete result of these changes is that war between sovereign states—interstate war—is becoming less and less frequent. Wars are usually defined as conflicts that cause at least 1,000 battle deaths per year; according to this definition the last interstate war was the three-week invasion of Iraq in 2003 (Goldstein and Pinker, 2011). The annual number of interstate conflicts in the new millennium has been between zero and two (Pettersson and Wallensteen 2015). Overall, there is an almost complete absence of interstate war since 1945. Jack Levy calculated that 'the probability of no war occurring between the handful of leading states in the system [for such a long period] is about .005' (Levy 1991: 147; see also Mueller 2009; Vayrynen (ed.) 2005; and Fettweis 2010).

Since anarchy (and the connected security dilemma) is always marshalled as a master explanation for the recurrence of interstate war, I need to explain why that condition is not as unsettling as it may seem to be.

Anarchy and the security dilemma

Anarchy means insecurity; states can never be certain of the intentions of others. The absence of central authority causes states to 'compete for power' (Mearsheimer 2001: 414). They do so in order to survive and remain secure, 'to maintain their territorial integrity and the autonomy of their domestic political order' (Mearsheimer 2001: 31). Power competition ignites the security dilemma: 'Striving to attain security from attack, [states] are driven to acquire more and more power in order to escape the power of others. This, in turn, renders others more insecure and compels them to prepare for the worst. Since none can ever feel entirely secure in such a world of competing units, power competition ensues, and the vicious circle of security and power accumulation is on' (Herz 1950: 157).

Supporters of these views differ in terms of how power-hungry states really are but that is less important here. They converge when it comes to seeing anarchy and the security dilemma as the core logics that lead to war, or always entail the risk of leading to war breaking out among sovereign states. Not only realists, but a large number of observers of other theoretical stripes, including English School theorists, social constructivists, and even Marxists and some liberals, support this basic line of thinking. But they differ substantially when it comes to the extent that anarchy and the security dilemma can be mitigated or even transcended (Booth and Wheeler 2008).

John Herz characterized the 'peculiar nature' of the modern territorial state by the fact that it was 'surrounded with what may be called its "hard shell" which protected it from foreign penetration; it is this factor which rendered it defensible and, at least to some extent, secure in its relation with other units' (Herz 1959: 40). This line of thinking connects directly with Thomas Hobbes. Hobbes taught that security—and ultimately other essential social values—derives from the state. The overriding purpose of the state is to provide a sufficient level of protection from external as well as from internal threats. Without the state, there can be no protection, no security; people will live in a 'state of nature' where anarchy will reign because egoistic humans will be at each other's throats. Life will be 'solitary, poor, nasty, brutish and short' (1946: 129). By contrast, under protection of the state, people can enjoy relative safety and thus pursue happiness and well-being, 'felicity' in Hobbes's term. Instead, anarchy and insecurity are moved to the level of the international system and the relations between sovereign states.

In sum, anarchy and the related security dilemma are not trans-historical entities with universal validity across the ages. They emerge only under specific conditions, because they require the existence of a system of autonomous, sovereign states, where domestic order is provided by the state and where the 'hard shell' of the state protects it from external security threats. For most historical periods before and after the emergence of the modern state, these specific conditions were not met. Consequently, in these historical periods anarchy and the security dilemma were not the major problems in relation to security and the threat of violence. Differently put, domestic security was not provided by the state and the threat from outside was not the major problem for the people.

For the state to be a successful provider of security, a Weberian monopoly of violence is required (Sørensen 2001). In the history of state-making in Europe (and elsewhere), that came relatively late. In its absence, security was supposed to be provided by local rulers, the knights and nobles who had sufficient power to protect their towns, castles or fiefs. But people at the bottom were as much or even more threatened from the rulers within as they were from external dangers. They endured 'the imprisoning of local leaders as hostages to the local community's payment of overdue taxes, the hanging of others who dared to protest, the looting of brutal soldiers on a hapless civilian population, the conscription of young men who were their parent's main hope for comfort in the old age' (Tilly 1990: 99).

In earlier days, then, there was no comprehensive domestic protection of individuals behind a barrier of the 'hard shell' of the state. For a long time, there was no 'peace within' and the violence in the domestic sphere was not qualitatively different from violence inflicted by external parties. Peace was not a core value; the societal elite were rather a warrior class for whom violence and battle was 'the central purpose of its existence' (Porter 1994: 25). Patterns of punishment at the time reflect the low price put on human life. Killing someone could often be absolved by paying a fine, whereas even 'quite trivial' crimes could fetch capital punishment. 'Regarding murder as the peak of the scale of crimes ... and separating murder unequivocally from the killing of alien populations in times of war, are attitudes peculiar to the past two past centuries or so' (Giddens 1992: 187).

In sum, the societal structures of earlier days did not correspond to the conception of domestic order as defined in relation to anarchy and the security dilemma. There was no domestic order in the sense of safety and security provided by political and military elites. On the contrary, those same elites were often the major sources of insecurity and unsafety for ordinary people who then had to look for alternative ways of protection. For example, when Spain increased the burdens of war on Catalonia in the 1640s, demanding increased tax revenues and manpower, the population called upon Louis XIII of France to assume sovereignty over the area (Tilly 1990: 101).

In other words, this was not anarchy and the security dilemma in action because the preconditions of, on one hand, domestic order, protection and safety and, on the other hand, international anarchy and mortal danger from the outside were not present. It was rather a situation of double jeopardy where people and groups had to calculate whether the uncertain protection afforded by the ruler was sufficient to warrant the hardships and insecurity imposed in return.

Anarchy and the security dilemma did emerge in the context of modern, consolidated states, but not to the extent proposed by some observers. As we shall see, there are many states in the present international system where the threat of interstate war is not a major security problem.

The security community of liberal democracies

Advanced liberal states ought to be the exemplary cases for the anarchy and security dilemma logic leading to interstate war. In security terms, these states function as expected by Herz and assumed by Hobbes: they are strong states both in military, economic and other respects, and the accumulation of state power translates meaningfully into security of the realm and protection of the citizens. Externally, however, these states compete with each other.

True to this logic, a number of realist observers predicted the return of intensified power competition among Western allies when the Cold War ended, including European great powers such as Germany and France (Mearsheimer 1991; for an overview, see Fettweis 2004). But power competition and rivalry did not emerge, rather to the contrary: intense cooperation and integration continued to build and develop. The liberal democracies in Western Europe, North

America and Japan make up a security community, that is, a group of states that have become integrated, meaning that 'a sense of community' has been achieved. Members of the community may have disagreements, but they will not get into violent conflict 'but will settle their disputes in some other way' (Deutsch et al. 1957: 5; Adler 2008; Laporte 2012).

In other words, anarchy and the security dilemma have been transcended; interstate war between members of a security community is out of the question. How could that happen? What are the driving forces in the creation of a security community? Before answering this question, we must first note a point made repeatedly by Alexander Wendt: anarchy, the lack of world government, does not compel states to be enemies or rivals in a world where states are always left to their own devices, to self-help. In processes of social interaction, states can develop different identities; they can become friends instead of enemies (Wendt 1992, 1999). The security community has developed shared identities based on norms of non-violence. John Mueller made the point already in 1989 when he ventured that 'at first war becomes rationally unthinkable—rejected because it's calculated to be ineffective and/or undesirable. Then it becomes subrationally unthinkable—rejected not because it's a bad idea but because it remains subconscious and never comes up as a coherent possibility. Peace, in other words, can prove to be habit forming, addictive' (Mueller 1989: 240). This is the optimistic and benign liberal view made against the sceptical realist stance of recurring violent conflict because of anarchy and the security dilemma.

Denmark and Sweden, for example, have been at war 29 times; some claim they hold a world record in that respect. Eleven of those wars were after 1521 (Historienet 2010). In other words, it took a while for war between the two countries to become rationally unthinkable; today war among them is surely subrationally unthinkable.

But how could this change take place? How could a comprehensive security community comprising several of the leading powers of the world emerge from a past of violent conflict and incessant rivalry? The question is important for two reasons. First, it will tell us something about the strength of the security community; sceptics will always say that friendship among states is nothing more than skin-deep not least because uncertainty in anarchy will always make it difficult to get trustworthy information about the motives and intentions of other states (Copeland 2000). But if there is a solid foundation for the security community these concerns can be put to rest. Second, the answer will tell us something about the extent to which the security community will be able to expand, or has already expanded, to other countries.

The original idea of a liberal security community goes back to Immanuel Kant's (1992 [1795]) reflections on a pacific union among liberal republics. Three elements make up the foundation for a pacific union (Doyle 1983; Russett and O'Neal 2001); first, the mere existence of democracies with their culture of peaceful conflict resolution; second, the common moral bonds that are forged between democracies because of their commitment to common values and their cooperation in international institutions; third, the bond of economic interdependence, that is, the democracies' economic cooperation towards mutual advantage.

As for the first point, it sounds immediately plausible that the core of democracy—peaceful resolution of conflict with regard to common rules and norms—would be a basis for peaceful relations between democratic systems. But Kant's reasoning on this point is potentially problematic (Sørensen 2008: 136–43); many systems in earlier phases of democratization have seen more rather than less violent conflict in relation to their political transformations.

So more work needs to be done on the domestic mechanisms of democratic restraint; at the same time, an empirical test of the argument basically supports it. It is difficult to come up with valid examples of war between consolidated democracies (for the debate see White 2005). It is a complex task to specify the exact domestic mechanisms that lead to peace (Hegre 2014) yet the general claim of a relationship between consolidated democracies and peaceful relations is difficult to reject. (At the same time, several democracies have gone to war against non-democracies since the end of the Cold War; see Geis, Brock and Müller 2006.)

The second point moves attention from the domestic scene in democracies to the relations between them. It is clear that democracies support common values and that they work closely together in international institutions. Values of freedom of expression and open communication promote mutual understanding internationally; governments resting on a popular mandate invite more trust and confidence compared to autocracies that are in a state of potential violent conflict with their own people.

The United States was the leading architect behind the setting up of institutional cooperation among the liberal democracies after 1945; it was also the United States that pushed for a tight institutional relationship among the former adversaries in Europe. Integrating a democratized Germany firmly into a Western alliance and network of institutional commitments was an important part of this undertaking. Integrating Japan into the liberal order was another important element. Even if the United States did not make the same supra-institutional commitments that came to characterize the European Union (where in some areas, the EU institutions have the right to write rules for member states), it did set up a system of bargaining, consultation and coordination with the other liberal democracies, enabled by a network of international institutions (Ikenberry 2011).

Close cooperation between liberal democracies is a move away from anarchy and the security dilemma. Realists claim that states want to maintain 'the autonomy of their domestic political order' (Mearsheimer 2001: 31). States involved in close institutional cooperation clearly move away from that principle; they commit themselves to networks of governance across borders, some of them with supranational elements. The 'hard shell' of the state is gone, replaced by a variety of relationships between what used to be insiders and outsiders. Differently put, the preconditions for interstate war have been replaced by preconditions for peaceful relations.

The third element in the security community is ties of economic interdependence. What Kant called 'the spirit of commerce' means possibility for mutual economic gain from involvement in economic exchange. Today's economic flows represent a much higher level of integration between countries than earlier. Traditional trade is arm's-length exchange between independent firms of different national economies, what is called 'shallow integration'. Contemporary flows represent a high level of 'deep integration', that is, economic activity organized in a cross-border system by transnational corporations who carve up the production process among locations optimized in terms of market proximity, labour cost and so on.

The Bretton Woods system created a political framework that liberalized economic relations especially among liberal states in Western Europe, North America and Japan. High levels of trade to GDP and high levels of deep integration characterize these countries in particular but are also rapidly spreading to many other countries (Nayar 2003).

Economic development pushes changes in the relative value of territory. In advanced economies, economic returns depend less and less on the possession of territory, because land is no longer the decisive factor in production. Technological, managerial, scientific and other competences matter more. It is more profitable to exploit those skills in relationships with other countries than it is to pursue territorial gain. The 'trading state' option becomes progressively more attractive than the classic 'territorial' option; Japan and Germany have prospered peacefully after World War II (Rosecrance 1986: 16; 1999).

Still, economic interdependence in earlier days was not enough to ensure peace. There was a significant degree of interdependence among the major contenders in World War I (Copeland 2015), but today's economic interdependence in the liberal security community is much higher and qualitatively deeper than earlier. Even the combined force of the three Kantian elements presented here does not add up to an ironclad guarantee that members of the security community will never again go to war against each other. There continues to be a lively debate about the prospects for a peaceful liberal security community (e.g. Hegre 2014; Schneider 2014; Dafoe, Oneal and Russett 2013; Gartzke and Weisiger 2013).

What can be said with utmost certainty is that such war cannot take place in absence of dramatic changes in the conditions discussed here. Should countries in the security community engage in war, they would first have to cast themselves as enemies; otherwise the choice of war which is now subrationally unthinkable cannot be brought on the table again. In other words, the identities and interests of states would have to move in dramatically different directions.

For that to happen, the conditions which underpin the security community would have to change for the worse. In one or more countries democracy would have to deteriorate towards autocracy, institutional cross-border cooperation would be built markedly down and interdependencies would be seriously reduced. There are no examples of such a development within the security community. The nearest possible candidate would be the cooling down of the transatlantic relationship after September 11. US policies became more unilateral, culminating in the National Security Strategy of 2002 that endorsed the need for pre-emptive action. Several European states were against this development, but the quarrels never went very deep. There was no serious breakdown of transatlantic institutions. Dense interdependence in economic and other areas and common basic (liberal) values were not seriously affected by the disagreements. The quarrels are now over but the security community was never in serious danger (Sørensen 2008b).

The more interesting question, then, concerns the extent to which the mechanisms leading to peaceful relations in the liberal security community have spread to other states in the international system that are not consolidated democracies.

Modernizing states and interstate war

In the liberal security community anarchy has been transcended and former enemies and rivals are now friends; interstate war among these states is out of the question. What about the modernizing states and the non-democratic great powers, China and Russia?

The first relevant issue concerns the global strength of the 'liberal factors' identified in relation to the liberal security community. If liberal democracy, common values plus institutional cooperation, and economic interdependence are spreading to the entire system, the basis for a global security community ought to be in the process of emerging.

Let us begin with democracy. On first glance, it looks very good. There were 20 countries ruled by democratic regimes in 1946; by 2015 there were 88. But there are two problems here; the first concerns measurement: what does it take to be a democracy? The second was mentioned earlier: how much democracy is enough for the pacifying effect to kick in? Democracy measurement is an industry of its own (Coppedge et al. 2011), yet there is basic consensus that democracy is not a dichotomous concept (i.e. countries are either democracies or not) but a continuous one where countries have varying degrees of democracy. A relaxed definition gives us between 90 and 118 democracies in the world in 2013 (Freedom House 2013); a very demanding definition results in merely 25 democracies (*Economist* 2012).

As for the second problem, I have argued elsewhere (Sørensen 2008a) that the peaceful behaviour of democracies is predicated on the existence of a democratic culture concerning peaceful resolution of conflict. It is clear that the emergence of such a culture is a longer-term process which is only in its beginning with the opening phase of regime change and early elections. The good news is that in spite of this, states in early phases of democratization—as well as non-democratic states—have not engaged in interstate war. But it leaves us with a puzzle: why the pervasive interstate peace in spite of a large number of relatively shallow democratizations and the persistence of many non-democratic regimes?

This takes us to the next element in the liberal peace, common values and institutional cooperation. The short answer to the question is that even in spite of a less developed democratic culture, both new democracies and even non-democratic states do respect basic international norms and they do engage in institutional cooperation. The foundational norm here is article 2(4) of the UN Charter: 'All members shall refrain in their international relations from the threat or use of force against the territorial integrity and political independence of any state, or in any manner inconsistent with the Purposes of the United Nations.' This amounts to a territorial integrity norm: the proscription that force should not be used to alter interstate boundaries.

Mark Zacher records the development of this norm in his detailed analysis (Zacher 2001). It emerged after World War I in the League Covenant; its broader acceptance began with the UN Charter in 1945 but a comprehensive and strong backing for the norm came only in the 1960s and 1970s. Since 1976, Zacher noted in 2001, 'no major cases of successful territorial aggrandizement have occurred' (Zacher 2001: 237).

Even if this is the case, a number of interstate territorial aggressions have taken place since 1946; Zacher counts 40 up to the year 2000. Most of them did not result in territorial changes, but some of them did, including the creation of Bangladesh, of the Turkish Republic on Cyprus and the unification of Vietnam; the case of Russia and Crimea will be taken up in Chapter 5.

Institutional cooperation is a move away from the uncertainty created by anarchy. Institutions provide a forum for negotiation and exchange of information. Institutional cooperation also improves the possibilities for governments to monitor each other and thus to make credible commitments. It has increased dramatically over time. One analysis counts an 83% increase in the number of IGOs (intergovernmental organizations) between 1965 and 2005 (COW 2015). But this is only the tip of the iceberg, of course, and the sheer number of IGOs is not the most important part of the story.

Many IGOs have expanded their roles and have become increasingly important for member states.

As for economic interdependence, it has grown dramatically. Since the early 1980s, world trade has grown much faster than world output and international financial flows have grown even faster than trade. World trade almost tripled between 1980 and 2002, while output doubled (Dean and Sebastia-Barriel 2004). The growth in trade does not take place according to the classic notion of comparative advantage where countries with different factor endowments develop trade. Trade primarily takes place between developed economies: 80% of OECD trade, for example, is with other OECD economies. Intra-industry specialization, productivity gains and low transportation costs are major determinants of this trade growth (Dean and Sebastia-Barriel 2004).

At the same time, almost the entire world, including the non-democratic great powers, are now committed to market economies with private property and intensive participation in cross-border economic exchange. China is of course the primary example of these developments. When the Deng Xiaoping reforms were announced in 1978, China accounted for less than 1% of global trade. By 2010, China accounts for about 10% of global imports and exports, making it the world's largest commodity exporter, and second largest commodity importer (Li 2010). Around the world, then, economies are becoming more and more integrated into networks of economic exchange. Huge differences of course remain among them; the extension of capitalism to a global scale must mean that intra-capitalist variation increases (Buzan and Lawson 2014; see also Chapter 6).

Irrespective of these differences, the commitment to capitalism does create a substantial obligation to the institutions and the common rules and norms that are required for the capitalist system to function. China became a member of the WTO in 2001, Russia in 2012. The participation in a functioning global network of production, trade and finance is now a precondition for growth and prosperity in most countries. Opting out of the system, or even seriously disturbing it, can have seriously negative economic and social consequences.

Overall, then, the liberal factors are weaker when it comes to the entire system, including modernizing states. Democracy is not firmly established in many countries, nor is a democratic culture of peaceful conflict resolution firmly in place. But there is a high level of adherence to basic international norms, including the territorial integrity norm. Institutional cooperation has increased vastly and we are in a world of market economies participating intensely in economic globalization.

Is that enough to make interstate war obsolescent? Rosecrance claimed that among trading states, 'the incentive to wage war is absent' (Rosecrance 1986: 24). Mueller finds that 'war is unlikely if countries take prosperity as their chief goal *and* if they come to believe that trade is the best way to achieve that goal' (Mueller 2009: 317). It is clear that the level of community discussed here is lower than the level of community instituted in the liberal security community. The latter is a thick community, based on common values, institutional cooperation and interdependence. The systemic community is a thin community, where common values are less developed, as are institutional cooperation and interdependence.

But significant changes have taken place. The non-democratic great powers may not be best friends of the liberal–democratic West, but nor are they any longer direct enemies. They are rivals who may become friends but might also revert to become enemies.

Domestic anarchy in fragile states

In relation to fragile states in the Global South, anarchy has been transcended in the way that the international society adopted new norms which guaranteed the continued right to independence of fragile states. The problems they face concern domestic conflict, not interstate war.

Fragile states in the Global South are in a peculiar situation as seen from the perspective of anarchy and the security dilemma. They are very weak entities in political, economic and social terms. This is in no small measure due to a history of external domination. Most fragile states emerged from a colonial period which profoundly influenced every aspect of politics and society. In Africa, the colonial administrators became the ultimate source of power; local leaders had to obey even when their own people objected. At independence, an authoritarian and patriarchal form of government was bequeathed to the Africans, within territories demarcated by outsiders with no regard for people on the ground. The export-dependent mono-crop economies continued to be deeply reliant on the world market that quickly became the primary source of income (Brock et al. 2011).

According to the logic of anarchy and the security dilemma, sovereign states survive the international competition for power because they grow strong and improve their capacities for defending themselves against outside threat. Under conditions of anarchy, says Kenneth Waltz, states are simply compelled to emulate the more successful states in the system. That is their only option; the alternative is to 'fall by the wayside' (Waltz 1979: 18). Just like successful firms in the marketplace, states who prosper will share certain characteristics while those who lack them will go bankrupt.

But this logic clearly does not apply when it comes to fragile states. They are not required to enter into a competitive struggle for self-help and survival. They do not survive or persist because of their strength or their capability to compete successfully. For them, the international system is not one of insecurity and potential threat from strong states. If it were, they would have been swallowed by stronger states a long time ago. In short, anarchy and the security dilemma do not, in significant measure, pertain to fragile states.

What has taken its place? The short answer is: a profound change of norms in the international system in the context of decolonization after 1945. Before that time, colonialism, defined as 'control by one power of a dependent area or people' (Merriam Webster Online), was a major institution in international society. But it quickly became an 'absolute wrong: an injury to the dignity and autonomy of those peoples and of course a vehicle for their economic exploitation and oppression' (Jackson 1993: 48). After the war, the right of self-determination for colonies became the accepted international norm very fast. Ideas about equality had grown stronger during the war and ties to the colonies had weakened. Colonial dependencies had aided the allied war effort and looked for something in return. Asian and African states that achieved early independence started pushing for comprehensive decolonization. The new global distribution of power did not favour the old colonial motherlands. By 1960 the UN General Assembly declared that 'all peoples have the right to self-determination' (Resolution 1514).

In short, after independence, post-colonial states and regimes were not subjected to an anarchic international system and a virulent security dilemma. They did not face external threats that could amount to a matter of life and death for the state or the regime; instead, they were protected by new international norms which confirmed the right to independence and sovereignty, no matter how fragile they were ('inadequacy of political, economic, social or educational prepared-ness should never serve as a pretext for delaying independence' said UN Resolution 1514 of 1960). Consequently, the threat of interstate war connected with anarchy and the security dilemma was not a major concern of the newly independent fragile states, and it is not their major concern today.

This does not mean that newly sovereign fragile states are all of a sudden masters of their own destinies. Their political, economic and social weakness makes them highly dependent on the international society and in many cases, including Afghanistan, the Congo and Haiti, external aid makes up an important part of the state's resources. Both superpowers competed for influence in fragile states during the Cold War and to some extent such competition continues with the participation of new players, not least China.

Yet the overall point stands: interstate war is no major concern of fragile states because they are protected by a new normative frame-work of the international society: old-fashioned, imperialistic take-overs of fragile states are out of the question. Colonialism was a primary institution of international society up to 1945 (Buzan 2004: 181). Today, that institution has been replaced by the principles of self-determination and popular sovereignty.

Unfortunately, this did not—in most cases—bring security, safety and other basic social values to the peoples of the former colonies. The vast majority of post-independence political leaders were not enthusiastic about building strong and effective states because such institutions could be a real threat to their firm grip on state power. At the same time, the leaders did not face a nation, a community of peo-ple with a common culture and a history of integration. They faced a divided community with deep ethnic, racial, religious and other divi-sions. The connections between leaders and people were connections of clan, kinship and ethnic affiliation. That opened the way to clien-telism, patronage and nepotism.

It may be the case that the pursuit of self-interest by state elites has some positive spin-off in terms of security and order because state leaders need some basic support to remain in power but the trajectory of fragile statehood demonstrates that such self-interest did not solve the problem. Most fragile state governments are contested, illegitimate and not reliable sources of protection for the citizens. On the contrary, such governments are major sources of threat and insecurity.

Fragile states, then, do not have a major problem with interstate war. What they face instead are violent domestic conflicts which can sometimes be with external involvement (as presently in Syria) because outside parties have an interest in the outcome; there have also been a number of irredentist and secessionist conflicts in relation to fragile states (Ambrosio 2001). In any case, the root causes of conflict in these states are not related to anarchy and the security dilemma.

The role of nuclear weapons

According to several observers, nuclear weapons make a great contribution to peace among nations. That is because they make war between nuclear powers irrational; such a war cannot be won in any meaningful sense of the word since both sides would stand to suffer irredeemable destruction. Kenneth Waltz found that 'nuclear weapons have drastically reduced the probability of [a war] being fought by the states that have them' (Waltz 1990: 745). Therefore, 'the probability of war between America and Russia or between NATO and the Warsaw Pact is practically nil precisely because … the fear of escalation to general nuclear war keeps it that way' (Art and Waltz 1983: 28).

The problem is that other factors play a role in the absence of war among the great powers and that makes it necessary to evaluate the relative importance of nuclear weapons. In addition to the liberal elements already discussed earlier, it is possible that the costs of comprehensive conventional warfare are more than enough to deter a choice of the war option. Nuclear weapons or not, the destructions of World War II were sufficient to opt for deterrence in the post-war world. Alexander Haig made the point in 1982: 'The catastrophic consequences of another world war—with or without nuclear weapons—make deterrence our highest objective and our only military strategy' (Quoted from Mueller 1995: 64). A year earlier Michael Mandelbaum argued that 'the tanks and artillery of the Second World War and especially the aircraft that reduced Dresden and Tokyo to rubble might have been terrifying enough by themselves to keep the peace between the United States and the Soviet Union' (1981: 21).

At the same time, the building of nuclear arsenals has been accompanied by the emergence of a particularly strong international norm which sees the first use of nuclear weapons as an 'unthinkable' option (Schelling 2000). This 'nuclear taboo' is 'a prohibition, it refers to danger, and it involves expectations of awful or uncertain consequences or sanctions if violated' (Tannenwald 2005: 9). The norm emerged in the 1950s helped by policies that established nuclear weapons as weapons of a special kind that should be handled separately from conventional weapons. The taboo was institutionalized in multilateral agreements and in bilateral arms control compacts between the United States and the Soviet Union. The ABM treaty of 1972 formalized consent about the no-first-use of nuclear weapons, making them weapons for deterrence and not for use (Tannenwald 2008).

The doomsday clock reflects the relative success of the taboo. The Bulletin of Atomic Scientists has published a 'Doomsday clock' since 1947, indicating the proximity of a threat of comprehensive nuclear war. The clock remains concerned about the danger from nuclear weapons, but since 2007 it has included the perils of climate change and new technologies in other domains in its assessment. The 2014 report from the Bulletin put the clock at five minutes to midnight; it continued to be concerned about the nuclear threat but even more so about climate change.

With a strong nuclear taboo there is a contribution to peace from nuclear weapons. But on one hand, there is the question of how robust that peace is: being based on deterrence, the underlying assumption is that war may be a possibility; that is, nuclear weapons alone are not enough to create a security community with states that are friends instead of potential enemies. On the other hand, there is a possible element of instability: the agreement that nuclear war must and will be avoided at all cost can open to hostilities at lower levels because the parties are certain that the nuclear option is off the table (Jervis 2002).

In sum, nuclear weapons support peace because they help create caution and prudence. President Kennedy knew that 'stupidities, individual idiosyncrasies, misunderstandings, and personal complexes of inferiority and grandeur' played an enormous role in the outbreak of World War I; he had taken that lesson from Barbara Tuchman's book *The Guns of August*. In the context of the October 1962 Cuban Missile Crisis he was determined not to become a similar character in 'a comparable book about this time: "The Missiles of October"' (quoted from Mueller 1995: 73).

A total of 190 states have joined the treaty on non-proliferation of nuclear weapons (NPT). Four states have not joined: India, Israel, Pakistan and Sudan; North Korea withdrew in 2003. There are great worries that 'rogue states', such as Iran, or international terrorists, might acquire nuclear weapons. Concerning terrorists, the worries appear to be vastly exaggerated (Lieber and Press 2013); it is highly unlikely that terrorists can get access to and will use weapons of mass destruction (Pearlstein 2004). As for Iran, an agreement has been made with the great powers to restrict the country's nuclear programme. Further, in the unlikely event that it would acquire and eventually use the bomb, what can it accomplish 'except possibly the destruction of its own system?' (Shelling 2005).

Another rogue state, North Korea, obtained a nuclear capability some years ago; nothing much happened (Pinker 2011: 375). 'What nuclear weapons have been used for, effectively, successfully, for sixty years has not been on the battlefield nor on population targets: they have been used for influence' (Shelling, Nobel lecture 2005).

A complex peace: The problem of overdetermination, ideas, structures and causation

The steep decline of interstate war is overdetermined: several different forces or elements are relevant for understanding this development. A major debate about the primary generator of peace is between idealists and structuralists. The former believe in the autonomous force of ideas and give credit to ideational change; the latter emphasize change in material and social structures. Idealists focus on actors and changes of their ideas; structuralists focus on material and social contexts that compel actors towards certain forms of action. This section will argue that the separation between actors/ideas and social and material structures is misguided and not helpful in understanding interstate peace. The two sides are part of a totality, a social whole, and we need to focus on the interaction between them in order to better understand the emergence of interstate peace.

A principal representative of the idealist view is John Mueller. Over several books and articles since the mid-1980s he has consistently argued that 'war is merely an idea, an institution that has been grafted onto human existence ... And the institution may be in pronounced decline, as attitudes towards it have changed, roughly following the pattern according to which slavery became discredited and then obsolete' (Mueller 2009: 320). The promotion of war aversion has taken place for more than a hundred years, according to Mueller (1995: 152). The anti-war idea entrepreneurs sought to demonstrate the futility of war and the advantages of peace; they were able to point to the benefits of peace in nineteenth-century Europe, but it took World War I for people to accept the message. The primary responsibility for World War II rests with Hitler; after that war, the peace lesson of World War I had finally been 'massively enhanced' also in Germany, Japan and Italy (Mueller 2004: 65).

According to Mueller, this dramatic change of ideas from war mongering to war aversion took place in the absence of any structural change whatsoever: '... without creating an effective world government or system of international law; without modifying the nature of the state or the nation-state; without expanding international trade, interdependence, or communication; ... without enveloping the earth in democracy or prosperity ... without altering the international system; without establishing security communities; ... and without doing much of anything about nuclear weapons' (Mueller 2009: 320).

The problem with this kind of thinking is that it creates an artificial division between actors and their ideas, on one hand, and social structures and material circumstances, on the other. Ideas do not emerge out of the blue; they are conditioned by social and material structures. The abolishment of slavery was part of a broader movement towards modernity, not a lonesome idea; the iPhone or Google's search engine could not have been invented in the nineteenth century, the technological context was not in place. And sure enough, Mueller submits that social and material circumstances such as the experience of World War I did heavily influence ideas of war aversion and peace. But curiously, he rejects that other social and material circumstances, such as democracy, economic interdependence, international institutions or nuclear weapons, had any influence whatsoever on ideas about peace.

Mueller is so determined to give priority to the autonomous role of ideas that he severely weakens his own argument. On one hand, if ideas stand alone in explaining peace, war could be back soon, because ideas can change very quickly. Mueller admits as much; the demise of war 'need not be permanent' because inventive entrepreneurs 'might be able to revive the idea' (Mueller 1995: 153). The spectre of great power war could return in the blink of an eye; some observers have indeed made just that claim in the context of the Ukrainian 2014 crisis (Roberts 2014).

By contrast, if Mueller admitted that ideas have consequences in terms of changing social and material structures, he could appreciate the embedding of war aversion in those structures and reversals at short notice would be much less likely. Furthermore, Mueller's argument compels him to reify social and material structures. He argues that anarchy remains in place because there is no world government and that states have not changed (Mueller 2009: 317). That is, when war aversion is merely an idea independent of structural context, one is bound to argue that only ideas have changed while structures remain in place. But since structures and agents do not exist in isolation (Hay 2001), such an argument cannot get off the ground. And sure enough, elsewhere Mueller submits that it is merely in a formal sense that anarchy remains in place (i.e. there is no world government) (Mueller 1995: 39). In other words, the change of ideas surely plays a role for the move towards interstate peace but it does so in a close interplay with changes in social and material structures.

The one-sided idealist view is matched by an equally one-sided structuralist view which is of course also deeply problematic. This is the neorealist position according to which war among states is always potentially imminent because of anarchy which must involve self-help and power competition. In John Mearsheimers formulation: 'The distribution of material capabilities among states is the key factor for understanding world politics. For realists, some level of security competition among great powers is inevitable because of the material structure of the international system' (Mearsheimer 1995: 91).

On this view, ideas and discourses don't really matter at all, because 'the system forces states to behave according to the dictates of realism, or risk destruction' (Mearsheimer 1995: 91). Ironically, Mearsheimer also reifies structure: having decided that structural change is out of the question and that ideas cannot influence structures, we are left with nothing but the war option. But this is clearly wrong; ideas as well as structures can change; states can become friends instead of enemies (Sørensen 2008). And realists themselves admit that the existence of nuclear weapons makes a difference in terms of opting for peace.

In sum, structures, on one hand, and agents and their ideas, on the other, interact and it is misleading to artificially isolate them from each other, just as it is misleading to claim that they do not affect each other. This view of interstate peace as something emerging from a social whole which includes ideas as well as structures, and something which is both a dependent and an independent variable, is surely a step forward but it will not solve the problems of overdetermination and of clarifying causal relationships. Both agents and their ideas and several structural elements play a role in the emergence of interstate peace; once established, peace surely has positive feedback effects on the structures and the agents which helped bring it about in the first place.

Conclusion

We return to the debate between sceptical realists and optimistic liberals. War among states is ubiquitous says realist Kenneth Waltz in his analysis of the causes of war; attempts to eliminate war 'have brought little more than fleeting moments of peace' (Waltz 1959: 1). The history of states and the history of war are weaved together (Tilly 1990) and the received wisdom is that this will always be the case. But states can change and there is no law built into history which stipulates that states must always go to war with each other. What supposedly must lead to war among states— anarchy and the security dilemma—are historical constructs and it is only under specific conditions that they are active in ways that can lead to war.

Even when there is anarchy in the sense that there is no world government, states can become friends and live peacefully together in security communities; and they can change international norms to the effect that territorial conquest such as colonialism is made illegitimate and replaced by other norms that confirm the right to independence of states, even very weak ones.

This is exactly what has happened since 1945. The liberal democracies in Western Europe, North America and Japan have built a security community and war among them is out of the question. At the same time, colonialism is no longer an accepted institution in international society. Postcolonial states may be weak and fragile but they are protected by strong international norms which secure their independence.

Modernizing states, including the non-democratic great powers, are not members of the liberal security community, but there is peace among them anyway. First, there is a high degree of respect for the territorial integrity norm, that is, the prohibition of the use of force to alter interstate boundaries. Second, they participate strongly in networks of economic interdependence and institutional cooperation. Third, there is a common commitment to the capitalism market economy including its rules and norms. Finally, the nuclear arsenals of great powers support peace in the sense that they help create caution and prudence.

In some parts of the international system, then, there is a stable, unbreakable peace among members of the liberal security community. In other parts of the system there is a thinner, but still robust peace based on international norms, institutional collaboration, economic integration and nuclear weapons.

So interstate war is of significantly decreased importance; peace is overdetermined, based both on social and material structures and on the ideas and convictions of actors. That does not mean it can never be broken; just as there are no laws of history guaranteeing recurring war among states there are no laws guaranteeing permanent peace. But it is a fairly solid peace which means that it cannot be undone in the short and medium term; it would have to involve a process of breaking down the social and material structures which support peace. It would also have to involve abandonment of the conviction that peaceful relations are in actors' primary interest. The current conflict in Ukraine will not lead to a great power war (see Chapter 5) but it is an example of a situation where institutional cooperation, economic interdependence and mutual trust among the great powers is eroding.

In the larger debate among optimistic liberals and sceptical realists, this is a development favouring liberal optimism, even if realists themselves point to the peace-enhancing role of nuclear weapons. But liberal optimism must not be exaggerated. The decreasing importance of interstate war does not pave the way for a peaceful and harmonious world. Fragile states in the Global South may be protected by norms of respect for self-determination and independence but they are plagued by serious domestic violent conflict. Some conflict is also looming in the near-abroads of the nonliberal great powers, Russia and China. States must also face new risks connected with international terrorism, economic crisis, transnational crime and environmental problems. Still, a consensus on the futility of interstate war, especially among great powers, is a big development. No more Sommes and Verduns; no more Stalingrads; no more Nankings.

4

The Distribution of Power and World Order

Introduction

The two previous chapters have outlined the basic international and domestic parameters for the present world order. Interstate war is becoming increasingly obsolete; at the same time most states have major problems with socio-political cohesion leading towards increased fragility. This chapter is about the third and final framework condition in the present study of world order: the distribution of power in today's world. The issue is important because a stable and effective world order needs to be backed by sufficient economic, military and other forms of power.

Under present international and domestic conditions, where does power lie in the international system and what are the implications for world order? These are core contested issues and there is little agreement about them. On one hand, power has been a central concern of IR at least since Thucydides and Machiavelli; on the other hand, concepts of power have seen systematic scrutiny only over the last several decades (Berenskoetter and Williams (eds) 2007; Acharya 2014). Since nothing of this has led to any consensus about the nature of power and its current distribution among actors, the best way of proceeding is to sketch the major positions and define the views of the present analysis on that basis. Realists tend to focus on the concentration of material power in the hands of strong states; liberals tend to underline the dispersion of a variety of different forms of power in the hands of many actors. Both positions contain insights and shortcomings; on that basis, I will present my own view.

Power, according to the most popular distinction, is what one actor (A) has when she gets another actor (B) to do something he would not otherwise do (Dahl 1957). This is power in action: in a conflict between two actors the most powerful prevails. It is clear that power may be at work even when there is no clear conflict on the table. The actor that controls the agenda may prevent issues from coming on the table at all. That is a form of structural power: the ability to define the rules within which others operate (Strange 1988: 24). Structural power often goes even further because it also operates in absence of any recognized conflict: powerful actors are capable of setting the frameworks and shaping the structures for interaction with the less powerful; that is what Steven Lukes (2005) calls domination.

This is the background for a series of debates about power in IR. Examples include Michael Barnett and Raymond Duvall (2005) who suggest a taxonomy of four fields of power; David Baldwin (1979) discusses the relationship between potential and realized power and argues for the importance of focusing on the scope, weight and domain of power, a theme followed up by Joseph Nye (2002). Barry Buzan (2004b) explores the issue of polarity (who are the great powers and superpowers) in the post-Cold War world and argues that this has to be studied in its interaction with identity; the contributions in Berenskoetter and Williams (eds 2007) bring together a variety of different theoretical perspectives on power (see also Acharya 2014; Weber and Jentleson 2010).

Against this background, it is perhaps no surprise that the debate about power in the post-Cold War international system is characterized by some confusion. It is sufficient here to mention two extreme views: one argues for the total concentration of power; the other argues for the total dispersion of power. The former view emerged strongly when the Cold War ended and only one superpower was left on the stage; it appeared a logical assumption that power in the system was now extremely concentrated in that leading state. Historian Paul Kennedy spoke of an 'enormous power gap' between the United States and the rest of the world: 'Nothing has ever existed like this disparity of power; nothing. I have returned to all of the comparative defence spending and military personnel statistics over the past 500 years that I compiled in *The Rise and Fall of the Great Powers* and no other nation comes close' (Kennedy 2002). Six years later, Stephen Brooks and William Wohlforth found that the assessment remained true: 'Even when capabilities are understood broadly to include economic, technological, and other wellsprings of national power, they are concentrated in the United States to a degree never before experienced the history of the modern system of states' (2008: 27).

As to the latter view, Susan Strange argued already in 1996 that the domain of state authority was shrinking because states were losing power, especially to markets; the state was becoming 'just one source of authority among several, with limited powers and resources' (Strange 1996: 73). Sociologist Jan Aart Scholte speaks of power being dispersed among 'a patchwork of actors in a multipolar system' (2013). This view is taken even further in the recent book by Moisés Naím introduced earlier (see Chapter 1). He argues that 'micropowers are beating the megaplayers'; power is shifting downwards because 'people are harder to control and more apt to question authority' (2013b: 1).

These contrasting positions can be better understood by placing them in their appropriate theoretical context. The concentration view draws on a realist understanding of power which emphasizes material power in a hostile international environment. The dispersion view draws on a liberal/constructivist understanding that underlines a social/non-material conception of power in a cooperative international environment. Both views have a point but none of them are fully accurate depictions of power in the present order. This argument is developed in what follows.

Concentration of power: Material power and anarchy

Realist analysis is based on the assumption that the international system is made up of sovereign states (we need not be concerned with the different strands of realist analysis here). States control the means of violence; they set the rules of the game for all other actors, including corporations, individuals and organizations. The international system is anarchic (see Chapter 3); anarchy means insecurity. States cannot be sure of each other's intentions. In order to defend themselves, states need power, especially military power, but also size (population and territory), as well as economic, technological and other capabilities.

This is the thinking behind the view which gives priority to sovereign states and in particular to material capabilities as the major source of state power. States are the core units that make up the international system. The military power of states is particularly important because that is what is put to use should a violent conflict erupt, but military strength requires other material power resources as well, including economic capacity. On this view a strong power is a country with 'substantial industrial and military potential' (Posen and Ross 1996-7: 17). John Mearsheimer emphasizes military strength when he claims that 'a state's effective power is ultimately a function of its military forces ... because force is the *ultima ratio* of international politics' (Mearsheimer 2001: 55–6).

Realists are well aware that there is a difference between possessing, for example, a strong military capability, on one hand, and putting it to effective use in specific situations, on the other. But they downplay this distinction because of the danger inherent in anarchy. When violent confrontations are always a possibility, the ultimate measure of power is the capacity to prevail (war-winning capacity) and that must give top priority to military and economic capabilities. Furthermore, sovereign states are considered to be unitary and coherent actors, rather like the billiard balls rolling on the table that is the international system. They are unitary in the sense that state leaders speak and act on behalf of their respective states. They are coherent in the sense that the power of the government and the power of the state as a territorial unit with population and resources are seen as one and the same thing. State leaders/governments are always under pressure from the system because anarchy means insecurity and insecurity can lead to violent conflict with fatal consequences for the state. In such conditions of imminent conflict, it is simply assumed that state leaders will be able to put the military and other material resources of the state to good use. In other words, putting capabilities to use is not a problem and therefore we may focus on the material capabilities of states in our analysis of who has power.

This view of power, then, compels us to focus on the material power resources of states in order to discover who has power in the international system. Particular attention should be paid to military power but other power resources, including economic capability, are important too. If we follow this view, are those realists who claim a colossal concentration of material power in the hands of the United

States then right? The short answer would appear to be 'yes' if we look at some of the most important numbers.

- Military expenditure: if we take the 15 states with highest military expenditures in 2013, the US share was 37%, China's 11%, Russia's 5%, while each of the remaining 12 countries accounted for less than 4% of the total (SIPRI 2013). That is to say, the United States is way ahead of everybody else in terms of military expenditure; at the same time, this expenditure amounts to only 3.8% of the US GDP. In 1988, the United States spent 5.7% of GDP; during the Vietnam War it was nearly 10% (Brown 2013: 36). This overwhelming military capability is generally agreed to grant the United States command of the global commons, the sea, air and space 'that belongs to no one and provide access to much of the globe' (Posen 2003).
- Economic capability: the US share of world GDP in PPP terms was 19.3% in 2013. The Chinese share stood at 15.4% (Quandl 2014). In per capita terms, the picture is much different of course: the United States stands at US$53,101 per capita and China at US$9,844; that is to say, the Chinese per capita GDP is less than 19% of the level of the United States.
- Innovation and technology: US expenditure on R&D vastly outnumbers that of any other nation in absolute terms ($408 billion, PPP in 2010, see NCSES 2013). As a percentage of GDP (2.81) the figure is less impressive; the numbers for such countries as Japan, South Korea and Finland are higher, though not for China (1.77). Yet the United States again takes the lead when it comes to the share of world high-tech production (39% by 2003). The United States also leads in terms of patents and science/engineering degrees (Brooks and Wohlforth 2008: 32–3).

In sum, a look at major aspects of the material capabilities of sovereign states does convey a picture of concentration, even of an enormous power gap, with the United States as the leading power in the system. There are observers who are sceptical about this; instead of current figures, they emphasize current trends. Emerging powers, especially China, are catching up fast and will in due course surpass the United States. Twenty-five years ago, the Chinese share of world GDP was 3.81%; the US share was more than 25% (Quandl 2014). But as we saw above, the gap is closing and in a few years' time the

Chinese economy will be the largest; by 2030, the Chinese economy is expected to be 1.5 times as large as the United States (Investopedia 2013). As for military capability, it basically follows economic capacity, says Charles Kupchan, because 'the foundation of military power is ultimately economic strength'; therefore, 'a more level playing field economically will ultimately translate into a world in which military power is more equally distributed' (Kupchan 2012: 80, 84; see also Layne 2009).

These different projections have given rise to a large debate for and against the idea of American decline (summarized in Acharya 2014: 12–32). Those who go against the notion of decline argue that the rise of China and other emerging powers is exaggerated. For example, the challenges to the Chinese economy are serious, as we saw in Chapter 2; it is not merely a question of upholding the extreme growth rates of previous decades; there are elements of a ghost economy where quantitative progress is not matched by qualitative changes and where the environmental and other problems connected to the present model of accumulation are rapidly increasing. Second, the connection between material capability and great power status is overly simplified in these projections. One aspect of this is whether there are specific kinds of economic strength (e.g. high-tech competence, steel industry) or military strength (e.g. nuclear weapons; air, sea or land forces) that are relatively more important than others. Another aspect concerns the ability to convert economic capacity into military and economic power (Zakaria 1998).

Both sides in the debate have a point. On one hand, the United States remains a leading power in material terms. On the other hand, its position is less dominant than earlier and—even more important— the overwhelming American lead in military power is less useful for influence and dominance than earlier, as will be discussed below. First, however, the 'diffusion of power' view must be introduced.

Diffusion of power: Non-material power in a cooperative environment

We now turn to the view which moves in another direction and emphasizes the dispersion of power. Liberal analysis does not begin with states; it begins with individuals who are citizens of states. States are not primarily power containers as claimed by realists; they are amalgamations of individuals and their primary purpose is to protect the rights of citizens to life, liberty and property (Greenberg and Mayer 1990). It follows that states cannot be all-powerful: states rest on the consent of individuals and states are not alone in creating relations across borders. Transnational relations, meaning relations across borders between individuals and groups of 'non-state actors', have always existed; they have become of much increased importance in a globalized world of fast-moving travel and communication. Furthermore, there is a global marketplace where transnational corporations and other economic actors conduct business across borders.

Power, then, is dispersed among many different actors at several levels (Nye 2002: 46; Guzzini 2012): there is a subnational level of local government, local business and local groups. There is a supranational level of international organizations, transnational corporations and non-governmental organizations; and there is a national level of central government, of national corporations and national third-sector organizations. All of these entities have relations across borders; they influence individuals, groups and organizations elsewhere and are in turn influenced by them; that opens to a highly complex power structure.

At the same time, sovereign states are not the unitary and coherent actors that realists claim them to be. National governments are complex entities, just like the societies they represent, and relations between states take place on many levels and through multiple channels (Keohane and Nye 1977: 24). In other words, there is a multifaceted network of transgovernmental relations. This is related to the fact that very little in international relations today is connected to the 'high politics' of potential military confrontation. Most of what goes on in international affairs is rather connected with the 'low politics' of social and economic issues.

In terms of power resources, liberals do not disregard material power but they emphasize the importance of non-material, intangible sources of power, such as national cohesion; a universalistic culture; and influence in international institutions. National cohesion is the ability of society and state to stand together; a universalistic culture is a culture with universal appeal. The United States remains powerful in the sense that 'the values of democracy, personal freedom, upward mobility, and openness that are often expressed in American popular culture, higher education, and foreign policy contribute to American power in many areas' (Nye 2002: 11). Joseph Nye calls this soft power: 'getting others to want what you want' (Nye 2002: 9) through attraction, not by the use of force or threat.

Liberals see power resources as much less fungible. Power resources in one area, whether for example, shipping, computer technology or international trade, cannot necessarily or easily be put to use in other areas. That of course makes the power structure a great deal more complex because it is necessary to specify what kind of power we are talking about in which domains. Small states, such as Denmark or Norway, may be powerful in shipping or oil; conversely the military might of large states is generally of little use in non-military affairs. In short, power is distributed among many actors across a vast range of issue areas.

At the same time, liberals underline that international relations are often non-antagonistic. In a world where democracy and interdependence has moved forward, states can be friends instead of enemies. And even if not all states are friends, they do not have to be enemies: the violent conflict foreseen by realists is not always merely one step away (cf. Sørensen 2008b). For these reasons, military force is not of the supreme importance that is claimed by the realists.

In sum, the liberal views move attention away from material capabilities and focus instead on the use of power in concrete situations. Since there are many different participants in international relations, numerous actors are involved in the power game. And since violent conflict is most often unlikely, many different sources of power are relevant, not least the less tangible ones, such as soft power. This opens to a fuzzy power structure where a great number of actors wield a large amount of different forms of power.

Power in the present world order

So where are we in power terms in the international system? It is an old question in IR which has preoccupied the attention of scholars for quite a while. The major debate during the Cold War took place between realists and liberals in the late 1960s and 1970s (Jackson and Sørensen 2016: 114–22). Liberals emphasized the fuzzy power structure among Western democracies that were heavily integrated economically and otherwise; realists pointed to the East–West confrontation and other types of enmity (e.g. India and Pakistan) where military confrontations were far from unthinkable and repeated that such confrontation could pop up anywhere. It is true today as well, of course, that some parts of the world (e.g. the Middle East) are much more conflict-prone than other parts (e.g. North America, Western Europe), but since today's world is a closely linked and tightly bound international system we must have some idea of the overall structure of that system in relation to power.

First, when we study world order it is appropriate to focus on sovereign states as the major actors. They are the basic units of the international system and they set the rules for other actors. But the special role for states does not make others irrelevant. States are not acting on their own, in splendid isolation from everyone else. They are deeply influenced by people and groups from society; Chapter 2 demonstrated how domestic conditions in states affect what states can do in relation to world order. So individuals and groups from civil society are important; so are the market players, corporations and labour, when it comes to the economy. The point is that states and 'non-state actors' should not be seen as separate from each other.

When we focus on the strength of states we must include the conditions in markets and civil societies. They are integrated parts of the states from which they emerge; being a leading power, in other words, is not merely about the state in the narrow sense of the state apparatus and its resources; it is also about 'non-state actors' as emphasized by Stuart Brown: 'In addition to its policymakers and the organs of government, a hegemonic power, by definition, features a broad array of such influential, globally oriented non-state actors including philanthropies, foundations and religious charities, professional associations, transnational non-governmental organization, universities and corporations' (Brown 2013: 8). In sum, a focus on the state must not exclude non-state actors.

If we begin with military force, there can be no doubt about US pre-eminence. It is not merely that the United States spends more on defence than all other major powers combined; it is also the quality of the equipment and the capacity to deploy it. No-one else has a fleet of aircraft that could 'pick up all the tanks in a heavy division and move them … to the Persian Gulf in 36–48 hours' (Odom and Dujarric 2004: 79). It is the same picture across all military sectors: drones, land forces, blue-water navy, nuclear weapons and so on. US supremacy is enhanced by a string of forward bases that allows it a global reach nobody else can begin to match.

When we move to economic capability, the picture is more nuanced. The European Union was the world's largest economy between 2007 and 2012. In 2013, due to the euro crisis, the United States again went ahead with an output of $16.7 trillion compared to the European Union's $15.8 trillion. China was a close third in 2013, at $13.34 trillion. No other economy comes close; India is in fourth place with $4.96 trillion closely followed by Japan at $4.73 trillion (CIA World Factbook). So while the distribution of military power is 'largely unipolar' according to Joseph Nye, economic power 'has been multipolar for more than a decade, with the United States, Europe, Japan, and China as the major players and others gaining in importance' (Nye 2010: 3).

But there is reason to reflect on the general figures. The question is whether economic power can be measured purely in terms of GDP. One aspect of this discussion is the measurement of GDP itself. Some scholars claim that projections based on PPP vastly overstate China's economic size because it makes it possible to manipulate calculations and cloud the real picture. At the same time, GDP is not tantamount to national power: China was by far the world's largest economy in 1820, for example, and remained so during most of its 'century of humiliation' when it was dominated by Britain and Japan (Beckley 2011).

The decisive point, however, concerns the relationship between, on one hand, the overall size of the economy and, on the other hand, the disposable amount of power resources. When more than one billion Chinese increase their output and also their consumption that makes a big difference in terms of GDP but not in terms of resources disposable for national purposes. What is of interest is rather GDP per capita, and in this regard the average American, for example, is about $25,000 richer than the average Chinese, compared to the situation in 1991 (Beckley 2011: 59). As for the future, within the next two decades China will have 300 million pensioners, 'the most severe aging process in human history'; the ratio of workers per retiree will shrink from 8:1 today to 2:1 by 2040 (Beckley 2011: 61).

So the general figures need scrutiny; but it is safe to conclude that the United States vastly leads in military capabilities and is also economically strong. That would make it a dominant superpower according to the 'concentration' view presented above. This view is based on a realist world where states are enemies and war is always an option and so the state with the greatest war-winning capacity always wins the day. But compared to the present world order this view is overly simplified. Interstate war is of decreasing importance. We are not in a raw anarchy world of enemy states constantly banging into each other. We are in an international society, a world of international norms and rules. To be a sovereign state is not merely about the material characteristics of military and economic power. It also requires recognition from other states and obligations to follow certain rules as a member of the society of states (Bull 1995: 13). States are not always enemies and that reduces the relative importance of military power (Weber and Jentleson 2010; Buzan 2004b; Acharya 2014).

There can be different cultures of anarchy and friendship can play a much greater role. Alexander Wendt suggests three major ideal types of anarchy (Wendt 1999: 257) where states can be enemies, rivals or friends. We are presently in an international society where there are several friends, many rivals and rather few enemies. Things may change of course, as they have done across history. Any given international society is always under construction in the sense that the participating states develop it through their behaviour and interaction. I argued in Chapter 3 that world order has moved towards greater friendship and more peaceful relations; that was the reasoning behind the increasing obsolescence of interstate war. Things can go the other way too; relations between Russia and the West have moved towards more enmity rather than towards closer friendship during the most recent period.

But the more powerful move since the end of the Cold War has been towards friendship rather than enmity. That supports the liberal view that military force is becoming less crucial as a source of power whereas economic power and less tangible forms of power, including soft power, have become more important. It does not mean that we should embrace an extreme 'end of power' (Naím 2013a) view where power is so diffused among many actors at different levels that any talk of a power structure becomes meaningless. But it does mean that a range of different forms of power, including political, economic, technological, cultural and ideological forms become relevant in the overall evaluation of who has power (Brown 2013: 22). In short, we need a more comprehensive view of power than the traditional focus on 'war-winning capacity'.

There is of course no agreement on which precise sources of power are relevant in this more comprehensive analysis, or on their relative importance. In a classic analysis Robert Keohane focused on the economic aspects; he argued that a leading power needed a number of economic power resources in different sectors, including raw materials, capital, markets and a competitive advantage in the production of high-value goods (Keohane 1984: 32). For Joseph Nye, power today unfolds on three different levels: the military level where the United States dominates, the economic level, which is multipolar, and the realm of transnational relations, which includes anything from bankers to terrorists and where power is 'widely dispersed' (Nye 2002: 39). The point is that a wide range of power resources, including soft power and institutional power, are needed to steer in that complex context. Stuart Brown discusses power in relation to military, political, economic and cultural dimensions (Brown 2013).

I cannot pursue this discussion about types of power, nor is it relevant for the present argument to do so. Even if there are disagreements about the precise power calculation, most observers agree that 'the United States will likely remain the world's single most powerful country well into this new century' (Nye 2002: 39; Brown 2013: 24). The US preponderance of military, economic and technological power has been noted. US power in these areas is combined with a strong position in other areas: the existing multilateral institutions, including the UN system, were conceived and developed under US leadership. These institutions are based on liberal principles that expound the liberal values which form the basis of US (and Western) societies. They are the values that make up the foundation for the soft power of these states.

But this view does not tell the full story about the distribution of power; therefore, it is potentially misleading. It does not tell the full story because power is not merely about various material and other resources. It is also about the ability to make use of these resources in relation to other actors. In these respects, the United States is distinctly weaker than earlier, for several reasons. First, the overwhelming lead in military power is less useful in a world where interstate war is increasingly obsolete. In such a situation, says Barry Buzan, 'superpower status hangs much more on the ability to create and sustain international societies ... than on warfighting ability' (Buzan 2004b: 139).

Second, economic power is multidimensional. In some areas, such as machine industry, Germany is a world leader; in container shipping Denmark punches above its weight. The United States may be economically strongest overall, but that does not translate into predominance in every economic domain. Third, even if international institutions are based on liberal principles, liberal states, including the United States, cannot have their way in these institutions if they want to move in a direction most other states would consider going against their interests (see Chapter 7). Fourth, the US may be powerful in soft power terms but at the same time, the liberal model for which it stands has also experienced economic and political problems in recent years (Chapter 2, Chapter 8). It may not be as attractive to others as earlier; that is a threat to the soft power of the United States (and the liberal West).

In sum, the United States leads in terms of material and other power resources, but that does not translate into dominance over other actors. The United States—and the established Western democracies—remain strong, but they cannot have their way in the world any longer without the consent (and often the active support) of other powers.

A stable and legitimate world order

I have discussed two aspects of power in today's world: on one hand, a wide range of different power resources; on the other hand, the ability and willingness to put the resources to use in the creation of an order that is also legitimate and therefore stable. A nation can be extremely powerful in terms of power resources; at the same time, it can put these resources to use in ways that will undermine rather than enhance its overall power position. That is because we are in a world where even a superpower needs the cooperation of others to achieve its ends and that requires legitimacy. Sebastian Mallaby made the point already in 1999: 'The paradox of American power at the end of this millennium is that it is too great to be challenged by any other state, yet not great enough to solve problems such as global terrorism and nuclear proliferation. America needs the help and respect of other nations' (Mallaby 1999).

This view of power as having a resource aspect as well as a social aspect can be related to the issue of world order with the help of a theoretical framework suggested by Robert Cox. On his approach, a stable and legitimate world order is based on a fit between a material power base (Cox emphasizes military and economic capabilities) on one hand, and a social side expressed in prevailing ideas (values and norms) of order as well as a set of appropriate institutions, on the other. Power flows from the material side; legitimacy flows from the support for common values and common institutions. In Cox's formulation, such order is based on 'a coherent conjunction or fit between a configuration of material power, the prevalent collective image of world order (including certain norms) and a set of institutions which administer the order with a certain semblance of universality (that is, not just as the overt instruments of a particular state's dominance)' (Cox 1996: 103). We then get the following requirements for a stable and legitimate world order (see Figure 4.1).

This analytical starting point puts the debate about who has power in larger perspective because it focuses both on power as different resources and the ability to employ these resources in the construction of a legitimate and therefore stable world order. It has been noted earlier in this book that the aspirations for world order have grown considerably over time. Current aspirations as formulated by UN declarations are for a 'thick' order which can provide the framework for the good life of all people. The question to be pursued in coming chapters, then, is whether such order is under construction or not. Differently put, are we moving towards a better, more effective and stable world order in terms of these aspirations, or are we rather moving in the opposite direction, towards a less effective, more unstable and frail order that cannot meet the grand expectations formulated in the UN declarations?

Figure 4.1   Requirements for a stable and legitimate world order

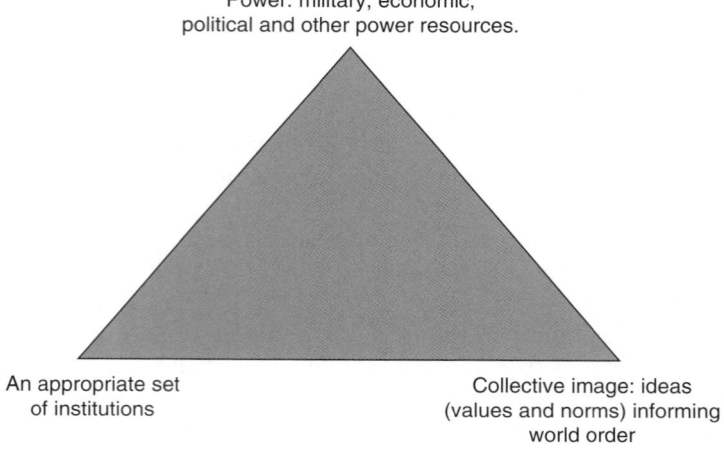

Power: military, economic, political and other power resources.

An appropriate set of institutions

Collective image: ideas (values and norms) informing world order

Cox identifies the *Pax Americana* after 1945 as a successful Western order. The United States provided security protection from the Soviet threat and it set up a framework for the economic and social reconstruction of Western Europe and Japan. The order was based on common (liberal democratic) values and an appropriate set of international institutions (NATO, the Bretton Woods and the UN systems). The question is whether such an order is possible today on a world scale.

Who has power to pursue an effective, stable and legitimate world order today? The argument above was that it is only the United States, or the US/Western coalition of liberal democracies, who have the necessary power resources to take the lead in such a project, further expanding the liberal order that was constructed after 1945. The challenge from the emerging powers is not that they can take over the system and construct an alternative world order, because they cannot. On one hand, they do not have the necessary arsenal of power resources; on the other hand, they have no ambition to take the lead and act as constructors of world order. Should they get the upper hand in any alternative project, it would probably be a regionalized order, dominated by the respective emerging powers of each region (for a scenario, see Acharya 2014).

The challenge is rather that the rising powers are now strong enough to demand substantial influence in the international institutions and on the international rules. At the same time, they must be successfully incorporated into a reformed order which is also legitimate. The big question is how far the emerging powers will be willing to cooperate in the construction of an ambitious, 'thick' order. On one hand, there has been a general movement towards greater cooperation. Chapter 1 argued that the world has made a significant move away from a 'thin' order of peace based on a relatively stable balance of power, towards a 'thick' order with the ultimate goal of providing the good life for all people.

On the other hand, not all countries are embracing exactly the same values and institutions even if almost all states, including the non-democratic great powers, are committed to some version of a capitalist market economy, substantial integration in a globalized world and some substantial participation in institutional cooperation. In November 2000, President Jiang Zemin declared that a nation's participation in economic development and globalization is an 'objective requirement' for economic development, but this should certainly not be taken to mean an embrace of liberal values. China sees integration into a liberal order as necessary for the promotion of national greatness and power; China is not committing itself to a common value foundation of political freedom, democracy and human rights, nor is Russia. Even more democratic emerging powers, including Brazil and India, emphasize state sovereignty and the right to take their own decisions (Kupchan 2012: 194).

And of course, there is the question about the extent to which the liberal Western states themselves actually work for the construction of a 'thick' order, as exemplified by the Bush presidency after 9/11. The US National Security Strategy of 2002 pledged to 'defend liberty and justice because these principles are right and true for people everywhere' (NSS 2002). It also emphasized that the United States must be unconstrained in responding to threats and this must include preemptive use of force; the wars in Afghanistan and Iraq followed. The Iraq war was particularly controversial because it was not sanctioned by the international community; the UN Security Council would not support it. The United States had to make do with a 'coalition of the willing' which included the United Kingdom and a string of lesser powers, including Georgia, Norway and Denmark.

Therefore, an overwhelming power position can lead towards unilateralist arrogance where the unipolar power requires the world to subject itself to an order that leaves the United States entirely unconstrained while requiring commitments to rules and regulations from everybody else. Such order lacks legitimacy; it is a form of liberal imperialism, that is, 'a neoimperial vision in which the United States arrogates to itself the global role of setting standards, determining threats, and meeting out justice' (Ikenberry 2002: 44). It is not a coherent and stable recipe for a post-Cold War liberal world order. Several close allies of the United States (Germany, France) would not accept it, nor would other great powers such as China, Russia and India. In other words, an unconstrained liberal power may adopt policies that undercut a stable liberal world order because it will not itself comply with the principles and values that it demands from others.

There is also a risk that the external behaviour of emerging powers will be strongly linked to domestic purposes, that is, to create legitimacy at home (James 2008; Serfaty 2011). 'The BRICs will look for compensating power, and military and strategic influence and prestige, as a way to solve internal problems' says Harold James (James 2008). As Chapter 2 demonstrated, the emerging powers face substantial internal weaknesses. But looking for compensating international power will most often not be a strong contribution to the building of world order. An example is Russia's behaviour in relation to Ukraine and China's behaviour in the South China Sea. (For further treatment of the emerging powers in global governance, see Chapter 7).

While any US or US/Western project of world order creation faces challenges from emerging powers, conflict-ridden regions (the Middle East) and human catastrophes in fragile states, it is also constrained, or even driven, by domestic politics, as examined in Chapter 2 Reduced social cohesion, a squeezed middle class and political polarization and gridlock have created domestic situations in the US/Western liberal democracies that are not very conducive to the pursuit of hegemonic projects that will also involve some holding back on the pursuit of narrow national interests for the larger purpose of a stable and effective order. So even if the US/West would be able to pursue a hegemonic project for a stable, 'thick' world order, would it be willing to do so and does it have some coherent scheme for how to proceed with the project? In sum, is a stable and legitimate world order at all possible today?

Conclusion: Power and world order

There is a comprehensive and long-standing debate about the concept of power and about power in relation to the international system and to world order. The 'concentration of power' view focuses on power as material resources with special focus on military and economic capabilities. On that view, there is an enormous concentration of power in the present system in the hands of the one remaining superpower, the United States. The 'diffusion of power' view, by contrast, argues that power is dispersed among many actors at several different levels, including subnational, national and supranational levels. Since war is no longer imminent, it is relevant to move focus to non-material, intangible sources of power, such as soft power.

It is true that sources of power other than military, economic and additional material capabilities are relevant for our analysis. But even when we expand the power calculation and include the widest range of material and non-material resources, the United States remains the leading and most powerful country in the present order.

Yet power resources are not enough for building a stable and effective order. There is a social side to power which turns on the ability to create and sustain an order which is legitimate in the sense of being seen as beneficial to all rather than an instrument of dominance of a leading state.

When these aspects of power come together we have a situation of what Robert Cox called successful hegemony: a coherent fit between an arsenal of power resources, ideas, and a set of appropriate institutions; this is also a fit between power and legitimacy. It is the purpose of the chapters that follow to interrogate the extent to which such order has been achieved or is under construction.

There are other possibilities than a successful hegemonic order. One is a more fragmented system with regions as the major units. That would amount to a more regionalized world where emerging centres of power led the way in the making of a 'Euro-capitalist', a 'Sino-capitalist', a 'Latino-capitalist', a 'Russo-capitalist' and maybe an 'Afro-capitalist' order where intra-regional networks would be much stronger than extra-regional ones. Regionalism has surely become more important after the end of the Cold War (Söderbaum 2015). But a world of regions is not in the making: emerging powers are involved in setting up regional networks but they also remain tightly enrolled in capitalist and institutional networks on a global scale.

A stable and legitimate order as sketched in Figure 4.1, on one hand, and an order of regions, on the other, can be seen as ideal types. The present order is surely somewhere in between, with elements of both these types. But what is the mix exactly? Amitav Acharya suggests that we are in a 'multiplex' order which is a world of 'diversity and complexity, a decentred architecture of order management, featuring old and new powers, with a greater role for regional governance' (Acharya 2014: 8). In other words, a multiplex order has a more pronounced role for regions, but it also contains a significant element of interdependence across regions, and a role for a 'constrained but still significant US power' (Acharya 2014: 8).

There is much to agree with in this vision; 'multiplex' sounds like an adequate metaphor for the current order as of 2016. But I miss two elements in the analysis. First, I have argued in Chapter 2 that the domestic dimension needs a place in the analysis of world order: whether or not states are increasingly fragile plays a role for the kind of order that we have. Second, Acharya appears quite happy with the multiplex order: it can be a rather well-functioning and effective order provided that the United States shows more willingness to share power instead of monopolizing it, and that emerging powers make a greater contribution to world order-building in a spirit of not merely demanding a greater say but also showing more willingness to work for common world order goals (Acharya 2014: 112).

But the happy prospects for a multiplex order are not really followed through by an analysis of the extent to which the current order gets the job done. How effective and well-functioning is it in major areas? That takes us back to the overarching theme of this book: sceptical realists versus optimistic liberals. The current debates about world order are not in agreement about where we are headed in these terms: towards a reformed Western order, or towards increasing crisis and instability. On the optimistic view, a global order project has basically been pursued by the United States since the end of the Cold War. In close cooperation with Europe, a large number of 'new' democracies in Eastern Europe and elsewhere have been incorporated into the liberal world order as participants in Western regional and global institutions. They have become integrated players in economic globalization, and members of the Western security networks, including NATO. The emerging great powers of China and India have to a large extent been successfully invited to join this order at several levels. Granted, there was a deviation from the multilateral path after September 11 where the United States was more bent on going alone and displayed a variety of unilateralist impulses. But the United States is now on track in pursuit of alliances, partnerships and multilateralism.

The other view is much more sceptic. It claims that globalization has helped create a 'governance gap' (Held and Roger (eds) 2013) which is now seriously undermining world order. Security, economic, environmental and other problems are not being looked after because states, including the emerging powers and in particular Russia and China, are unwilling to make bargains that go against what they see as fundamental national interests. And there is nobody to entice or cajole, push or threaten them into compliance because 'for the first time in seven decades, we live in a world without global leadership' (Bremmer 2012: 3).

In the chapters that follow, this debate about world order will be pursued along four major dimensions. The security dimension is the subject of Chapter 5. The economic dimension will be discussed in Chapter 6. Chapter 7 focuses on the institutional dimension of world order and interrogates the current standing of global governance. Finally, Chapter 8 is about the value dimension of world order, in particular the tension between *in*dependence, on one hand, and *inter*-dependence, on the other.

5
Security: Intervention, Order and Legitimacy

Introduction

We want to know what kind of security agenda emerged from the end of the Cold War and what the consequences are for world order. For four decades the global security structure was defined by the Cold War. Two superpowers, heavily armed with nuclear weapons, confronted each other; they were backed by networks of alliances and bent on taking their confrontation to all corners of the world. The Cold War ended when Mikhail Gorbachev ceased to support the communist dictatorships in Eastern Europe; they fell one by one. In his own country, the reform policies of *glasnost* and *perestroika* eventually led to the collapse of the Soviet Union. As noted earlier in this book, there was no agreement on the magnitude and wider significance of the end of the Cold War. Some commentators thought it was pretty much business as usual because the state system endured with all its well-known problems of international relations. Others embraced notions of much more radical change. Today, 25 years later, the debate lingers on (Lundestad 2013: 9).

The focus in this chapter is on security. In this area, the sceptics have a point: 'old' issues of power balancing, of nuclear weapons, of rivalry between states in the Middle East and elsewhere, and of rising and declining powers remain in place. But I have also argued for a thesis of 'the decreasing importance of interstate war' and that indicates some significant modifications of the security agenda. These changes involve an increased emphasis on collective security and human security.

The post-Cold War security agenda is concerned with human security due to the predominance of intrastate conflict and the increased emphasis on human rights and democracy. According to this view, the most important security problem in terms of human cost and bloodshed is domestic conflict within fragile states. A second security problem emerges from the human security focus: it is the extension of the security agenda to include a range of different threats to individuals, including physical security issues such as terrorism, environmental and economic challenges, infectious disease, drugs and arms trafficking and a host of other risks. Human security then includes concerns about citizens in all countries, including well-ordered states in the North that are normally considered safe for their citizens.

Collective security is more important as well. During the Cold War, any initiative towards collective security could be blocked by a great power. It was this stalemate that came to an end with the termination of the Cold War. The concrete turning point was the international society's response to Iraq's invasion of Kuwait on August 2, 1990. A series of UN Security Council Resolutions called for Iraq's unconditional withdrawal and the restoration of Kuwait's independence. The US-led operation 'Desert Storm' defeated Iraq's forces in less than two months. President George H.W. Bush declared that a 'new world order' was in the making, 'a world in which the strong respect the rights of the weak' (Bush 1990).

Regardless of the president's rhetoric, it was clear already at the time that this was not a full-fledged turn to a system of collective security. The Gulf war came at a high point of Soviet/Russian compliance and Arab states were ready to support the coalition (Clark 2001: 201). In many other cases, conditions were not so forthcoming. At the same time, most operations require a substantial commitment of resources which depends on the willingness of the great powers to participate. Collective security then becomes 'selective security' because operations require great power consent and active support.

But nor is it business as usual. There has been a major turn to what Ian Clark calls 'the collectivization of security' (Clark 2001: 193–216). All states, including great powers, seek to justify their actions in order to be able to claim legitimacy. This is also the case when they are in breach of international norms, as the United States in Iraq in 2003 and Russia in Ukraine in 2014. This turn to collectivization and quest for legitimacy is tied in with a much higher concern for human security than was the case during the Cold War. Meanwhile, the traditional security agenda has not gone away; it concerns a stable security order among states in various regions in the face of changes in the balances of power and emerging conflicts. Focus will be on Asia-Pacific, Russia's near abroad and the Middle East.

The approach to these items on the security agenda will be that of the prospects for a stable order. Such order was defined in the previous chapter as resting on a combination of power and legitimacy. A stable order must be based on power because enforcement is necessary when rules are under attack or in process of breaking down; and it must be based on legitimacy, which derives from consent among the participants about support for the values and institutions of that order. Without legitimacy, the order will always be contested and at risk of breaking down (Kissinger 2014; Ikenberry 2011, Buzan 2014).

The necessity of power as well as legitimacy for building a stable order can be demonstrated by reference to core dimensions of the Cold War order. The Western order, based on US hegemony and involving liberal democracies in Western Europe and Japan, was stable both in terms of power and legitimacy. It was secured by US power but also supported by common values and institutions. The Eastern order was secured by Soviet power; but it was never legitimate in terms of popular support for values and institutions. Eventually, even the Eastern European elites lost faith in their own right to rule, their own legitimacy (Ash 1990). When Soviet power went out of the equation due to Mikhail Gorbachev, the Eastern order lacked power as well as legitimacy, and quickly dismantled.

In sum, there are three major items on the new security agenda; they concern violent conflict in fragile states, the traditional security agenda of order among states, and the larger horizon of human security. They will be discussed in what follows with the aim of assessing whether a stable order, based on power and legitimacy, is under construction (or already in place) in the security domain. If a stable order is emerging, it will support the optimist liberal view discussed earlier; if it is not, the realist sceptics will have the upper hand.

Fragile states

Fragile states in the Global South were briefly introduced in Chapter 2. The typical fragile state has a history of state formation which is radically different from the consolidated states in the North. Their history is one of external domination, most often in the form of colonialism (Brock et al. 2011). Colonial administrators set up authoritarian and patriarchal forms of governance playing a game of alliances that sharpened divisions among domestic groups. At independence, the local elite that won the power game took over administrative and institutional structures that were lacking capacity, competence and resources. The new rulers appealed to national unity and community, but this was mostly rhetoric, covering forms of elite rule based on patron–client relationships (Jackson and Rosberg 1982) to the benefit of the state elites and their allies.

The link to domestic violent conflict is clear: rulers profoundly lacked legitimacy in the population and that led to authoritarian rule and the reliance on coercion to remain in power (Sørensen 2001: 103–25). Patron–client relationships favour certain ethnic groups over others; access to material and other benefits becomes connected to ethnic (or ethno-religious) identity, both for insiders and outsiders. The principal issue of the most intense conflicts, said Ted Gurr already in 1994, is 'the contention for state power among communal groups' (Gurr 1994: 364). In other words, domestic violent conflict in fragile states is not a new development of the post-Cold War world; it has been a serious problem since the wave of decolonization around 1960.

During the Cold War there was a reluctance to intervene in fragile states; the ideology of anti-colonialism was strong in the North, the newly independent states could argue their case for sovereignty in the UN system, and they could play on the competition between East and West in the context of the Cold War. There was an emerging development aid regime, but outside of that the great powers primarily looked after their security interests. The lack of progress in economic development did lead to demands for so-called structural adjustment programmes in the 1980s but always through negotiations with incumbent governments (World Bank 1994).

It was the *Agenda for Peace* by UN General Secretary Boutros Boutros-Ghali in 1992 that opened the door to a new phase of international involvement in making peace. In Cold War times, focus was on peacekeeping, getting to end hostilities and monitor ceasefires in interstate conflict. The new agenda argued for peacebuilding, a wider set of actions that aim at bringing about a more solid, sustainable peace. This includes political, economic and social reforms aimed at the root causes of violence. Emphasis then moves away from the acute conflict, towards the wider societal framework. That opened up to projects of state-building, democratization, good governance and economic development (Newman, Paris and Richmond 2009: 3–26); a new era of the international society comprehensively addressing violent conflict inside countries appeared to be in the making. Current UN operations are a mixture of peacekeeping and peacebuilding missions (UN 2014).

The international terrorism of 9/11 added a national security concern to the focus on fragile states. The US National Security strategy of 2002 explained the lesson of 9/11: '...weak states, such as Afghanistan, can pose a great danger to our national interests...' (NSS 2002: 9). However, national security concerns and humanitarian concerns seldom overlap; in general, the security factor has not helped strengthen the humanitarian factor (Jentleson 2007: 284). In addition, the justification for the Iraq war was not supported by most great powers; in other words, the national security concern remained contentious as a justification for violent intervention in fragile states.

In terms of human cost, fragile states are the major security problem today. Is the problem being handled in a way which points towards a stable and effective order? For an affirmative answer, the international society's response to the problem must be based on sufficient power and legitimacy, as explained earlier. Let us first look at intervention in fragile states from the vantage point of power, with a focus on military power. Intervention with force requires a sufficient volume and quality in order to stabilize the security situation and to be able to build and enforce peace. The issue of how much is enough is of course deeply contested. The standard recommendation is 20 troops per 1,000 population (Dobbins et al. 2003) but much depends on the size and geography of the country and the situation on the ground. A study in the context of the US army reaches a number of 13.26 soldiers per 1,000 population, including police forces (McGrath 2006: 106). Almost all peace operations come nowhere near that number (Kosovo and Bosnia are exceptions). Worst of all, the beginning of the Rwanda genocide in 1994 caused the Security Council to reduce UN presence in the country to a symbolic force of 270 troops; (the 13.26 standard would have required close to 108,000 troops). One analysis of peacebuilding in Africa found that the most concentrated operations are in small countries with small populations: they have more than one peacekeeper per 1,000 population. The UN is consistently pressed for funds and compelled to end peace missions quickly (Englebert and Tull 2008: 131).

The belated response to the Rwanda genocide was partly due to the mishaps in Somalia less than a year earlier. Operation 'Restore Hope' was a response to the civil war in Somalia, following the overthrow of Siad Barre's regime. With 38,000 troops, of which the United States provided 28,000, it was initially successful, but when the mission expanded from relief to peace- and state-building, militias began attacking peacebuilders. The 'Black Hawk Down' confrontation in Mogadishu in 1994 caused 18 American casualties and led President Clinton to announce the withdrawal of American forces (Brock et al. 2011: 104).

With the break-up of Yugoslavia, state failure moved to Europe. Humanitarian relief operations by Western countries were powerless in face of the Srebrenica massacre in 1995. When NATO did intervene militarily it was in the context of air strikes against Serb military forces in Kosovo and Serbia, a high-risk operation in terms of exposing people on the ground. Substantial ground-force intervention came only in the context of implementing peace agreements.

The national security concern after 9/11, especially in the United States, changed the agenda and removed some of the hesitation concerning intervention with force. It led to the wars in Afghanistan and Iraq, which, upon regime change, were transformed into peace- and state-building operations. But even here, the commitment of military power was less than might have been expected, falling well short of the ratios mentioned earlier. Since these are wars that have been going on for over a decade and there are ongoing efforts to increase the number of local security forces, any exact calculation is complicated. It is certainly clear that for some time the American debates have been about bringing troops home; that has been nearly completed with respect to Iraq (by late 2011). By 2015, the plan for US troops in Afghanistan is less than 10,000; all troops are expected to leave by the end of 2016.

In sum, there was increased commitment to forcefully intervene in fragile states after the end of the Cold War, but this was always tempered by reluctance and concerns of human and material cost. Interventions in humanitarian catastrophes in Sub-Saharan Africa, for example, have tended to come late, as in Rwanda, and to be too small for high impact. Nowhere is this more clearly demonstrated than in the Democratic Republic of Congo, where more than five million people have been killed since the start of the second Congo war in 1998 (North 2012; Brock et al. 2011: 123). Iraq and Afghanistan are different in this regard, because of the leading role of (perceived) national security interests. But they then raise the question about the extent to which the national interest can be mobilized towards peace- and state-building in far-away foreign lands, that is, activities that go clearly beyond looking after more urgent national security interests.

This takes us to the legitimacy issue in relation to intervention in fragile states. Legitimacy is relevant at four levels in this context. The first is legitimacy at home: in democracies, support for costly operations that may take place over several years must be able to command substantial domestic support. The second level is that of international society; the starting point is that to be legitimate, intervention must be in accordance with international law. As indicated already, international norms have moved towards greater readiness to accept intervention. The third and fourth levels concern legitimacy at the receiving end: those intervened upon—both national elites and the local population—must accept and support, or at least tolerate, intervention if it is to achieve any amount of success.

Legitimacy at home has been brought about by a combination of human security arguments concerning innocent people in mortal danger and national security arguments about the connection between a fragile state and security at home. Substantial commitment of resources to any operation has always tended to emphasize national security concerns. In the United States in particular, the experiences of Afghanistan and Iraq, together with the legacy of Somalia and other humanitarian efforts, have not been helpful in terms of legitimacy at home. 'In my opinion, any future defense secretary who advises the president to again send a big American land army into Asia or into the Middle East or Africa should "have his head examined", as General MacArthur so delicately put it' said Secretary of Defense Robert Gates in his 2011 farewell address (Luján 2013: 6). Congresswoman Jackie Spier gave ten reasons to bring the troops home from Afghanistan in 2011; they were all about the irrelevance of the war for US national interests. In particular, 'there are fewer than 50 al Qaeda operatives in Afghanistan, so who are we exactly fighting?' (Spier 2011). The focus on national interests may bring legitimacy at home but it is not well suited to provide legitimacy in the country that is intervened upon, because victory in war is not at all the same as a stable peace; winning the peace is a quite different undertaking than winning the war.

International legitimacy derives from international law and the prevailing norms connected with it. In this regard, the adoption of the 'Responsibility to Protect' (R2P) in 2005 is significant because it calls upon the international community to act when a host state does not meet its obligation to protect its own people. The intervention in Libya in 2011 was hailed as 'a textbook case of the R2P norm working exactly as it was supposed to' (Evans 2011). But the R2P does not obligate members of the Security Council to take a certain action in the event of a humanitarian crisis. It is not a legal obligation but a political framework which makes it possible for the great powers to undertake or accept action, provided they are willing to do so in a specific case. Libya set no precedence for future action. The Security Council was not able to agree on condemning the violence in Syria in 2013; nor was any measure taken to protect the Syrian population. Perceived national interest will continue to be decisive. Military interventions will probably continue to be few and far between. Intervention of the kind undertaken in Libya will depend on national interest shaped by a number of peculiar circumstances tied to the single case (Hehir 2013).

The third level of legitimacy concerns national elites in the host country. All observers are in agreement that successful processes of peace- and state-building require local ownership (e.g. Kahler 2009; Krasner and Risse 2014; Richmond 2012). Outsiders must eventually go home; insiders must be the primary drivers of lasting change. This creates a delicate relationship between outsiders and insiders. The former come with power and resources and specific agendas of liberal peace- and state-building; the latter are clients and must be ready to accept the plans and priorities of outsiders in order to get access to the resources they control. But at the same time, insiders are the crucial gatekeepers of any peace- and state-building process; without them, no success.

Outsiders want to build institutions that are effective, accountable and democratic (but also in harmony with their own national security interests). They must do so in a context of incoherent state structures based on patron–client relationships. Local elites do not represent 'the people' because socio-political cohesion is lacking; any nation-building process is in the early stages. Their position is tenuous, their popular power base limited to certain groups and they must compete with others for resources and influence. In short, outsiders face local elites that may formally accept their agendas, but their substantial interests are quite different: they want to survive, strengthen their power and maximize their control of public resources. Insiders may formally consent to the transition schemes of outsiders but then proceed to divert them for their own purposes (Barnett and Zürcher 2009; Englebert and Tull 2008; Lake and Fariss 2014; Lemay-Hébert 2009).

Given the conditions in fragile states, outsiders have not been able to effectively confront these problems. The result is prolonged and expensive peace- and state-building operations with very limited success in terms of the ambitious liberal goals set by outsiders. At the same time, it cannot be assumed that competing national elites represent the interests of the population. This is where the fourth level of legitimacy—the local population, people on the ground—has received increasing attention in recent years (Richmond 2012). The ultimate goal of peace- and state-building operations is, after all, to improve the conditions for ordinary people. But most often operations have been top-down, focused on national elites in the capital city, and on the construction of national institutions (Roberts 2011). Violence in the Congo, for example, is motivated primarily by local agendas, but the UN, diplomats and journalists have focused on the national and regional level, whereas the appropriate course should really be a 'bottom-up' approach (Autessere 2008, 2014).

Local focus sounds logical but it is also potentially problematic. In some cases the security situation is not sufficiently stabilized to carry out local projects. The underlining of a 'grassroots' and 'bottom-up' approach is at risk of romanticizing a highly heterogeneous and complex reality that does not easily lend itself to intensive engagement (Simons and Zanker 2014; Billerbeck 2009; Donais 2009). The bottom-up emphasis requires personnel which is highly competent with regard to local socio-cultural conditions. There is a top-down version of local focus which looks for local participation as compliance with external projects, but this is different from 'genuine bottom-up', a situation where any project would emerge from a consensus among local constituencies. The latter might involve a significant step away from the liberal principles brought in by outsiders.

In other words, local preferences and international preferences may clash. On that issue, the UN position has most often remained on liberal ground: 'Local norms and practices must be taken into consideration and weaved into emerging democratic institutions and processes to the extent possible, while at the same time promoting internationally agreed norms and principles' (UN 2009: 4). There is a potentially sharp conflict between local norms and international (liberal) norms. In sum, local legitimacy is highly desirable but difficult to achieve in practice.

Overall, approaching intervention from the vantage points of power and legitimacy reveals a number of tensions and complications that may serve to undermine these operations. At the same time, many claim that humanitarian intervention has come of age and that the international community 'has grown increasingly adept at using military force to stop or prevent atrocities' (Western and Goldstein 2011: 49). How serious is the security problem of domestic conflict in fragile states at the present time?

A first point is that the old 'too little, too late' problem in relation to humanitarian intervention remains on the table. In August 2013, the French president warned that a 'Somalization' of the Central African Republic (CAR) was taking place due to fighting between militias as government forces. The international estimate is that 2.7 million— over half of the population—were in need of humanitarian assistance by April 2015 (OCHA 2015). The UN has been slow to react for budgetary reasons, lack of great power support and interorganizational rivalry between the AU (African Union) and other regional organizations (IRC 2015; Mitchell 2014). Elections in January 2016 hold some promise of the country finally being able to turn the page on three years of ethnic violence (AFP 2016).

Second, the early enthusiasm for the Libya intervention in 2011 (see for example Western and Goldstein 2011: 48) has cooled substantially as chaos and violence have returned to that country. On one hand, NATO misperceived the situation and vastly overstated the regime's intention of committing 'bloodbaths'; this was helped along by opposition propaganda. On the other hand, the intervention encouraged the uprising to escalate in the pursuit of regime change and that created a dynamic which increased the threat to civilians before intervention could protect them. Finally, the tendency to demonize the Gaddafi regime prevented a negotiated settlement that would have been preferable on humanitarian grounds (see the analysis in Kuperman 2013).

Third, there is no doubt that the UN is overburdened by the challenges of humanitarian crises. The open-endedness of R2P plays a role in this regard: it sets the bar rather low in calling for international action in a large number of situations, but at the same time it is also very ambitious in terms of calling for peace-, state- and nation-building. Robert Pape has called for a less ambitious 'pragmatic standard of intervention' that would limit international measures to cases where there is an 'ongoing campaign of mass homicide' (Pape 2012: 43) while at the same time creating a system much more capable of rapid response.

There are probably no magic blueprints for conducting intervention. In spite of the many difficulties, there is no doubt that interventions have saved many lives. But they have most often not been able to 'win the peace' in terms of successful peace-, state- and nation-building. This is closely connected to adverse conditions in the countries in question, but also to the inherent limitations of intervention.

The problems involved in intervention and the poor record of fragile states in terms of creating order and safety for their populations have helped put more radical proposals on the table. One is to 'Give War a Chance' (Luttwak 1999), that is, let them fight it out inside and among fragile states until a winner emerges who can provide a lasting solution. Aside from the human cost of this pathway, recent decades of fighting in fragile states have not led to high payoffs in terms of creating order and state-building. It is possible that 'states made war and war made states' (Tilly 1985) in European history but that experience does not readily apply to today's fragile states (Sørensen 2001).

Another proposal concerns changing the rules of secession, making the formation of new states easier; or the 'decertification' of states by the international community so that 'ineffective' states should no longer be considered sovereign by the international community (Herbst 1996–7: 142). Aside from the fact that the international community is highly sceptical about these pathways, the experience with 'new protectorates' (Mayall and Oliveira, eds, 2011) and the recent experience of newly independent South Sudan—which has decayed into anarchy and violence—demonstrate that there are no simple solutions to the problems of fragile states.

Human security has moved much higher on the international agenda since the end of the Cold War; that has led to the international concerns for human misery in fragile states. But sovereignty remains a fundamental institution of international society: outsiders only react under certain conditions, connected to their perceived national interests. And when they do react, it is clear that there are limits to the long-term transformation they can engender in host states. The continued comprehensive humanitarian problems in fragile states mean that the present order is not a success in terms of the ambitious goal of providing for the good life of all people. Such an order will not emerge in the foreseeable future.

The problems in relation to fragile states have become more urgent recently. That is because of two direct connections between violence within fragile states, on one hand, and the security situation in the advanced liberal democracies in Europe and North America, on the other. The first connection concerns acts of terrorism, as in Paris in 2015. The roots of such terror are complex; radical movements in fragile states, such as ISIL, clearly play a role, but so do the social conditions among less integrated minorities in Western urban centres. Western democracies have not found effective answers to this challenge. After Iraq and Afghanistan there was an emerging consensus that a 'war on terror' was not a sufficient or even appropriate response, but significantly better answers have not been found. The bombing campaign against ISIL in Syria remains a centrepiece of the Western response to the attacks in Paris (Bouzis 2015).

The second connection between domestic turmoil in fragile states and the security of the advanced Western countries is the flow of refugees heading north. Millions of refugees want shelter in Germany and other EU countries. The European Union does have an agency with responsibility for the external frontier of the Union, but member countries have so far been unable to devise effective common answers to the problems raised by the large number of people from fragile states knocking on the door of the Union (*Financial Times* 2015).

The traditional security agenda: Global and regional order

Elements of great power rivalry and competition between states persist in the present world order. They can be amplified both by a presently leading power and by emerging great powers. Rapidly rising powers, like China today, may entertain ambitions of increased influence and control that may lead towards conflict with other states, including the United States. Putin's Russia has already embarked on a decisively more aggressive course towards the West than was the case even a short while ago. The unilateralism of the Bush administrations after 9/11 reconfirmed the United States' unparalleled material power, but it was entirely unable to produce the legitimacy required for a stable order.

The early liberal vision of warm friendship between all in an increasingly liberal world has not come to pass. But nor are we in a world of great power enemies. Russia was on the way to becoming a friend of the US/West; it presently defines itself as a rival; it could become an enemy. China is a rival, mixed with elements of friendship and potential enmity. Neither China nor Russia has design for an alternative to the present US/Western-constructed order; their aim is to modify that order in ways that better conform to their interests. I develop this argument in what follows with the aim of characterizing the present security order among the great powers.

Three regions are in focus in what follows: the Asia-Pacific, Eastern Europe and the Middle East. We begin with the Asia-Pacific. For the United States, the first decade of this century was defined, in security terms, by 9/11 and the two wars in Afghanistan and Iraq. By 2013, the United States declared its intention to rebalance its strategic focus towards Asia-Pacific. This involves strengthening alliances in Asia, deepening partnerships with emerging powers, building a constructive relationship with China and bolstering regional institutions (Kurata 2013). The agenda indicates the complexity of the Asian regional order. It is made up of bilateral security bargains combined with a host of minilateral and multilateral arrangements (Loke 2010; Ayson 2015).

The United States has sustained a successful hegemony in the Asia-Pacific for several decades. Based on US power, its legitimacy derives from goods that this order has provided in terms of stability, security, management of regional conflict, and attention to the economic interests of the states in the region. Its early foundation was the reconciliation with China in 1972 and the bilateral alliance system mentioned earlier. The accord with China could no longer rest on a common anti-Soviet posture once the Cold War ended. By then, however, China needed reconciliation with the West for other reasons, not least its ambitions for economic expansion based on participation in globalization.

For quite some time, China chose to constructively underwrite the US-led order instead of mounting a challenge to it (Goh 2013). It has helped build and expand multilateral organizations such as the Shanghai Cooperation Organization, has agreed with ASEAN on a 'conduct of the parties' in relation to the South China Sea, and participates in numerous other regional institutions (Goh 2013; Loke

2010). Second, the ASEAN countries have played an active role in bringing about this result by pushing the great powers in the right direction: 'They have functioned as willing allies and military partners, political "middlemen", institutional brokers, and the suppliers of legitimacy for a variety of major power decisions and positions [including] the United States to maintain its military presence, [and] China to demonstrate good neighbourliness and assurance through institutional and economic engagement' (Goh 2007/08: 156).

Only a few years ago, it appeared that China continued to be ready to accept US military primacy in the region and to live with the United States as the 'hegemonic power' (Zhang and Tang 2005: 53). Today, after costly American wars and an economic crisis, Chinese commentators find that the US 'has begun to degenerate from a "leader" to a "balancer"' (Wang 2014: 4), which, again, challenges the stability of the Asian security order. At the same time, there is increased security competition between China and Japan, and between China and several ASEAN countries; in other words, it is a more volatile situation than earlier.

In this situation, the future for a stable order hinges on the ambitions of China for the accommodation of its interests and the willingness of the United States and its allies to make adjustments. There are two competing views on this issue. The liberal view is that regional security must be seen in context. It is not a fundamental struggle over liberal world order because China fundamentally supports that order and benefits from it in its pursuit of economic growth and transformation. For that reason, and because the long-term trend in modernizing China is in a liberal direction, China will not seek regional revisions that create serious conflict with the United States. Conflict will jeopardize its economic priorities (Ikenberry 2014; Deudney and Ikenberry 2009). The realist view claims that China is committed to seeking regional hegemony and that may easily combine with an offensive posture in the near future, leading towards conflict with the United States (Mearsheimer 2010; Ayson 2015).

Both views have a point, but also a weakness. Liberals are right that the overriding concern of China is continued stable economic development. That requires a reformed growth model which is set to further entrench China's integration in the capitalist world economy. But at the same time, Xi Jinping's plan for re-vitalization of the Communist Party by no means includes a movement in the direction of liberal democracy (Rudd 2013). Realists are right that China is looking for a 'new type of major-country relationship' with the United States (Campbell and Murray 2013). Yet this 'new relationship' is not only defined by the promotion of Chinese key security interests, but also by the expansion of economic, institutional and even military cooperation. At the present time, the United States and China know that they are rivals and they actively seek to avoid becoming enemies; whether this is a sufficient basis for a stable order in the Asia-Pacific is as of yet unclear.

We turn to Eastern Europe with a focus on Russia. The relationship between Russia and other great powers is at present overwhelmingly shaped by the situation in Ukraine. In November of 2013 the cabinet of Ukrainian president Viktor Yanukovych rejected an agreement on close trade ties between Ukraine and the European Union. Popular protests in Kiev soon followed, culminating in early December when 800,000 people attended a demonstration and protesters occupied Kiev city hall. Further protests were followed by restrictive anti-protest laws and clashes between police and activists. On 19–20 February, close to a hundred people were killed. A 21 February compromise between Yanukovych and opposition leaders stipulated constitutional reform, presidential elections and the formation of a national unity government.

The next day, President Yanukovych disappears, parliament votes to remove the president from power, and an election is set for 25 May. Parliament speaker Oleksandr Turchynov is appointed interim president. By the end of February, pro-Russian gunmen take control of strategic buildings in the Crimean capital, Simferopol. On 6 March, Crimea's parliament votes to join Russia and sets a referendum for 16 March. Official results say 97% of voters back a proposal to join Russia. The European Union and the United States impose sanctions on Russian and Ukrainian officials. Moscow vetoes a UN draft resolution criticizing the referendum and Putin signs a bill to incorporate Crimea into the Russian Federation.

EU leaders meet in Brussels and condemn Russia's 'annexation'; both the United States and the European Union extend the list of individuals targeted for sanctions. In late March, signs of a build-up of Russian forces on the Eastern border of Ukraine are criticized by President Obama. Vladimir Putin orders a 'partial withdrawal' of troops and declares Russia will not interfere in Eastern Ukraine. Pro-Russian protesters occupy government buildings in the Eastern Ukrainian cities of Donetsk, Kharkiv and Lugansk.

In mid-April, the foreign ministers of Ukraine, the European Union, the United States and Russia meet in Geneva. The result is a declaration aimed at de-escalating the tensions in Eastern Ukraine and preventing them from turning into open conflict. All sides are called upon to refrain from violence, armed groups are to lay down their weapons and occupied public spaces must be vacated. Further, a broad national dialogue and international aid to Ukraine is envisaged. But de-escalation is so far not very successful and Russia and the West have not reached a consensus about future developments in Ukraine.

Do these developments amount to a return towards the 'old world' of interstate war? Some observers appear to think so. *The Economist* (March 22, 2014) finds that 'Mr Putin has driven a tank over the existing world order' and displays a return to 'revanchism' and an 'anarchic, mistrustful world'. Former US ambassador to Moscow, Michael McFaul said in March 2014 that the Russian president 'embraces confrontation with the West ... [and] has made a strategic pivot' (McFaul 2014).

There is surely a colder climate between Russia and the West than was the case before the Ukrainian crisis. As recently as September 2013, Vladimir Putin had this message to the world speaking in the context of the Syrian crisis: 'We need to use the United Nations Security Council and believe that preserving law and order in today's complex and turbulent world is one of the few ways to keep international relations from sliding into chaos. ... The law is still the law and we must follow it whether we like it or not' (Putin 2013). Whatever the disputes over Russian activities in Ukraine, they have not respected international law.

But is this a return to imminent dangers of interstate war? Certainly not at the present time; Obama has emphasized that the West does not want to go war with Russia over Ukraine and Putin knows very well that Russia has neither the military capability nor any substantial interest in a military confrontation with the West (Shuster 2014). So if it's not a situation of imminent great power war, what is it? And will the situation eventually lead to a new Cold War between Russia and the West?

First, the current situation emerged primarily from domestic developments in Ukraine. The country is a fragile state in the sense that the political system is corrupt and ineffective, the economy is weak and dependent, and national coherence is increasingly challenged by divisions between Russian-oriented and Western-oriented groups. The presidency of Victor Yanukovych severely aggravated these problems. His inner circle, 'the family' grouped around his son, formed a clan that attempted to take control over government and persecuted political opponents. Together with the issue of Ukraine's leaning towards the West or towards Russia this led to the confrontations with the opposition.

Second, Russia has been active in this process by characterizing anti-Yanukovych forces as 'fascists' presenting a threat to the Russian-oriented population similar to the Nazi threat of World War II. The West, meanwhile, was quick to accept the ousting of Yanukovych and the abandoning of the 21 February compromise (signed by three EU foreign ministers) which promised a unity government. This plays into the larger context of mistrust between the West and Russia. The West sees Russian activities in Ukraine and the annexation of Crimea in particular, as a dramatic breach of international law. Putin defends the Russian actions in Crimea as a 'humanitarian intervention' and argues that it is the West which has ignored international law for quite a while (Walker 2014).

Will this then lead to a new Cold War? In earlier days, the fall of a pro-Soviet government would have triggered a Soviet invasion in Ukraine immediately; Russia has not undertaken any such invasion but it has put military forces on the ground in Eastern Ukraine and it certainly would like a friendly regime in Kiev or, at the least, a federalization of Ukraine which includes the rights of regions to their own foreign and economic policies. On the Western side, it is not surprising that the NATO General Secretary would like a tighter transatlantic alliance and an increase in European defence spending. But the long-term solution for Ukraine and the other countries in Russia's 'near abroad' is surely strong relationships with both Russia and the European Union. That requires a democratic and effective Ukrainian government which serves the interests of ordinary Ukrainians of all stripes. It also requires that the channels for economic and political cooperation with Russia are kept open (Slaughter 2014).

As indicated earlier, there will not be great power war. But nor will there be an easy pathway to a stable order based on power and legitimacy (for recent in-depth treatments of the Ukraine crisis, see Wilson 2014 and Menon and Rumer 2015). In power terms, Russia cannot take on the West, and the economic consequences would be disastrous for the country. But Russia is strong enough to assert its influence in the 'intermediary zone' of Ukraine, Belarus and Moldova. At the same time, two understandings of legitimacy confront each other in this zone: on one hand, the Western view that these countries must enjoy a free choice of closer economic, political and military relations with the West; on the other hand, the view of Putin's Russia that the country has legitimate special security interests in the 'intermediary zone' (in the same way the United States has had special interests in Latin America since the Monroe doctrine) and that Westernization of the zone is a policy of containment and a threat to Russian security (Götz 2013; Zubok 2013).

In sum, this is not a new Cold War, but it might eventually lead to a significantly cooled relationship between Russia and the West depending on what the parties choose to do. The structural setting points in the direction of moderation: neither party is deeply interested in cutting off economic interdependencies or abandoning institutional networks. But real progress in the direction of moderation still depends on a successful de-escalation of the crisis in Ukraine and that remains a complex task (on Russian 'isolationism', see Chapter 6).

We turn to the greater Middle East. After more than ten years of intense engagement in Afghanistan and Iraq, the United States had begun to wind down its military engagement in the region. But then came the civil war in Syria in 2011; together with increased fragmentation of Iraq into Kurd, Shia and Sunni areas, the war has given new life to a violently radical Islamism, the Islamic State of Iraq and the Levant, ISIL. The US runs a bombing campaign against ISIL, but will not put boots on the ground. The great powers have not been able to agree on an effective way of approaching the Syrian conflict, which has produced an estimated 7.6 million internally displaced people and 4.4 million refugees (IDMC 2015; UNHCR 2015).

Most states in the Middle East suffer from lack of socio-political cohesion. Syria, for example, is an Arab country with a majority of Sunni Muslims; but there are Kurdish and Armenian minorities and some 10% Christians. President Bashar al-Assad belongs to the Alawite minority, an offshoot of Shia Islam. Nevertheless, in the past most authoritarian Arab rulers have been able to consolidate themselves and to contain domestic violence. One important element in this is the control of oil resources that have brought the means to co-opt and suppress their populations. The major exception is the Israeli-Palestinian conflict which can be seen as a domestic struggle defining patterns of enmity and amity between Israel and the Arab world (Buzan 2003).

At the same time, important Arab states in the region have weakened over the last decade, becoming less able to control sectarian conflicts. The US invasion of Iraq effectively led to the dissolution of the authoritarian state; the ruling party was banned, the military dissolved, and the bureaucracy purged of party members. When the state collapsed, religious and ethnic divisions became dominant in the struggle for power. It also opened to the influence of strong regional powers, that is, Iran and Saudi Arabia. The classic case of a weak state in the region is Lebanon, but Syria and Yemen are other examples. State weakness opens to outside influence. According to one recent analysis, the regional powers are key players in the current conflicts in Syria and Iraq: 'Saudi Arabia and Iran did not create the state weakness and sectarian identities in these countries, but they are certainly taking advantage, advancing their own interests in a classic balance of power game' (Gause 2014: 11; see also Lynch 2012 and Valbjørn and Bank 2012).

In contrast to Europe and Asia-Pacific, no great power has been willing or able to establish a stable security order in the Middle East. The Soviet Union and the United States competed for influence in the region during the Cold War, but were not able to create stable alliances, even when it came to client regimes. Egypt shifted to the United States after 1973 and close ally Iran fell out of American influence after 1979. The strongest and most permanent alliance is between Israel and the United States. The US has pledged an 'unshakable commitment' to Israel's security (NSS 2010: 24); it also acknowledges the 'legitimate aspirations' (NSS 2010: 25) of Palestinians for security and dignity, but the latter has never stood in the way of the former. Russia is an ally of the Assad regime; it operates a naval facility in Syria (Tartus) and is the major arms supplier of the regime. This is not an alliance in the class of US–Israel but Russia has stood by the Assad regime since the beginning of the civil war in 2011.

So the United States and Russia have been active in the Middle East since the beginning of the Cold War, but not severely beyond protecting core interests and even that has proven sufficiently complicated. American oil interests have pulled in the direction of close relations to Arab countries; the pledge to Israel has pulled in another direction. When it made sense to ally with one state—such as Iraq in the context of the Iraq/Iran war in the 1980s—there were often negative consequences in terms of other commitments, such as the alliance with Israel. The war in Iraq strengthened the position of Iran in the region; the current operation against ISIL indirectly supports the Assad regime. It is not a simple task, not even for a great power, to operate in the Middle East.

There is one current area where the great powers have demonstrated some cooperation. It is in relation to blocking Iran's nuclear programme. Iran assures that the programme is for peaceful purposes. The great powers (United States, China, Russia, United Kingdom, France and Germany) suspect that Iran is seeking the ability to build a nuclear bomb. Negotiations concern the future of the programme including international inspection, and the lifting of sanctions against Iran.

In sum, the great powers have competed in the Middle East, but they have not aggressively confronted each other and none have been able to control or even heavily determine the security situation in the region. Their role as arms suppliers, alliance partners, and interveners has helped create, fuel and sustain regional conflict as often as it has been able to dampen it. With Palestinians in the state of a semi-intifada and Israelis continuing settlement and discrimination policies unabashedly (Dugard 2007; Makdisi 2014), no end of this unrelenting conflict is in sight. Syria and Iraq are being torn apart by violent conflict that may lead to long-term divisions within the countries and have serious consequences elsewhere in the region.

There will be no hostile great power conflict in relation to the Middle East but nor is any great power able or willing to establish a stable and legitimate security order in the area. The one realistic candidate for the job, the United States, is preoccupied with its alliance with Israel and the struggle against radical Islamists. A legitimate order needs to accommodate not only Iran, Saudi Arabia and Israel, but also the Palestinians, Islamic groups, and several large minorities. Neither the United States and other great powers, nor the local players, are moving strongly in that direction at the present time. For a very large number of people in the region, even a rudimentary version of the good life is nowhere in sight.

The larger horizon of human security

The traditional view of security concerns the protection of states from military attack by other states. The focus of human security is on the protection of individuals and groups of people from the hazards that really affect them. One major aspect of this is threats from violent conflict inside fragile states as addressed in a previous section. But human security addresses other types of threat that not only have to do with physical violence; human safety is also endangered by hunger, disease, repression, environmental degradation and more. Compared with the traditional approach to security, then, the referent object changes from states to people, and the list of possible threats to people is dramatically expanded.

The concept was first prominently launched in the *Human Development Report* issued by the United Nations Development Programme (UNDP 1994). The relevant question in the present context is about the extent to which the larger agenda of human security has affected world order. The broad agenda of human security has not significantly found its way into political practice. This can be seen especially in the case of the European Union. The European Union formally wants to promote the concept of human security, but also notes that 'further reflection is needed to identify the thematic areas in which this approach can best show its added value' (EU priorities for the UN General Assembly, June 2011, cited from Christou 2014). This basically means that traditional national security issues continue to dominate the EU common security and defence policy.

The United States has generally 'defined its security policies in terms that are largely distinct from the human security agenda' (Payne 2004). China maintains a traditional view of security, emphasizing national sovereignty and non-intervention. At the same time, China looks to integrate itself into international society and become a legitimate great power. This has led to consideration of human security issues, both in China's own development and in connection with its international engagements (Tow et al. 2013). So human security has entered the official Chinese language of security, but most of that debate is focused on domestic conditions. In the international sphere, the national security outlook remains vastly dominant. India has a debate on human security but, even more than in China, it is entirely domestically focused; traditional security concerns dominate the international outlook.

Overall, both established and emerging great powers nod kindly towards the larger agenda of human security but this has not meant a real shift in security priorities. Focus remains on the traditional national security agenda, as reflected in the levels of military expenditure compared to levels of development aid. This is behind the critical claim that human security has not made any difference in relation to business-as-usual (Booth 2007: 323–24).

But the lack of great power muscle behind the broad human security agenda and the tendency to define human security threats in traditional terms does not make the human security agenda irrelevant or even marginal. There has been a major change in relation to legitimacy. The classic notion of national security is primarily concerned with territorial integrity. The human security focus on individuals and groups makes it abundantly clear that the security of people may not be looked after by the classic focus. The human security focus requires states to be alert to environmental, health, food and economic security. The legitimacy of states internally, in relation to their own populations, and externally, in international society, is now much more clearly connected to the human security agenda than used to be the case. In that sense, it is not business as usual.

The point can be amplified by reference to the institution of sovereignty. It is the classic imperative in relation to sovereignty that states acknowledge 'the sovereign equality of all states, respect for territorial integrity and political independence ... [and] non-interference in the internal affairs of states' (UN Millennium Declaration 2000). This is the emphasis on sovereign autonomy and the principle of non-intervention. At the same time, the Millennium Declaration, as does the UN Charter, requires states to 'respect human rights and fundamental freedoms' and 'equal rights of all' (UN Millennium Declaration 2000; UN Charter 1945). This is the emphasis on human security for all people.

Sovereign autonomy was always the first principle while the human security emphasis came second. It is this relationship which has changed to upgrade human security concerns and to downgrade sovereign autonomy concerns. This is reflected in numerous UN declarations and reports (Gómez and Gasper 2012), and in the international debate which much more clearly includes concerns about inequality, environmental degradation, health and food problems, and political security, not merely in fragile states in the Global South but in all states including the rich countries. The peace- and state-building activities mentioned earlier are part of this picture as well.

A great amount of human misery remains unaddressed because many states are not able or willing to take care of their own. The broad notion of human security has put this item on the agenda. States whose people fare poorly are in worse standing and lose legitimacy in the international society. This is not least due to the increased salience of the human security perspective on the international agenda. It has not solved the problem of human security and there is no consensus about best ways forward, but at least there is now a much increased focus on it in international as well as national debates.

Conclusion

The present security agenda differs dramatically from that of the Cold War, but there is no agreement on exactly what has replaced that period. I have identified three items of importance. First, there are several fragile states with high levels of domestic violence. Significant moves have been made in the direction of a security order that addresses violence in fragile states. The 'Responsibility to Protect' creates a framework for intervention towards the protection of people and numerous peace- and state-building operations are under way in fragile states. But the UN remains weak and dependent on support from resourceful countries and these countries are concerned about human and material cost. At the same time, international terrorism and large flows of refugees have emerged as major problems in relation to fragile states.

Perhaps the largest challenge concerns the combination of peace-building and state-building. The former requires *ex*clusion of groups that act as spoilers in the peace process, such as the Taliban in Afghanistan; the latter requires *in*clusion of all significant groups in society in pursuit of democracy and effective statehood, so one part of the task is divisive and the other part of the task needs to be inclusive. The creation of legitimacy and support for state-building, both in relation to national elites and in relation to people on the ground, comes with a number of complex challenges that are not easily handled.

It is an open question whether sustained progress can be made in terms of peace- and state-building in states where local conditions are adverse and outsiders face a number of obstacles that prevent them from effective operations. They may be able to save lives in the short and medium term, but they cannot reconstruct fragile states or build them from scratch if local conditions are not forthcoming. Their operations must, by necessity, be constrained both by lack of power and lack of legitimacy.

The second item concerns the traditional security agenda of global and regional order, and great power contention. In Asia-Pacific, the United States has retained its major role in the establishment of a revised security order. The order is increasingly challenged by China's rise but there are possibilities for accommodation. By early 2016, China had moved away from a confrontational course in the East and South China Seas, towards diplomatic efforts in relation to Japan, Korea, Vietnam, the Philippines and Taiwan. Whether this will lead to a stable order in the area is still an open question. Russia's relationship with the West is deteriorating because of the crisis in Ukraine and will depend on a de-escalation of that crisis. There was less violence in Eastern Ukraine by late 2015; this has been combined with increased Russian involvement in the Syrian conflict. It might mean that Russia is embarking on a more negotiation-friendly course towards the West, but it is still uncertain what Russia's future international role—a rival, an enemy or a friend—will be. There are several crises in the Middle East; the great powers are heavily involved, but there is no great power hegemony in the region which is characterized by an arch of fragile states and competition between strong regional players.

Third, the human security agenda concerns a variety of threats to people everywhere. This larger security agenda has not become dominant; in that sense states continue to focus on traditional security concerns. But human security matters anyway because both rich and poor states are now judged—and their domestic and international legitimacy affected—by the ways in which they are able and willing to look after the general safety of their own populations.

Does all this add up to a functioning security order? Not in terms of the ambitious goal of access to the good life for all people. But a case can surely be made for 'security governance in pieces': the issue of fragile states is being addressed, not always and not very effectively, but to a much larger extent than earlier. Traditional security issues have not been resolved, but with the partial exception of Russia, emerging non-democratic great powers have an acknowledged place in the present security order; it is not an all-out Cold War confrontation anymore. Human security in the broad sense is an acknowledged item on the agenda.

Sceptics will surely find this a much too rosy picture. The US/West has been able to make very little headway when it comes to the largest security problem in terms of human cost: violence in fragile states. Both domestic and international conditions (including perceived Western security interests) heavily constrain what can be done in fragile states and the results, over more than two decades, have not been impressive. Human security is talked about, but there is little in terms of concrete measures. We will not see a violent great power confrontation, but regional security complexes, including the Middle East, Russia's near abroad and Asia-Pacific, present enough of current security challenges. US preponderant power is not enough; a stable security order must be able to claim legitimacy among other relevant actors as well. How this will be done, in particular in the Middle East and in Russia's near abroad, remains unclear.

I put the general question earlier, whether we were headed towards a liberal scenario of a reformed Western order with global reach, or towards a realist scenario of increasing crisis and instability. In terms of the security structure discussed in this chapter, the latter scenario dominates the former at the present time. The present order was developed by the US/West, and in some respects it has been able to accommodate the non-liberal great powers and to address violent conflict in fragile states. But serious problems also remain. A stable and effective order based on sufficient power and legitimacy is not in place.

6
Economics: The Dynamics of Globalization

Introduction

The principal characteristic of the economic structure is the ongoing process of globalization. Globalization is the intensification of economic, political, social and cultural relations across borders (Holm and Sørensen 1995: 4). The focus in this chapter is on economic globalization in all of its aspects, for example trade, production, investment and financial flows. The aim is to identify the major features of current processes of globalization and to evaluate their consequences for world order.

During most of the Cold War, it was relevant to think of the economic world in terms of three areas: the industrialized capitalist countries; the developing countries in Asia, Africa and Latin America; and the centrally planned economies of the communist world. But in 1979, China (and Vietnam) began a move away from central planning and towards international markets; the Soviet Union began a similar move by the mid-1980s and when the Cold War ended the entire Eastern Bloc followed suit. Developing countries had focused on domestically driven economic development in the 1960s and 1970s; with the debt and oil crises of the late 1970s they chose, or were pushed by donors, in the direction of economic openness. A severe balance of payment deficit took India in the same direction in 1990. The industrialized world, meanwhile, was compelled to reform the fixed exchange rate regime connected with the Bretton Woods system; that opened to floating exchange rates and the massive growth of international financial markets (Frieden 2012).

These transformations in the political economy of nations were combined with other changes that set the stage for economic globalization: mass transportation technologies made movement of goods and people across the globe much faster and cheaper than earlier; production technologies made it possible to carve up the production of various components of a complex product (a car, a smartphone) and situate each in locations where conditions were optimal in terms of labour cost, technological environment, proximity of markets and so on. Finally, communication technologies have opened up to organizing and managing all this on a global scale. In short, political, economic and technological developments gave way to a much intensified process of economic globalization.

In a brief period of time, economic globalization has become so taken for granted that it appears to be a juggernaut out of control. According to one observer, 'the impact of this *Juggernaut* upon the countries of the world is unstoppable, as it is driven by the most powerful incentives among human beings, namely the search for economic gain' (Lane 2008: 8). But this view is misleading, because as we have just noted, economic globalization is shaped by a host of political and economic factors and when they change, globalization changes with them. Two examples: intensified regional cooperation, such as the European Union, tends to promote regional as opposed to truly global economic exchange; some European countries have actually 'de-globalized' in recent years in the sense that regional flows have replaced global flows (Ghemawat and Altman 2014). Further, technological developments can change the economic calculation away from globalizing and in favour of 'staying home' or even domesticizing activities that were previously outsourced. A substantial amount of 'reshoring' has been taking place of late (*The Economist* 2013). Several other elements of course affect economic globalization, such as the financial crisis from 2008. Joachim Fels, head of global economics at Morgan Stanley, worried in 2013 about 'a creeping trend towards de-globalization of economic activity and capital flows' (quoted from Ghemawat and Altman 2014: 22; for additional views of economic globalization, see Glyn 2007, Boltanski and Chiapello 2007, Nee 2005, and Bhagwati 2007).

One way of measuring economic globalization is the Global Connectedness Index (GCI) which looks at trade, capital, information and people flows (Ghemawat and Altman 2014). In terms of overall connectedness, nine out of the ten most connected countries are in Europe (the exception is Singapore); but it is in the emerging economies where global connectedness has increased the most in recent years. The level of countries' international flows relative to the size of their economies remains smaller than most people think: in most cases the international share is less than 10–20%. Only the trade share and the share of portfolio equity stocks score over 30%. At the same time, the intra-regional share of international interactions remains high, at more than 40% of the total (Ghemawat and Altman 2014: 14).

At the same time, this should not be mistaken for a general process of de-globalization. It is not surprising that especially larger countries retain a major share of economic activity at home. Nevertheless, globalization is now the defining economic context for almost all countries in the world. Three basic trends underline this state of affairs (Dervis 2012); first, many emerging and developing economies have practised catch-up growth compared to the advanced market economies. This is due to strengthened trade links and high levels of foreign investment. That has led to a new tendency towards convergence among what used to be the rich 'North' and a group of the less developed 'South', even if the catch-up process is far from complete. The sharp distinction between 'developed' and 'developing' countries (where China and Brazil were included among the latter) was finally abandoned in the 2014 Lima meeting on climate change (Jacobs 2014).

Second, intensified trade relations, integrated financial markets and a tendency for convergence of economic expectations have led to a harmonization in terms of cyclical interdependence. That is to say, the cyclical links between all advanced and developing economies have become much stronger, in particular over the last two decades (Dervis 2012). Finally, a tendency towards higher inequality within all types of countries, including advanced, emerging, and developing economies, has become a feature of current economic globalization. There is increased income concentration at the very top, combined with a vast bottom in the developing world, where many millions have not seen improved real incomes (Milanovic 2012). This is due to a variety of factors, including an increased skill premium, technological change, the mobility of capital versus the relative immobility of labour, and the declining influence of unions (Dervis 2012: 13).

In short, the world hangs closer together in economic terms and we want to know what that means for world order. Chapter 2 argued that interstate war is of decreasing importance, but it did not embrace a liberal scenario of harmonious cooperation. A range of different forms of rivalry, competition or cooperation are possible. The benign scenario would be one of 'common fate' where a world of capitalist economies cooperate in facing shared challenges of economic stability, environmental balance, and the management of security threats. The malign scenario, by contrast, would be one of economic rivalry and competition, which might entail geopolitical rivalry and competition as well.

The liberal idea that trade and other economic intercourse are good for cooperation and peace goes back to Baron Montesquieu and Richard Cobden. Norman Angell's book from 1909, *The Great Illusion*, further developed the argument. The illusion, said Angell, is to believe that war serves profitable purposes and that success in war is beneficial for the winner. The opposite is true: in modern times territorial conquest is extremely expensive and politically divisive because it severely disrupts international commerce. The liberal argument is that economic globalization—a high division of labour in the international economy—increases economic interdependence among states, and that this discourages and reduces conflict between them (for a contemporary version of the claim, see Rosecrance 1999).

The problem for the argument was that comparatively high levels of economic interdependence among European powers did little to prevent the devastations of World War I. The war appeared to support the realist argument which has no faith whatsoever in benefits of economic interdependence when it comes to cooperation and peace: on the contrary, economic networks across borders create vulnerability and dependence. For these reasons, states will attempt to minimize and to control these relationships. States that require vital goods from the outside will seek 'to expand political control to the source of supply, giving rise to conflict with the source or with its customers' (Mearsheimer 1992: 223).

The debate has been revisited many times, also by scholars who pursue large-N quantitative analyses. The disagreement about the major effects of economic interdependence—cooperation or conflict—remains, but there is increasing consensus on an important point: economic interdependence alone does not determine the outcome. The effect of economic interdependence is tied in with the larger context in which it unfolds. The further specification of that context continues to divide liberals from realists, of course. The former emphasize additional liberal elements that help create cooperation and peace; the latter underline elements that help create conflict (for an excellent overview, see Copeland 2015). I begin with the expanded liberal view after which the supposedly cooperative and conflictual elements in economic globalization will be discussed.

The benign view: Globalization leading towards 'one world'

The classic liberal view is based on modernization theory: the process of economic, political and social modernization undertaken by the advanced capitalist countries will eventually come to all societies. The progressive journey from a pre-industrial, agrarian society towards a modern, industrial, mass-consumption society is well under way in many countries in the world, driven in no small measure by the process of economic globalization. This is where economic interdependence can be put in context: the general process of modernization involves a host of other changes in terms of mass politics and democratization, higher levels of education and information, institutional and social connectedness, and so on (Jackson and Sørensen 2013). They combine with economic interdependence to produce a new, modern context which is much more supportive towards cooperation between countries.

With an intensified economic globalization in recent decades, there is no doubt that elements of these processes are taking place in many countries. The question is how far they have progressed and how sustainable they are. One recent liberal analysis suggests that they have already progressed sufficiently so as to produce one world in practice, if not in theory. Kishore Mahbubani (2013: 51) quotes political leaders in support of this view, including Bill Clinton, who calls for 'an ethic of interdependence rooted in our common history', Al Gore ('We are now in a Global Age. Like it or not, we live in an age where our destinies and the destinies of billions of people around the globe are increasingly intertwined ... Our future is dependent upon increasing cooperation and interdependence in a world tied ever more closely together by technologies of communication and travel') and Tony Blair ('Under the momentum of globalization, the world is opening up and countries and cultures are coming closer together at an astonishing speed. ... In a shrinking world we must be global citizens as well as citizens of our own countries').

On this basis, Mahbubani (2013: 55) suggests a 'comprehensive theory' of one world. It rests on four pillars of convergence that 'are driving humanity to acknowledge that we live in one world'. The four pillars are economic, technological, environmental and aspirational (the following draws on Mahbubani 2013: 51–89).

The economic pillar: the financial crisis of 2008–09 demonstrated the existence of a single, global economy. But political leaders responded by underscoring short-term, narrow national interests instead of global interests. They are supported by economists who claim that a single, global economy only exists when there is also a single, global government, elected by a global electorate emerging from a global society. But even in the absence of global political institutions, we do have a single, global economy. US Federal Reserve decisions on monetary policies deeply influence the prospects for other countries. Manufacturing companies such as Apple are compelled to outsource jobs from the United States in order to stay globally competitive; narrow, national efforts can no longer fix national economies. The march of economic liberalization will continue to strengthen the emerging global economy.

The technological pillar: the advance of technology helps to bring about a new global identity. Cell phones, computers and aircrafts help bring people closer together. Governments are now much less able to control access to information. International travellers will be globally educated citizens. The previous connection to the village, city or country will be overlapped by new layers of identity, drawn from the connections across borders.

The environmental pillar: the growing threats to the environment are possibly the strongest factor which unites the inhabitants of the globe; we need to preserve our one home. The dangers connected to climate change and global warming are vastly important but they are accompanied by a large number of additional hazards related to resource depletion, water and air pollution, land degradation, deforestation and so on. There is a growing environmental awareness, but because national leaders primarily defend national interests, there is a glaring lack of governance of global issues such as the environment.

The aspirational pillar: the vast majority of the world's population now share a common set of material aspirations. They help create common interests which override differences in ideology or religion. People want their government to focus on economic development, not on war. Educational aspirations also unite people; in combination, we are moving towards a one-world dynamic where our common aspirations are greater than our differences.

In sum, according to Mahbubani it is already the case that the theory of one world is driving global affairs, pushed by the four pillars of convergence. 'This is why we urgently need to equip the minds of policymakers with new mental maps. National considerations will have to be balanced with global considerations, national interests with global interests ...' (Mahbubani 2013: 87). In the following sections, the validity of this view is examined.

What sort of convergence?

Mahbubani speaks of a process of economic convergence leading to a single, global economy. But capitalist development is by definition uneven (Smith 2008). The same goes for the process of economic globalization under capitalist conditions; it is uneven in terms of intensity and geographical scope, in both the international and the domestic dimension. The unevenness of economic globalization means that the idea of convergence towards a single global economy is highly contested. Paul Hirst and Grahame Thompson make a distinction between two ideal types of economic globalization that help clarify the debate. The first is a growing level of interconnection between two national economies, for example in the form of investment or trade; this could be called 'intensified interdependence'. The other is a shift towards 'true economic globalization' with a global economic system no longer based on autonomous national economies but on a 'consolidated global marketplace for production, distribution and consumption' (Hirst and Thompson 1992: 199).

It is quite clear that we have not arrived in a world where 'true economic globalization' in the sense described by Hirst and Thompson has been created; there is not a unified, homogenous and totally integrated global economy. The question is rather whether processes of 'intensified interdependence' have led to a very high level of convergence and thus to a 'single global economy' as indicated by Mahbubani. Some developments surely point in this direction, as already indicated. Today's level of economic globalization is unprecedented in the sense that we have, for the first time in history, a situation where all three circuits of capital—trade, finance and production—are strongly globalized (Went 2004). During the previous peak of economic globalization, the decades before World War I, it was only trade and finance that were highly internationalized. The inclusion of production in globalization relates to convergence in the sense that all countries increasingly become part of the same globalized production system.

Second, the involvement of almost all countries in the pursuit of economic globalization has made capitalism truly global for the first time in history. Third, finance capital has become the dominant engine of the global capitalist system. In particular, the advanced capitalist economies have undergone a process of 'financialization' (Tabb 2012) in three ways: industrial and commercial undertakings increasingly involve themselves in financial transactions not related to productive investment but with a view to extracting financial profit; big banks are less classic lenders of capital but seek profit by transacting in financial markets; and households and individuals are increasingly also involved in private finance in relation to housing, pensions, education and health (Lapavitsas 2013). The overall ramifications of financialization are contested, but it is clear that they increase the volatility of the economic system due to speculation and that single countries are more exposed to 'a globalized regime of accumulation with financial predominance' (Went 2004). The convergence aspect of this is that countries must comply with the rules and demands of the financialized system and this reduces the scope for national variation in countries' participation in the global economic system (Went 2004: 343).

A final aspect of convergence relates to the role of transnational corporations, companies with activities in several countries. There were 78,000 TNCs by 2006, with 780,000 overseas affiliates (Spero 2010: 129). But only a couple of thousand corporations account for half the world's trade in goods (Went 2004: 344); one analysis went further and argued that a mere 737 companies control 80% of the global economy (Vitali, Glattfelder and Batiston: 2011). On this view, convergence is driven by a process of increasing international concentration and centralization of capital, whereby a small number of companies wield global economic power.

But is all this truly a process of convergence towards a 'single global economy'? There are sharp limits to convergence. First, even if almost all countries aspire to participate in a global economy, the actual level of involvement if highly uneven. As already indicated, it is the advanced capitalist countries in Western Europe,

North America and East Asia that are mostly involved in economic globalization. Many developing countries, especially the least developed countries, are minimally involved. A key indicator of this state of affairs is the stock of FDI. The global stock of FDI was $25 trillion in 2013; developed economies accounted for 67%, developing economies took 33%. The lion's share of the latter went to a limited number of emerging economies, including China (11%), Brazil (8.5%) and Mexico (4.5%). The total share for all of Africa was 8.5% (calculated from UNCTAD 2014).

Behind these figures on the distribution of total *stocks* of FDI are several new trends in the *flows* of direct investment. China is the top preferred destination for FDI in the 2012–14 period; the United States is second on that list, with India, Indonesia and Brazil next in the ranking. In sum, a core reason for economic globalization being uneven is related to the preferences of investment capital: some locations are very interesting for a host of reasons, others much less so. Seen from recipient countries, there is a clear hierarchy: emerging economies are favoured over a host of less developed countries struggling on the margins. The increased investor interest in some African countries in recent years has not basically changed this picture.

Second, even if countries are heavily involved in the global economy, any process of convergence is limited by the fact that economic globalization—and capitalist development in general—takes place under very different political, cultural and other conditions in various countries. Participation in economic globalization does involve convergence in the sense that the involved countries must conform to basic standards of a capitalist market economy, but in any country, such a system cannot possibly create itself. It can only be brought about through political regulations which construct the necessary enabling framework. In other words, the road to a capitalist market economy is paved with political regulation, containing the variety of rules and principles which enable the market to function. That regulatory framework is an integrated part of what capitalism is in any given national context. The point is that the resulting model of capitalism is deeply conditioned by the politics, power configurations, social traditions and so on, that prevail in the single country.

Against this background there is a large debate about 'varieties of capitalism', but most of this literature is focused on neoliberal versus social democratic varieties of capitalism in the advanced Western countries (Becker 2014) making it less suited for looking at capitalist varieties in a global context. In order to get at the issue of global capitalism and convergence, I briefly discuss economic variation in today's world, followed by reflections on the consequences for world order.

A primary feature of many of the recent additions to the capitalist world system is that the countries are not democratic. China, Russia and many others have embraced a capitalist market economy (or substantial parts of it), but the political systems remain autocratic. Economic modernization and Westernization understood as political liberalization are not the same. Buzan and Lawson (2014) make a distinction between 'competitive authoritarian capitalism', which favours state control over the market and constrains democratic governance, and 'state bureaucratic capitalism', where democracy is rejected outright and there is a mix of state ownership and market relations. Kupchan (2012) differentiates between 'communal autocracy' with a partnership between the private sector and the state apparatus (China), 'paternal autocracy' with a hierarchical relationship between the state and the private sector (Russia), and 'tribal autocracy' where tribe and clan define political community (the sheikdoms of the Persian Gulf). The point is that there are many different and complex combinations of state–market relations within various shades of autocracy.

Since China was introduced earlier (Chapter 2), it is relevant to focus on Russia as a case of transition towards capitalism with definitely peculiar characteristics. The dissolution of the Soviet Union was an experiment on many levels; many commentators focus on the huge challenges to democracy and political pluralism but perhaps the greatest challenge was to introduce capitalism into an already industrialized society under complete state control (Mann 2013: 207–17; see also Tikhomirov 2000 and Aslund 2002). The destructive phase—dismantling the powers of the state and the Communist Party—went quickly, but the constructive phase—building an effective market economy under sensible liberal regulation—never really got off the ground. The neoliberal 'shock therapy' promoted by Boris Yeltsin from 1992 immediately liberalized prices, currency, foreign trade and restrictions on capital flows. But there was no new system of rules to take over, no cohorts of entrepreneurial venture capitalists waiting in the wings. Prices went up—inflation was 900% in 1993—when subsidies were cut and production went down because state enterprises lacked orders and means of financing; unemployment soared; so did imports, threatening many Russian firms. Overall production declined by half and investment declined by two-thirds; shock therapy was a catastrophe.

The policy of allowing nomenklatura members to acquire control of industries and banks had begun already under Gorbachev; it was continued and strengthened under Yeltsin. On one hand, the newly-turned capitalists continued to receive state subsidies because state firms were in dire straits; on the other hand, with no restrictions on capital flows it was possible to move ample funds into foreign bank accounts. The result had very little to do with a classic capitalist system. In the latter, the production and distribution of commodities is controlled, regulated and directed by the market. This implies an institutional separation of economics from politics. That separation is substantially absent in the Russian system; it is political crony capitalism, a kleptocracy, where state and market are integrated in ways unknown to the classic system because more than anything else economic power is based on political connections, monopoly and theft. In that sense, it is a system of 'capitalists without capitalism' (Eyal et al. 1998).

Vladimir Putin came into power in 2000. He was widely credited with shifting power back to the state, renationalizing some industries, bringing inflation under control, securing economic growth and raising living standards, all within a context of cracking down on political opponents and reining in earlier democratic reforms. The restored order is Kremlin's order; it is not the rule of law because there is not an independent judiciary. The power of oligarchs and of regional governors has been cut and those that have not been arrested now toe the line of the government. Even if democracy suffered, this looked like a substantial achievement in terms of bringing order to Russia. Putin was *Time Magazine*'s Person of the Year 2007 for his 'extraordinary feat of leadership in imposing stability on a nation that has rarely known it and brought Russia back to the table of world power' (*Time Magazine* 2007).

Today's picture of Putin's achievements is less rosy. Economic growth was helped along by rising energy prices and ruble devaluations. The weak rule of law and insecure property rights remain a problem, and inequality remains high (Hanson 2003; Voigt and Hockmann 2008). The sharpest indictment of Putin comes in a recent analysis by Karen Dawisha (2014) titled 'Putin's Kleptocracy'. The claim is that ever since his KGB days in the 1980s, Putin has strived to create a 'kleptocracy' led by himself, a system where risks are nationalized and rewards are privatized, as in the Sochi Olympics project where $50 billion of state expenses were awarded as no-bid contracts to people close to Putin who made billions. Putin's personal worth was estimated to be $40 billion already in 2007 (Blomfield 2007), a claim Putin denounced as 'trash'.

In addition to kickbacks from such contracts, the system thrives on bribe-taking from companies, privatization deals rigged to enrich cronies, illicit exports of raw materials, real estate scams, money laundering and off-shore accounts, all within a framework where tycoons must demonstrate absolute loyalty to the president. There are surely limits as to how far this system can go: it has to deliver some benefits to the population in order to retain its legitimacy. But so far any setbacks here have been mitigated by promoting a rally-around-the-flag effect in relation to Russia's near abroad, especially Ukraine.

The general point is that there are sharp limits to the amount of convergence that emerge from Russia's participation in the global economy. Domestic economic, political and social structures shape the nature of distinctive national trajectories of development. The convergence that does take place from integration in the global economy is a two-way street: it produces benefits as well as problems. Russia was boosted economically by integration but the shock therapy also had highly destructive consequences. Inside Russia, the old order was tailored to a centrally planned economy with more benefits to some regions and much less to others.

Transition to a market economy involves substantial spatial restructuring in order to reflect the logic of the market; but that creates resistance from the interests of the old order. Further, some regions would benefit from global interactions bypassing Moscow but that plays against Kremlin's aspirations for central control. As for people on the ground, they surely entertain the material aspirations outlined by Mahbubani; but in a Russian context, this is not always easily combined with the introduction of the liberal rules of a market economy. In short, there are limits to convergence and the process will create tensions and conflict even if all people, in a general sense, can be said to share material aspirations. Russia may be an extraordinary case because of the shock therapy but even more successful transitions towards a market economy experience great difficulties, as demonstrated by the case of China (Chapter 2). Arriving at 'one world' is not nearly as simple as foreseen by Mahbubani.

Hidden worlds of globalization

There is a less visible part of the global economy which must go into our analysis. A significant aspect of the current process of economic globalization is the development and change of the informal economy. Focus here is not on the large number of farmers in subsistence agriculture who concentrate on growing enough food to feed themselves and their families, but on the situation outside agriculture. The informal economy is 'off-the-books' in the sense that it involves employment in producing goods and services which generate an earned income, but such employment is not registered, taxed or regulated, which means that it violates 'tax laws, labour codes and other regulations' (Weiss 1987: 219).

In search of new opportunities, many millions of people have migrated to cities where they have been unable to find work in the formal economy, but had to seek refuge in the informal economy. The conventional liberal view is that once development gets firmly under way, the modern economy would undertake fast growth and thus absorb the surplus labour in the informal economy. But this has not happened nearly to the extent expected; the situation is rather that the formal sector increasingly depends on the persistence of the informal sector. The two develop together in complex ways which are also affected by the structure and activities of the state. Therefore, the size and nature of the informal economy varies greatly between countries, and economic globalization has not led to convergence in this area.

The advanced capitalist countries have the smallest share of the labour force in the informal economy—the OECD average is around 12% of workers outside of agriculture—but informal employment is still pervasive in some countries (Huitfeldt and Jütting 2009). When Spanish export-led industrialization was hit by the oil crisis and government cutbacks around 1980, unemployment soared and formal sector employment dropped; but there was a high increase in the hiring of 'unregulated' labour. Cutbacks in larger firms went together with a growth in subcontracting where small, informal firms supplied their erstwhile employers. In Italy, patterns of state clientelism and patronage have impeded the growth of the formal sector. Consequently, a large share of the labour force (upwards of 25%) works in the informal economy (Weiss 1987).

In emerging and developing countries the informal economy is much larger. A recent survey by the ILO (2012) puts the percentage of informal employment outside of agriculture at 84% in India, 73% in Indonesia, 54% in Mexico, 42% in Brazil and 33% in China. The question is how these numbers are related to economic globalization. It is clear that globalization involves the segmentation of complex production processes and that labour-intensive operations are often subcontracted to undertakings in the informal economy. This is the case in all sectors of the economy. Horticultural production (Kenyan flowers, Zambian flowers and vegetables, South African fruit) are produced in the informal economy and delivered to European buyers in export chains. But also more technologically advanced production is now taking place in the informal economy, leading to a greater heterogeneity of the latter.

At one extreme, there are the traditional, one-person household undertakings such as personal services, market vendors or small scale manufacturing. At the other extreme are informal enterprises with some capital and hired workers, producing standardized goods. In other words, they look like small-scale formal enterprises but they do not comply with the legal regulations and worker conditions of the formal sector. Subcontracting in relation to economic globalization is primarily related to this more modern part of the informal economy. Entrepreneurs active in the informal economy avoid the costly procedure of setting up a formal business and they do not have to comply with formal labour regulation (Moreno Monroy et al. 2012).The benefits of the informal sector in terms of easily getting people employed must be weighed against the costs of no legal protection for workers with very low wages and really unsafe or directly dangerous working conditions. Economies with a large informal sector undertake a form of lumpen development which reinforces a hierarchy among more and less economically developed countries.

Processes of convergence in relation to economic globalization, then, are mediated through conditions that must necessarily be uneven among countries: the number of people coming into the cities in search of employment; the local conditions for national and transnational enterprises in the setting up of subcontracted activities in the informal economy; and the regulation of enterprises and labour in the formal economy. There are huge informal sectors in some developing and emerging economies but there is also great variation among them. The notion that the informal economy will be reduced, or even disappear, when economic growth gets under way has not held up. It rather grows in new ways in relation to economic globalization.

Informalization works in other ways as well, bringing us closer to the criminal economy. A major part of Chinese foreign investment abroad has not been made for the traditional purpose of exploiting the comparative advantages of Chinese firms in a new context. It has instead been made in order to transfer property from state ownership to private possession, the process called informal privatization. In the context of moving abroad, public ownership is changed to private ownership. For example, by the mid-1990s there were more than 3,500 Chinese firms in Hong Kong and Macau, most of them state firms (Ding 2000: 124), but now under private control by members of the nomenklatura. It is one way of laundering money illegally gained in China; these transfers are possible because central control is ineffective and coastal regions have extensive connections with overseas Chinese communities.

Internationalization then becomes a vehicle for the illicit creation of private ownership. The most successful capitalists belong to the nomenklatura; the transition to an open market economy provides them with ample opportunity 'to make a fortune quickly and easily by pocketing state assets' (Ding 2000: 144). China, as is the case with Russia, also displays major aspects of economic globalization that are little in line with the usual set of rationalities connected with a standard version of a liberal market economy.

Turning to the criminal economy in more general terms, it is clear that economic globalization helps produce transnational 'bads' as well as transnational goods. There was always an illicit international political economy (IIPE) existing in tandem with a 'legal' IPE. The classic understanding of transnational organized crime (TOC) basically involves some form of profit-driven smuggling across borders (Andreas 2004: 643). In today's terms important examples of these activities include the drug trade, sex trafficking, smuggling of migrants and of natural resources, money laundering and illicit traffic in arms (Pankratz and Matiasek 2012). US Senator John Kerry has argued that this type of crime is sharply on the rise, driven by five organizations: the Italian mafia, the Russian mobs, the Chinese triads, the Japanese Yakuza and the Colombian cartels, against which the international community must now strengthen its cooperation and resolve (Kerry 1998).

These entities surely present problems, but the question is whether current IIPE can be defined in this traditional way. A broader view is that in the current process of economic globalization, there is an interrelationship between licit and illicit economic exchange so that there is an illicit counterpart to every part of the licit economy (Naim 2005). Indeed, the structures which make up the backbone of economic globalization: the transportation and communication systems, the financial networks and tax havens, are vehicles for both licit and illicit transactions; and the global companies 'often engage in both licit and illicit economic exchange' (Andreas 2004: 644).

It is generally agreed that the increased scope and depth of economic globalization have involved 'a quantum leap' in illicit activities (Rotberg 2009: 3). This is not difficult to understand. The countries that have recently become more involved in globalization generally have a higher level of corruption than the advanced capitalist countries. The former Soviet Union is a special problem: some areas are outright criminal in that the state apparatus depends 'overwhelmingly on the returns from illicit trade'; they include Abkhazia, South Ossetia, Transniestr, and Nagorno-Karabakh. Others are 'criminalized' in the sense that the state has been captured for the exploitation of private interests; the business of the state is 'privatized'. Russia, Ukraine, Uzbekistan, Kyrgyzstan, Moldova, Armenia and Azerbaijan are examples (Legvold 2009). In general, the emerging economies in the BRICS have severe corruption problems. Transparency International's 2014 Corruption Perceptions Index lists Russia as no. 136 (out of 175 countries); China is no. 100, India no. 85, Brazil no. 69, and South Africa no. 67. For comparison, the United States is no. 17; the least corrupt countries are in Scandinavia.

Naylor makes the point that a black market cannot be tamed from the supply side. 'At best a few intermediaries get knocked out of business. But as long as demand persists, the market is served more or less as before' (Naylor 2005: 6). With recent developments in globalization, demand now comes from the heart of the very state apparatuses that are supposed to be in the frontline in the struggle against corruption. If Naylor is right, this can only be curbed by the creation of effective, responsive, democratic and non-corrupt states. In the best of worlds, that may eventually happen, but not sometime soon. Meanwhile, instead of convergence to ordinary market standards, global capitalism is presently being drawn in another direction which includes a markedly higher level of illicit activities.

Common fate? The environmental challenge and globalization

It is increasingly agreed that the world faces a serious and growing set of environmental problems. It is a complex set of challenges:
global degradation of land, water and air; the exploitation and gradual depletion of natural resources; the accumulation of all kinds of
waste, including radioactive waste, and so on. Climate change, or
global warming, is considered one of the most serious problems
because of its many negative consequences in terms of rising sea levels and flooding, extreme weather, droughts, wildfires, forest death
and melting ice. It is caused by the emission of 'greenhouse gasses',
in particular carbon dioxide (CO_2) into the Earth's atmosphere, trap-
ping the rays of the Sun and leading to heating of the Earth and the
atmosphere. There is now general consensus that this is an increasingly serious problem (IPCC 2014) and that most of it stems from
human activities, especially the burning of fossil fuels.

Liberal theorists argue in the vein of Mahbubani: the environmental challenge does not respect borders; it unites humanity in a
common fate and forces peoples and states to cooperate. National
leaders still need to look much more radically beyond the blinkers of
narrow national interests, but increasingly, they will come together
in a process of 'ever greater transnational cooperation' (Rosenau
1983: 74). There is some evidence of that taking place. The number
of multilateral environmental agreements has grown by leaps and
bounds, especially boosted by the UN environment conferences in
Stockholm in 1972 and in Rio in 1992. Since the mid-1970s the
number of environmental accords has more than doubled, reach-
ing 400–500 around 2008. As reported in Chapter 1, environmental issues have a recognized place on the international agenda, tied
in with the recurrent environmental conferences in the UN system
(O'Neill 2009).

The problem is that the activities and agreements on behalf on the
environment are no valid indication that the problems are being confronted in an effective way. In many cases goals are set so modestly
that the underlying problem will not really be addressed. There are
no clear and uniform rules for ratification or for the number of signa-
tories required before a treaty can come into force. The large number
of environmental accords is a sign of weakness, not of strength; there
is very little coordination, no common standards and no overarching
coordinating agency. Funding is insecure, made up of donations from

small groups of countries, and 'enforcement of global environmental treaties is practically nonexistent' (Susskind 2008).

Global warming is addressed by the international community in the Kyoto Protocol from 1997. It requires 38 industrialized countries to cut their greenhouse gas emissions (by 2012) at an average of 5%. The Protocol has not been ratified by the second-largest contributor of greenhouse gas, the United States. The single largest contributor, China, is exempted from the treaty together with India and over 100 developing countries. This is due to the notion of 'common but differentiated responsibilities and respective capabilities', meaning that while there is common responsibility for global warming, developed nations are primarily liable because they have benefited from the industrialization that is mostly responsible for global warming in the first place. The 35 least developed countries accounted for about 1% of the total carbon dioxide emissions while six countries (by 2011) were responsible for 70% of the world total (China, United States, European Union, India, Russia and Japan) (Union of Concerned Scientists 2014).

The Protocol was extended to 2020 in Doha in 2012, but Canada withdrew from the treaty in 2011 and several other industrialized countries have not taken on new targets for this new commitment period (2012–2020); they include Japan, New Zealand, Russia and several European states. China, India and the United States have all indicated that they will not ratify any treaty which legally commits them to reduce emissions. The climate agreement reached in Paris in December 2015 was widely considered a great step in the right direction. It pledges to limit global warming to well below 2 degrees Celsius above pre-industrial levels and that is indeed a new global ambition. But the deal is little more than an expression of good intentions; countries are to set their own targets for carbon emissions and the financial aid commitment to developing countries for energy reforms remains voluntary (Cassidy 2015).

The situation illustrates how environmental issues may well contain an element of 'common fate' inducing cooperation but at the same time there are several elements which draw countries apart and impede their coming together in a unified effort. This is especially the case as regards the division between developed, industrialized countries and poor, less developed nations in the Global South. The 'ecological footprint' of the rich is so much more massive than that of the poor and it can even be combined with the legacy of 'ecological imperialism', the notion that European colonial expansion has taken over and suppressed peoples as well as ecological systems around the world (Crosby 2004). From a present-day perspective, any reduction in carbon emissions in the North must be seen in the framework that several high-pollution industries have moved from the North to the South. This means that the North today relies greatly on carbon-intensive imports (Mann 2013: 391).

Meanwhile, the BRICS and other emerging economies are confronting the environmental challenges in their own countries. By one calculation, it would require five planet Earths to upgrade the entire world to current Western lifestyles (Hulme 2009). But it is hardly a way forward to suggest that emerging and developing economies should stay poor; this is where environmental concerns crucially connect with economics: what kind of global economic transformations are necessary for creating models of development less harmful to the environment? For some time, this debate has taken place under the heading of 'sustainable development'; currently the concept of 'green growth' has become popular.

According to OECD's green growth strategy, the term means 'fostering economic growth and development, while ensuring that national assets continue to provide the resources and environmental services on which our well-being relies' (OECD 2011). In terms of global warming, the official target is now set at a maximum rise of 2 degrees Celsius by 2050; the International Energy Agency (IEA) projection is that this will require a cutting of current energy-related CO_2 emissions by more than half compared to 2009 levels (IEA 2014). This is a huge task; even at financial crisis growth rates (1.4% per year) and modest population growth (0.7% per annum) the required carbon intensity reduction must be 21-fold (per $ of production) compared to today's level (Jackson 2009; Hoffmann 2011).

Green growth strategies may be helpful in a number of ways but they are unlikely to be able to bring about the enormous changes required by an effective response to the global warming challenge (see Hoffmann 2011). First, there is very little time; it took 125 years to increase labour productivity ten-fold (1830–1955) during the Industrial Revolution in the US; the 'carbon revolution' must be squeezed into 2–3 decades (McKinsey 2008). Second, savings in the Global North will most probably be eroded by consumption increases in the Global South, neutralizing a substantial part of the global carbon reduction. Third, a significant part of the gains in the North emerge from the outsourcing of emission-intensive production to the South; for example, production in the United Kingdom reduced emissions from UK production by 14% between 1990 and 2008, but due to imports emissions from UK consumption increased by 20% (Peters et al. 2011). Fourth, the technical challenges to switch from fossil fuel to renewable energy are considerable. Wind and solar energy cannot replace transport fuel (biofuel will require enormous amounts of what is currently global cropland), and they are not reliable as 'base-load' electricity. Finally, the very substantial greenhouse gas emissions from agriculture (almost half of global emissions if packaging, transport, retail and food waste are included) are set to rise by nearly 30% until 2030; going against this trend through massive transformations of industrialized agriculture is a huge challenge (Hoffmann 2011: 6–7).

The detailed analysis by Ulrich Hoffmann argues that the serious problems involved in pursuing green growth leave three major policy options to the world: '(i) limiting population growth; (ii) reducing per-capita income growth in developed countries and giving up developmental catch-up in the South; or (iii) drastically changing consumption patterns' (Hoffmann 2011: 9). All three options indicate that the 'common fate' of the environmental challenge is little more than a thin veil over very deep tensions between countries and different parts of the world. The first option puts the problem squarely at the doorstep of the poorest countries, those who are least responsible for global warming in the first place. The second option goes directly against the core mechanism on which capitalism is founded, accumulation and economic growth: 'Growth is inherent in capitalism which means you can't have capitalism without growth, and you can't have a capitalist steady state economy' (Lockwood 2011). No growth means no jobs for the huge masses that are currently waiting to get access to the labour market not merely in the South, but in many places in the North as well. The emerging economies that have the capacities will surely continue their quest for economic growth and catching-up in the coming years.

The third option would tend to befall mostly on the Global North, where material consumption is already so much higher (the United States consumes 25% of the world total of oil with 4% of the population, for example). But lifestyles are not easily transformed in a profound way. George H.W. Bush famously declared that 'The American way of life is not negotiable' at the 1992 Earth Summit;

but even with more political resolve, dramatic changes will need to focus on 'societies and structures as a whole, rather than on individual actions' (Vermeulen 2009: 25).

There is a group of optimists who argue that the global warming problem can be handled in the way that capitalist development has handled previous great challenges: through technological innovation. Bjørn Lomborg (2007) is a prominent representative of this group, but also a controversial one (see for example Svoboda 2011). The optimists may of course be somewhat rose-colored about what can be achieved through innovation, but they also face a more general problem: even when innovation is successful it has to be put into practical use; that demands a smooth process of technology transfer, effective and well-functioning political institutions capable of an extraordinarily high degree of cooperation, and, maybe first of all, a sufficient political and financial interest in most countries towards giving priority to getting such projects under way. The present mood in the leading capitalist centres is geared towards getting economic growth going after the financial crisis slump; in comparison, environmental concerns play a secondary role.

Michael Mann notes that the environmental crisis is so profound because it is caused by the three great triumphs of the modern period: capitalism, the nation-state and citizen rights (Mann 2013: 95). Capitalism's focus on profit means that hefty regulation will be required in order to compel companies to turn to investment in low-emission industries. The nation-state remains obsessed with growth as well, even when it causes environmental degradation. A different system requires the reining in of political elites fixated on short-term growth in order to win the next election. Citizens, finally, have to give up a system where they consider it a right to demand continued growth in order to consume more. The prospect for environmental concerns to prevail in these three struggles is not bright. 'America is not only unwilling to begin any of these three struggles but it will not sign up to even minor emissions programmes. China does embrace emissions programmes ... but all their efforts are overwhelmed by the sheer pace of Chinese industrialization—as is also the case in India and other successfully industrializing countries. I would predict that little emissions mitigation will be undertaken until tangible climate change impacts begin to strike hard on the world at some point in the mid-21st century' (Mann 2013: 95). Meanwhile, President Obama did launch a 'Clean Power Plan' in August 2015 which—if implemented—is beginning to address the issue of climate change (Malloy and Serfaty 2015).

In sum, there is surely an element of 'common fate' in relation to the environmental challenge. That is behind the ever more frequent calls for much closer international cooperation. A comment by Gary Stix represents this way of thinking. He used to focus on technological challenges in relation to global warming; now he is convinced that the real challenge is the required 'fundamental reorientation and restructuring of national and international institutions towards more effective Earth system governance and planetary stewardship'. The institutions would have to be instilled with 'heavy-handed, transnational enforcement powers'; this is effectively a call for 'world government' (Stix 2012); nothing less will do if impending climate catastrophe shall be avoided. In a global economic structure deeply characterized by globalization, moreover, all countries dealing with the environment face the fundamental challenges identified by Michael Mann: capitalism, the nation-state and citizen rights.

But being part of the problem, capitalists, nation-state governments and citizens are also the crucial forces in forging any kind of stable solution. And this is where diversity, opposing interests, different outlooks and substantial differences in terms of local problems come to the surface. Climate change is mostly discussed in the Global North; the South is more focused on water- and food-scarcity, access to clean water, soil degradation and desertification (Hurrell 2007). The latter problems may be connected to climate change but they present themselves in different ways. Capitalists are divided both inside and across countries, sectors and industries: all are interested in accumulation and profits but some will want to support a 'green' while others will benefit from a 'black' economy. The poor countries will be hardest hit by the effects of climate change, but they are also the nations mostly in need of rapid economic growth and development. Nation states will increasingly enter the game already played by the Global South: minimize the cost incurred by the environmental challenge and maximize the room for manoeuver in the face of demands for international commitments. Many citizens, both in the North and in the South, will continue to give priority to growth and a higher level of consumption. Increasing income inequalities both within and among countries will exacerbate this problem.

There is 'common fate' for sure, but it unfolds in a context where centralizing approaches, even those falling markedly short of 'world government' will meet with sharp resistance. At the same time, the results of global negotiations tend to become so diluted that several governments increasingly turn to bilateral agreements that provide a more clear-cut environmental effect. Special subsidy of some countries could bring substantial gains; for example, if Brazil and Indonesia could preserve their rainforests better that would bring major benefits in terms of lower greenhouse gas emissions (Mann 2013: 391). Coming years will probably see more results from specific negotiations on particular problems than from global discussions of very large agendas.

What kind of economic model will move the world forward?

In the advanced capitalist economies, the post-war Bretton Woods system of 'embedded capitalism' was replaced during the 1980s by a much more deregulated, neoliberal model of capitalism where the financial sector plays a central role. This was the system that paved the way for the current process of economic globalization. Up to 2008, many thought the system to be virtually crisis free due to the inbuilt stability of a self-regulating market. Among the believers was the then chairman of the US Federal Reserve, Alan Greenspan (Andrews 2008). But it wasn't; the financial crisis of 2007 and 2008 shocked the economic system in a way that could only be compared with the profound crises of the 1930s and 1970s. It was clear that a group of advanced capitalist economies were hit the hardest while the emerging economies, including China and India, fared better. Still, the crisis has raised the question of whether the current model is a sustainable and robust framework for a continued process of economic globalization.

By 2016, the United States is back on a growth track, but the economy is based on extreme and still-rising levels of inequality, as we saw in Chapter 2. After several years of austerity policies, Europe is trying to fight its way out of a deflationary cycle that might turn into a sustained and painful recession. In all of the five BRICS countries growth has slowed markedly down. Further, China and India still face the restructuring away from models built on cheap exports, towards a more balanced growth pattern. And the advanced capitalist countries must face the prospect of not being able to rely on floods of cheap imports.

The outline of a different economic model as the framework for economic globalization has not emerged (Ougaard 2013). Unsurprisingly, a comprehensive debate began after 2008, concerning more regulation of finance both in the national and the international context, but it has been much talk and little action. New regulatory bodies have been made; the international Financial Stability Forum was turned into the Financial Stability Board with a wide set of coordination and monitoring tasks (FSB 2015). The Basel III agreement of 2010 is aimed at strengthening the capital requirement standards of banks; it is a voluntary agreement and implementation is expected by 2019. Nothing has come of the debates about tighter regulation of potentially toxic assets or short-term financial transactions. Both the United States and the United Kingdom have turned down proposals for a 0.1% Tobin tax on financial transactions. The financial sector remains strong, not merely in the United States and the United Kingdom, but in many other countries as well.

The transformation of the present economic model will depend on other power relations than those connected to finance. 'Green capital' is the sectors and companies that support a transition towards more environment-friendly models of development. They face opposition from 'black capital' centred on the oil, coal and gas industries. The 'green' faction has grown stronger in recent years as evidenced by the support from several international business associations for efforts against global warming. But as the previous section indicated, 'black' capital continues to have strong political support in most major countries.

There are also divisions among countries because they diverge in terms of levels and models of development. The standard liberal view is that participation in economic globalization is good for all countries and peoples in terms of promoting economic development and increasing material well-being (Bhagwati 2007; see also Mahbubani 2013). This is certainly true in some cases, but as we saw earlier in this chapter, international investment capital is particularly interested in some locations and not at all interested in other locations. The least developed countries in the bottom of the economic hierarchy are also the least interesting in terms of local markets, the supply of labour with adequate skills, physical infrastructure and geographical location. They are also the least capable in terms of creating the optimum framework for benefitting from foreign investment; this will often require sophisticated regulations concerning technology, profit transfers and relations to local firms. The latter is particularly important; if there is no local economic capacity, processes of competence transfer and upgrading will rarely take place. In short, participation in economic globalization alone does not pave the way for a successful process of development; that requires preconditions which the weakest countries often do not have to a sufficient extent (Sørensen 2004: 46–58).

Meanwhile, a number of what used to be considered developing countries have become successful industrializers. They include the 'Asian Tigers' of South Korea, Taiwan and Singapore; the BRICS countries; and maybe some, or all, of the group of 'Next 11' (N11), which includes Turkey, Mexico, the Philippines, Indonesia and Vietnam (O'Neill 2007). But economic globalization and economic development never stand still and the early successes now face a new set of challenges. South Korea, Taiwan and Singapore saw their earlier competitive advantages erode in the 1990s and their exports squeezed by the financial crisis of 2007 and 2008. All three countries concluded that they needed further technological and industrial upgrading; they began an ambitious drive to establish themselves in biotechnology (Wong 2011).

This move is significantly different from earlier upgrading. The initial industrialization in these states benefitted from the 'second-mover advantages' connected with late development; 'they were spared the uncertainty and the heavy lifting of creating, reaping at the other ends the benefits of creatively copying' (Wong 2011: 168). The wager on biotech is different because this is 'first-order innovation' with a much higher degree of uncertainty for both companies and policymakers. Wong's detailed analysis concludes that 'the prospective development of commercial biotech and the translation of upstream discoveries into commercially viable outputs remain obscured by technological, economic, and temporal uncertainty' (Wong 2011: 169).

As far as the BRICS and the N11 countries are concerned, they face new barriers for latecomers. Regulations of intellectual property rights make it more expensive and more difficult for these countries to get access to advanced technology. Trade-Related Investment Measures (TRIMS) prevent host countries from demanding performance requirements from foreign investors. The General Agreement on Trade in Services (GATS) stipulates market liberalization in services (e.g. banking, insurance, health care). Governments are not allowed to protect their service industries from foreign competition.

In sum, these agreements are favourable to the advanced countries in the sense that they constrain national development strategies for latecomers (Wade 2003).

The larger message in the present context is that different types of countries face a variety of different challenges in relation to economic globalization. Weak states will want better market access in the North, more support in terms of economic aid, and increased willingness of international firms to include them in economic globalization. They also face domestic struggles in order to improve local conditions for moving forward. The 'Tigers' want to upgrade further; they will face fierce competition from leading biotech and other advanced firms of the Global North. Another group of latecomers will have a harder time catching up than previous successes because they must handle new international constraints on the process.

In sum, current economic globalization continues to take place in the framework of a neoliberal model with a significant role for the financial sector. The question is whether this is a sufficiently solid and stable framework for economic globalization in coming years. Struggles have begun about how to revise or even deeply transform this model. They open to contestation among factions of capital both in the advanced countries and elsewhere; they also involve discords among groups of countries with different interests and demands in relation to globalization. There is both the issue of the concrete substance of a revised or transformed model, and the issue of the social forces and countries that will support it. Continued globalization is not a juggernaut; it needs an adequate economic, political and regulatory framework in order to thrive. The current framework has many shortcomings.

Conclusion

This chapter aimed to study major characteristics of economic globalization and to evaluate their consequences for world order. The liberal view is that economic globalization promotes closer cooperation and interstate peace. It drives a general process of convergence which has already progressed so far that we urgently need a theory of 'one world' which demonstrates how economics, technology, the environment challenges and common material aspirations drive us closer and closer together.

Some substantial convergence is surely taking place. In earlier days, the West and the East went their separate ways in terms of economic models of development and they were largely separated from each other while the former colonies in the developing world struggled with their own set of problems. Today, almost all participate in a global, capitalist system, devoted to a market economy and economic openness. A very serious financial crisis has not led to significantly increased 'inter-imperialist rivalry' or even serious economic tensions among the advanced capitalist countries. There have been no significant tendencies towards a replay of the economic protectionism and 'beggar thy neighbour' policies of the 1930s. Interstate war can largely be ruled out.

At the same time, this chapter has demonstrated how capitalist development as well as economic globalization is highly uneven and there are strong limits to convergence. The transition to capitalism and intense participation in globalization sharpens domestic social, political and economic tensions as demonstrated by the case of Russia; the informal economy remains very substantial in many countries, and the amount of illicit economic activity has grown conspicuously since the end of the Cold War. The environmental challenge contains an element of 'common fate' but it is not a game changer which completely reshuffles the existing economic agenda in a way that makes peoples and states come together. It will rather intensify contestation among groups of capitalists, among nation-states and among citizens about best ways of responding and moving forward. This will take place in a context where the disputes over the future framework for economic development and globalization are bound to intensify.

Overall, then, there is a peculiar, but significant, 'double movement' taking place when it comes to the economic structure and world order. On one hand, countries have converged on an economic model of capitalist development and globalization where there is common support for the basic rules of production, finance and trade. Economic interdependence is more intense than it ever was, both in terms of scope and depth. Almost all countries know and care about the importance of participating in economic exchange and networks of economic governance. Former Brazilian president, Fernando Henrique Cardoso, formulated the integration and upgrading imperative as a new form of dependence on the part of the Global South: 'Either the South (or part of it) enters into the democratic-technological-scientific race, invests heavily in research and development, and supports the transformation into an "information economy", or it will beccme unimportant, unexploited and unexploitable ... without any interest to the developing global economy' (Cardoso 1996, cited from Hurrell 2007: 341). Manmohan Singh, India's prime minister until 2014, noted that 'All countries must compete in global markets and such competition is not inconsistent with cooperation, nor is it adversarial' (speech 2008); Wen Jiabao of China confirmed that India and China have 'common interests in the global economic and trade system' (speech 2010, both cited from Mahbubani 2013: 146).

On the other hand, however, the very process of economic transformation, integration into globalization and participation in the networks of governance is not smooth and uncontroversial; it creates tensions at home and often underlines divergent interests among groups of people, among economic factions, and among political groups struggling for influence. In the case of Russia and China, the regimes of the two countries have supported and indeed led the integration of their countries in the globalized world economy; there can be little doubt about the long term benefits of such integration; compare the situation in desperately poor and isolated North Korea. But just as the North Korean regime rightly fears that any serious opening up to the outside world will quickly undermine its hold on power, so the Russian and Chinese leaderships are well aware that integration into the world economy is a double-edged sword. It might also help produce opposition and resistance at home which will threaten their holds on power. That opposition would come not only from people in the street but also from business elites increasingly integrated with the West and therefore less willing to be dominated by an autocratic regime. To counter this, the regime might seek, paradoxically, to combine integration with isolation.

In a recent analysis, Ivan Krastev and Stephen Holmes argue that such developments are the real reason for Putin's policies since 2012, where large anti-Putin demonstrations filled the streets of Moscow: 'Putin does not dream of conquering Warsaw or re-occupying Riga. On the contrary, his policies are an expression of "*aggressive isolationism*". They embody his defensive reaction to the threat to Russia posed not so much by NATO as by global *economic* interdependence. ... Putin controls everything in Russia except the things that really matter: the price of oil and gas, and the loyalty of the rich. His sway over an economic elite that does so much of its business offshore is very limited. This is why the re-nationalization of the country's globe-trotting business classes became one of Putin's major objectives, especially after 2012. The open confrontation with the West over Ukraine should be understood in this context as a strategy adopted well before the fall of Viktor Yanukovych. Crimea and Donbass are meant to scandalize the West in order to increase Russia's economic, political, and cultural isolation from the world' (Krastev and Holmes 2014: 6; see also Kupchan 2012: 111). Krastev and Holmes recommend that the Western answer should be to deepen 'Western engagement with all facets of Russian society' (2014: 9), rather than to press on with sanctions over the long term. For Putin, the problem with a policy of isolationism is that it obstructs economic growth, which remains an important source of legitimacy for the regime.

Russia may be an extreme example but there are variations of 'backlash' tendencies elsewhere. Greece has received massive assistance from eurozone countries and the IMF in order to stabilize its economy in the wake of the government-debt crisis. But domestic repercussions have been harsh in terms of negative growth, public sector cutbacks and unemployment. The political backlash came in the January 2015 general election victory of the radical left-wing party, Syriza. The party is not seeking to leave European cooperation entirely, but it wants deeply different—milder and growth-friendly—conditions on its economic support or it threatens to disengage from European cooperation.

A domestic backlash against globalization in the concrete form of EU cooperation has also emerged in Britain, where there is now open talk about 'Brexit', that is, Britain leaving the European Union altogether following a 2016 referendum. In this case the Conservative government led by David Cameron has been challenged by a the right-wing populist party, UK Independence Party, that wants to withdraw Britain from the European Union and replace membership with a Norwegian or Swiss model of retaining trading links and participation in the single market without treaty obligations or subscription payments. Again, continued economic interdependence is foreseen (which will entail commitment to the rules and regulations of the single market), but in a context of less institutional cooperation.

In sum, liberals are right that current processes of economic globalization help create economic interdependence which fosters substantial commitment to common rules and regulations and in that sense points towards increased cooperation. Many observers of economic globalization argue that an increasing demand for institutional cooperation is a logical consequence of the process; when countries hang closer together because of globalization, the amount of common problems increases and more cooperation is likely to follow (cf. Sørensen 2004: 60). The point is well taken, but liberals seriously underestimate the potential downsides of increased interdependence. The demand for more cooperation needs to be seen in the context of the backlashes against cooperation which pull in a different direction.

After the end of the Cold War, the upsides of economic globalization have clearly been dominant; a long phase of economic development in many countries has drawn hundreds of millions of poor people out of abject poverty. The backlashes discussed here do not amount to breakdown or chaos but nor do we have a stable and effective framework for continued globalization. A better framework for economic globalization will need to be ambitious in order to address, for example, the need for better regulation of the financial sector. But the ambitions for closer cooperation must also consider the reactions against globalization and intensified cooperation. The paradox is that these reactions emerge from instability within states, rather than from rivalry among them.

When the upsides of economic globalization dominated in many countries, it was relatively easy to drive cooperation forward and the liberal 'one world emerging' view was popular in many quarters. With the downsides of economic globalization coming to the fore, cooperation falters and backlash tendencies are on the rise. The growing contestation of globalization comes at a point in time where there is an increasing need for a reformed framework of globalization capable of addressing the several problems which the process has thrown up so far.

7

Institutions: Governance or Gridlock?

Introduction

Institutions are sets of rules, formal and informal, that states and other actors play by. In the international realm, such sets of rules have for some time been labelled 'global governance'. Government in the strict sense is not taking place because there is no world government. But nor do we live in a world of raw anarchy where states are always at each other's throats. Therefore, global governance is a 'halfway house' between anarchy at one extreme and a world state at the other (Weiss and Wilkinson 2014: 213).

'Global governance' is a slippery term for two reasons; first, far from all international rules have global reach but they are often included in the label anyway. Second, global governance can be taken to mean any sets of rules which have transnational repercussions, making it very difficult to decide what does and does not qualify as global governance (Finkelstein 1995). In principle, global governance can refer to activities everywhere—local, national, regional, global—involving regulation and control aimed at problems that transcend national frontiers. I use the term to broadly designate the subject matter of this chapter—an evaluation of the current standing of global governance and the consequences for world order. In a more narrow sense, focus is on the global institutions which have led the way in global governance since the end of the Cold War. To which extent are they, if at all, able to meet the current governance challenges of an intensely globalized world?

154

The basic institutions which have framed global governance in recent decades were put in place after World War II. At the centre was the Charter of the United Nations; it set impressive goals for global governance: 'Determined to save succeeding generations from the scourge of war ... to reaffirm faith in fundamental human rights ... to promote social progress and better standards of life in larger freedom ... to practice tolerance and live together in peace ... that armed force shall not be used save in the common interest' (excerpt, UN Charter 1945).

On that ambitious basis, global governance has developed by leaps and bounds. This process interacts with the vast growth of cross-border connections due to globalization. In the context of more intensified globalization, countries are now increasingly influenced by events and decisions made beyond their territorial reach. The result is an increasing demand for political and other cooperation across borders as a way for states and other actors to reclaim the regulative powers lost due to globalization (Zürn 1998). The development of cooperation provides feedback that stimulates even closer interdependence between countries in a self-reinforcing process (Hale, Held and Young 2013: 26).

Three major developments illustrate the development of cross-border cooperation. The first is the growth of *interstate* relations, in particular through cooperation in international organizations (IGOs). There were 123 IGOs in 1951; the number today is close to 8,000 (UIA 2013). The number of international treaties in force has grown dramatically, as has the complexity of single agreements. The *acquis communautaire*, which new EU members must accept, totals more than 85,000 pages; the NAFTA agreement runs some 26,000 pages. These quantitative aspects are only part of the story of course; many international organizations have expanded their roles so that they are of increasing importance for the member states. UN institutions have significantly developed international law in such areas as human rights and minority rights, and they are deeply involved in peacekeeping and peace enforcement in fragile states. The IMF and the World Bank monitor economic performance in all parts of the world and are central players in situations of economic crisis; membership of the World Trade Organization is considered a very high priority for states that want to integrate in the global economic system.

The second important development is the expansion of *transgovernmental* relations. Such relations are especially developed among national regulators, the officials responsible for corporate supervision, environmental standards, antitrust policies and so on. According to one observer, 'transgovernmentalism is rapidly becoming the most widespread and effective mode of international governance' (Slaughter 1997: 185).

The third significant development is the expansion of *transnational* relations, that is, cross-border relations between individuals, groups and organizations from civil society. International non-governmental organizations (INGOs) are active in all major areas of regulation activity, including trade policy, the environment, disarmament or human rights, where they often work alongside governments. INGOs help pave the way for global public policy networks, defined as 'loose alliances of government agencies, international organizations, corporations, and elements of civil society such as nongovernmental organizations, professional associations, or religious groups that join together to achieve what none can accomplish on its own' (Reinicke 2000: 44).

Taken together, the development of interstate, transgovernmental and transnational relations signify a development of global governance away from traditional territorial government by sovereign states towards global governance where national governments are increasingly enmeshed in a complex network of international organizations to which they have made a variety of commitments, some of them more binding in nature than previously. Non-state actors are not primary in this process but they are active participants in global governance; regulation and control is no longer a sole preserve of states. At the same time, the extent to which one or the other form of governance has developed in the real world varies greatly between countries and groups of countries.

In sum, globalization and interdependence increase the need for international cooperation; the supply of cooperation on many levels is itself a force for the creation of even closer interdependence. At the same time, globalization is uneven and may also contain impulses which work against cooperation, as we saw in the previous chapter. This is the context for the debate about the institutional structure and its relation to world order. There are two major views, as indicated earlier in this book.

The liberal optimist view is that the current order is in pretty good shape even if it faces a number of new challenges. When the Cold War ended, the 'inside' order that had existed among liberal democracies now became the outside order. There was only one order for the entire world 'bound together by multilateral rules and institutions, a globalizing form of capitalism and American political leadership' (Ikenberry 2011: 275). That liberal order is open to new participants, including non-democratic countries, and it is rule-based. Both China and Russia are deeply integrated in the liberal order, permanent members of the Security Council and members of the WTO, the IMF, the World Bank and G20. Global institutions may not always be perfect but that is increasingly compensated by networks and partnerships at many different levels, a form of piecemeal global governance that actually amounts to 'good enough governance' (Patrick 2014: 73).

The sceptical view finds many more faults with the current institutional structure. Realists are sceptical towards the emergence of any form of binding international cooperation because state interests will always get in the way. There are also observers of other theoretical stripes who are pessimistic about the future of cooperation. The argument is that while the need for international cooperation has never been higher, the supply of cooperation has stalled. The result is gridlock, 'a specific set of conditions and mechanisms that impede global cooperation in the present day' (Hale, Held and Young 2013: 3). So gridlock or good-enough governance? The situation might vary across issue areas, of course; surely some areas are better governed than others but this is not a big item in the debate among these positions. The optimist view that the institutional structure amounts to decently working global governance is presented in the next section. The elements that point to a much more severe crisis are then taken up.

Good-enough governance or gridlock?

The present institutional structure emerges from the order built after World War II under American leadership. It was not based on a fixed blueprint; US policies developed and changed in the context of an increasingly hostile relationship to the Soviet Union and the shifting demands of the European allies (Trachtenberg 1999). There were two basic pillars in that order. First, a security arrangement with NATO at its core aimed at containing the Soviet threat against the Western world, but also aimed at securing firm cooperation on the Western side. In Lord Ismay's memorable formulation, the purpose was to 'keep the Russians out, the Germans down, and the Americans in'.

Second, the Bretton Woods institutions, that is, the World Bank and the IMF, provided a framework for intensified Western economic and political cooperation following liberal goals of economic openness and political democracy. It was this successful order that oversaw the reconstruction of Germany and Japan, and the advent of European cooperation in a context of dramatic economic progress.

The end of the Cold War meant the end of the bipolar confrontation between two superpowers and their respective allies; it was a liberal victory because the forces for economic openness and liberal democracy prevailed. Since the Bretton Woods institutions were open to all countries in principle, it would appear a relatively simple task to roll out what had been a primarily Western order on a global scale. But the replacement of bipolarity by unipolarity propelled the United States into an entirely new situation of unconstrained power. Unconstrained power may lead to 'we can do whatever we want' policies of unilateralist expansionism or liberal imposition; it can also lead to withdrawal and isolationism (Sørensen 2011: 141–67). After a honeymoon period of moderate multilateralism in the 1990s came the terrorist attacks of September 11, 2001. The George W. Bush presidency turned the United States towards a period of unilateralism aimed at strengthening American power. The United States retreated from international institutions and agreements, rejecting accession to the Kyoto Protocol on global warming, the Biological Weapons Convention and the International Criminal Court, and abandoning the Anti-Ballistic Missile Treaty made with the Soviet Union in 1972. The resulting governance crisis, then, is generated 'primarily from choices made by the US government' said G. John Ikenberry in 2006.

According to the optimist view, the good news is that this was not a breakdown of liberal order even if it was a serious crisis. The core values of the order—open and rule-based—remained in place. It was an authority crisis that could be mended by a significant shift of US policies. The content of that shift ought to be clear: 'The United States is going to need to invest in re-creating the basic governance institutions of the system—invest in alliances, partnerships, multilateral institutions, special relationships, great-power concerts, cooperative security pacts, and democratic security communities. That is, the United States will need to return to the great tasks of liberal order building' (Ikenberry 2011: 349).

According to the optimist view, it was exactly such a shift that was declared by the Barack Obama presidency in 2008. He praised the legacy of the UN and the Bretton Woods institutions and claimed that 'instead of constraining our power, these institutions magnified it', but Obama also announced an overhaul of the institutions in order to 'keep pace with the fast-moving threats we face' (quoted from Patrick 2014: 58).

There has been no grand institutional reform, however. A reform of the UN has been on the agenda for more than three decades but old great powers, emerging powers and developing countries do not agree on the priorities of reform (Weiss and Young 2005), and there are great practical obstacles: a changed composition of the UN Security Council, for example, will require two-thirds approval by the UN General Assembly as well as domestic ratification by the five permanent members of the Council. Apart from limited voting reforms of the World Bank and the IMF, the major global institutions retain the ground structures of their creation.

Therefore, the case for good-enough governance lies elsewhere. The big institutions do remain in place but they are increasingly supplemented by regional institutions, ad hoc coalitions, global action networks, issue-specific arrangements and more. In other words, patterns of transnational and transgovernmental relationships have grown and proliferated giving a new diversity to cooperation across borders. Collective action, according to Stewart Patrick, 'is no longer focused solely, or even primarily, on the UN and other universal, treaty-based institutions, or even on a single apex forum such as the G20. Rather, governments have taken to operating in many venues simultaneously, participating in a bewildering array of issue-specific networks and partnerships whose membership varies based on situational interests, shared values, and relevant capabilities' (Patrick 2014: 62).

Examples abound (the following draws on Patrick 2014: 64–74).

Climate change: the 17 largest greenhouse gas emitters have created the Major Economies Forum on Energy and Climate, seeking breakthroughs outside of the lumbering UN Framework Convention on Climate Change (UNFCC). To date the forum has underdelivered, but more tangible progress has occurred through parallel national efforts, as states pledge to undertake a menu of domestic actions, which they subsequently submit to the forum for collective review.

Trade: given the failure of WTO's Doha round, the United States and other nations have turned to preferential trade agreements in order to spur further liberalization of commerce. Some are bilateral but others involve multiple countries. These include two initiatives that constitute the centrepiece of Obama's second-term trade agenda: the Trans-Pacific Partnership and the Transatlantic Trade and Investment Partnership.

Peacekeeping: alongside classic UN operations, we now see a variety of hybrid models in which the UN Security Council authorizes an observer or peacekeeping mission, which is then implemented by an ad hoc coalition (as in the African Union Mission in Somalia, AMISOM) or some combination of the two.

Health: the once-premier World Health Organization now shares policy space and a division of labour with other major organizations, including public–private partnerships, such as the GAVI Alliance (formerly called the Global Alliance for Vaccines and Immunization); philanthropic organizations, such as the Bill and Melinda Gates Foundation; consultative bodies, such as the eight-nation (plus the EU) Global Health Security Initiative; and multi-stakeholder bodies, such as the Global Fund to Fight AIDS, Tuberculosis and Malaria. The upshot is a disaggregated system of global health governance.

In sum, global governance was in an authority crisis during a period of American unilateralism, but under the Obama presidency the country has again turned towards multilateralism and order-building. This may not be happening on a grand scale but activities are blooming at many different levels and in several shapes and sizes. It is not a unified, streamlined structure of governance but it is getting a lot of things done; it is good-enough governance.

This benign view is discussed in the following sections against the critique of the sceptical view. The latter maintains that the extension of liberal order from a 'West–West' context to a global context is no simple matter at all. The Western order was held together by a common enemy, the Soviet Union; tensions between the partners always played out against the background of a larger, common threat. Countries participating in the Western order were all liberal democracies, supporting common values of democracy and human rights. And rising great powers—Japan and Germany—restrained themselves as participants in the liberal order. They sought economic and political reconstruction, but not military might or nuclear capacities that could challenge close cooperation. Today, important great powers are autocratic and they do not accept any restraints in their aspirations for a more prominent place in the global order. They are not animated by the same set of liberal values that tie Western countries together and the coherence provided by a common enemy is gone.

The sceptics argue that this new situation has already seriously impeded the creation of an effective institutional structure. The lack of common ground among established and emerging powers, on one hand, and the inability of a leading country or coalition of countries to impose solutions, on the other, makes for a world order where the challenges of global leadership cannot be met; we are in a gridlock or a 'G-Zero' world where 'no one is driving the bus' (Bremmer 2012: 10).

The next three sections examine the current status of governance in three major areas (economy, environment and security) against the contentions of good-enough governance and 'gridlock'. This is followed by a closer look at the behaviour and interests of emerging and established powers.

The financial crisis

Global economic governance involves a host of issues connected with the great variety of economic relationships across borders in a globalized world. Focus in this section is on governance in relation to the financial and economic crisis of 2008, arguably the most serious disruption of the global economy since the Great Depression some 85 years ago. The crisis itself is linked to the previous growth of financial and economic interdependence: the mortgage defaults of the US housing market bubble not only affected American financial institutions but the entire global economic system. Global capital flows dropped dramatically as financial firms tightened credit and focused on more secure financial assets in the rich, developed world (Hale, Held and Young 2013: 162–71).

There is no single cause of a comprehensive crisis, but a major element is the way in which banks and other financial institutions were involved in excessive risk taking that led to the near collapse of the entire financial system (for the following points, see Kapoor 2010). The system rewards risk taking. The higher risk the greater the prospects for profits (and bonuses). In earlier days, banks in the United Kingdom and the United States earned the same amount of return on equity as firms in the real economy, about 10%. When the crisis hit, bank returns had climbed to 30%. There are several ways of excessive risk taking. One is leverage: the more you borrow in order to invest, the higher the leverage ratio; the ratio is 1 when you put up half of your own money and borrow the rest. Around the time of the crisis, leverage ratios for banks such as Deutsche Bank or UBS exceeded 60.

A derivative is a financial product that derives its value from the performance of an underlying security. They are most often leveraged products that can be traded using only a fraction of their total profit (or loss) potential. High profits can then be generated by loading up on derivatives. Over time, these products became increasingly diversified and opaque. Option contracts, futures contracts, swaps (issuing bonds in one currency and swapping them for another), credit default swaps, portfolio insurance and securitization (bundling loans into packages that are then sold to investors) were the major products. Another motivation for getting into derivatives was that increasing market prices of the assets could immediately be booked as profits (and lead to the payment of bonuses) irrespective of whether market values would later drop and be translated into losses.

Maturing mismatch led to another form of excessive risk taking. Borrowing on the short term is cheaper than borrowing on the long term and, vice versa, lending on the long term is more profitable than lending on the short term. So banks increasingly financed their activity by short-term borrowing while increasing the duration of the loans they made; they also went into more risky loan-making to increase returns. This goes well as long as fresh short-term finance is readily available but it breaks down when liquidity dries up in times of crisis.

There are three major links between excessive risk taking at the firm level and systemic risk for the financial sector and the general economy. First, a failing financial institution can drag down other financial institutions, as in the case of Lehman Brothers. Second, financial sector breakdown freezes credits and thus halts activity in the real economy. Finally, since real economic meltdown is to be avoided, states tend to come to the rescue of the financial sector. In this way, the financial institutions always stand to win when risk taking goes well and do not overly lose when it goes wrong because they are bailed out by states. The direct and indirect costs to taxpayers of the financial crisis exceed $15 trillion according to the Bank of England, 'a sum far greater than any contribution from the financial sector to the real economy' (Kapoor 2010: 38).

In sum, a deregulated financial system provided a host of incentives for excessive risk taking which led to the most severe financial crisis the world had seen since 1929. In fact, the drop in industrial output and world trade levels was more serious in early 2008 than was the case in October 1929. But in contrast to earlier there was a much faster rebound after 2008. Industrial output, world trade volumes and aggregate economic growth had recovered by 2012, with Europe as a partial exception. This is the basis for the claim that global economic governance actually worked rather well in responding to the crisis (Drezner 2012).

Both national and international institutions contributed to this result. Central banks cut interest rates, promoted countercyclical lending and expanded credit facilities. The G20 emerged as a central forum in facilitating coordination and institutional innovation. It created the Financial Stability Board with the aim of developing new regulatory standards for financial institutions and made a Basel III agreement with more robust banking standards. To be sure, the G20 is an ad hoc institution with very limited powers but it did achieve something in terms of short-term recovery. In comparison, the World Economic Conference, convened in 1933 to deal with the Great Depression, achieved nothing.

The sceptical view is not impressed by this record. To begin with, in the early phases of the crisis, coordination among central banks was weak and ad hoc, focused on the rich developed countries. The coordination that emerged in the G20 lacked both the institutional power and the administrative infrastructure needed for implementation and enforcement of its proposals (Hale, Held and Young 2013: 170). The Financial Stability Board (FSB), arguably the most ambitious institutional innovation of the G20, faces a number of serious challenges in developing mechanisms for compliance and promoting effective international financial standards (Helleiner 2010; Kapoor 2010: 56). Basel III rules require an increase in the capital reserve requirements of banks; the rules are to be implemented step by step until 2019. But on one hand the new requirements are similar to those that applied to US banks already before the crisis (Hoenig 2012); on the other hand, the regulations may incentivize banks to shift assets 'off balance sheet' and thus stimulate the creation of a grey area 'shadow banking sector' (Gooptu 2012).

At the same time, the G20 has been plagued by disagreement among its members and has not succeeded in transforming itself from a short-term crisis manager to a longer-term steering institution for the global economy. The issue of effective supervisory structures at the global level is important because in order to address systemic risk, regulators need a system-wide view. The bodies that have been set up so far have limited capacities and little or no statutory powers. That is, there is an intensely globalized financial system but there is no effective global regulator (Kapoor 2010: 99).

The second major problem not addressed by short-term crisis management concerns the 'too big to fail' financial institutions, the excessive risk takers that were bailed out by tax payers at the height of the financial crisis. After six years of deliberations, the Financial Stability Board presented a proposal in late 2014 aimed at ensuring that the cost of failure would be borne by shareholders, not taxpayers. The proposal requires a number of 'global systemically important banks' to hold a certain amount of cash in order to be able to survive big losses on their own. The proposed requirement was 15–20% of the bank's assets, a much bigger cushion than under current rules.

Again, the proposal is a template that must be followed up by specific regulations, aimed to take effect by 2019. If eventually successful, critics worry that this will not be enough because the big financial institutions remain too big and too complex to allow for effective supervision, yet it is deemed a step in the right direction (Stanley and Beekarry 2014).

Finally, there is a set of problems connected with the utterly complex and opaque financial products, high-frequency trading driven by computers and algorithms, a shadow banking system of conduits and money-market funds, and the growth of a securitization industry. The common factor behind these elements is the incentive structure in the financial sector which encourages excessive risk taking and short-termism. Nothing much has been done in this area; 'the incentive misalignments at the heart of the financial sector are scarcely being addressed' (Kapoor 2010: 99).

In sum, the argument of sceptics is that while short-term crisis management in relation to the 2008 financial meltdown was relatively successful, the substantial measures aimed at reforming the financial system so as to avoid similar dramatic calamities in the future have been relatively weak and the multilateral institutional apparatus set in place to tackle these challenges does not possess the political clout and the administrative capacity to play more than a limited role when the next crisis comes around.

Climate change

The climate change issue was introduced in the previous chapter. The conclusion there was that 'coming years will probably see more results from specific negotiations on particular problems than from global discussions of very large agendas'. In other words, an indication that good-enough governance can be achieved through a multitude of much more loosely linked initiatives, what have been called 'a regime complex for climate change' (Keohane and Victor 2011). The arguments for and against this view are discussed in what follows.

The hopes for a climate change regime complex to do better flows from the relative failure of big, multilateral initiatives. One would immediately think that climate change, of all problems, is one that calls for grand, multilateral, concerted action. Many countries have long supported the establishment of a 'World Environmental Organization' (WEO) so as to create an institutional anchor for global endeavours for the environment, but little has come of it, even though major countries, such as Germany and France, have favoured the creation of a strong multilateral organization with more political clout.

The major problem remains divergent interests among many players, powerful states in particular. The proudest outcome of the multilateral effort has been the Kyoto Protocol (and its successors), an agreement on reduced emission targets. Its most important result so far is the Paris Agreement of 2015. But the deal is little more than an expression of good intentions; countries are to set their own targets for carbon emissions and the financial aid commitment to developing countries for energy reforms remains voluntary (Cassidy 2015). Nor is the core of the agreement—percentage reduction targets over a certain time span—an effective one because governments only partially control emission outcomes and they often evade their commitments when they prove too costly (Hale, Held and Young 2013; Victor 2011).

In the larger scheme then, Kyoto can be considered one element of what is a diversified regime complex for climate change. Another component of the regime is club-making efforts or 'a la carte multilateralism'. The most important forums are the MEF (Major Economies Forum) with 17 (16 states and the EU) members responsible for some 80% of global emissions; it was created by the United States in 2007. The other important club-forum is the G20, which has been pre-occupied with the financial crisis but has also taken some time to discuss environmental issues. In addition to these two forums, climate change is on the agenda in several other agencies of the UN system whose primary mandate is something else, including the World Bank, the United Nations Development Programme (UNDP), the Global Environment Facility (GEF) and the United Nations Environment Programme (UNEP).

A further major component of the regime complex consists of a variety of bilateral deals. Several countries, including the United States, the United Kingdom, France and Australia, have created bilateral partnerships with China concerning coal technologies and nuclear power. The United States also collaborates with India about access to nuclear technology. A large number of countries have signed bilateral deals concerning reduced carbon emissions, including a 2014 deal between China and the United States (White House 2014). Finally, unilateral initiatives abound in several countries, including the United States where individual states such as California have imposed state limits on emissions. Civil society organizations and several firms have also pushed initiatives for controlling emissions.

What is the track record of the climate change regime? Not overly impressive. Emissions have been reduced in a number of developed countries, but not sufficiently to offset the increases in the developing world. China alone added more than the sum of reductions between 1990 and 2009. Some developed countries contributed to increased emissions too, including Australia, Canada and Switzerland. The climate regime is therefore 'grossly inadequate' (CFR 2013) when it comes to stabilizing greenhouse gas levels. Current emission growth levels will cause an average rise of global temperatures by a minimum of 4 degrees Celsius in 2100, instead of the 2 degrees that is the current ambition (Carrington 2013).

The monitoring and enforcement mechanisms are weak. Developing countries in particular lack domestic capacity to monitor their own emissions and there are no precise ways, for example, to measure emissions from deforestation. Several developing countries, including China, resist international monitoring for national sovereignty reasons. Enforcement, meanwhile, is 'essentially nonexistent' (CFR 2013: 13).

Furthermore, there is no adequate financing. The calculation of total costs for a safe climate is of course difficult; the Stern Review (2006) put it at 1% of global GDP. There is consensus, however, that the cost of doing nothing will be much higher, 5% of GDP according to the Stern Review. The International Energy Agency estimated the cost of achieving climate goals by 2020 at \$5 trillion (IEA 2014). Developing countries are scheduled to need \$300 billion per year in 2020. There is a principled intention of providing \$100 billion by 2020 but no substantial framework for financing has been created.

Finally, there is the issue of climate-friendly economic development strategies and the related issue of development and transfer of new technologies. There are a number of small-scale projects under way in this area. For example, there is an EU–China partnership on Climate Change on developing 'Near-Zero Emissions Coal' (NZEC) plants in China using new technologies; there are also a number of UNEP initiatives on renewable energies focused on biofuels and solar and wind energy. At the same time, however, the 'climate-proofing' of larger-scale economic development models is in the very early stages, and the larger issues of technology transfer and international property rights remain contested (Wade 2003).

In sum, the climate change regime cannot boast a record of great success. To be sure, the problems related to climate change are intensely connected across borders, but the climate change regime is deeply fragmented. That is behind the call for a 'structural change in global governance ... both inside and outside the UN system ...' (Biermann et al. 2009: 38). In a sense, a 'constitutional moment' has arrived in the governance of climate change, because now is the time to do much more if catastrophic damage is to be avoided. Yet the major actors, including states, firms, civil society organizations and most individuals, do not fully recognize this to be a decisive point in time requiring fundamental change. Moreover, there is no firm guarantee that an integrated and overarching climate regime will produce better results than the currently fragmented sets of institutions. A case can indeed be made that the latter are more flexible and can boast higher adaptability (Keohane and Victor 2011: 15). Unfortunately, they can also be plagued by extreme fragmentation, chaos and gridlock. At the present time, there is no simple way forward for the climate change regime.

Security

At UN headquarters, one of the walls has a quote from former General Secretary Dag Hammarskjöld: 'The UN was not created to take humanity to heaven but to save it from hell.' The statement was made during the height of the Cold War and there is no doubt about what was the meaning of 'hell': a devastating war among the great powers. That never happened and the UN did play a role in that achievement. Cooperation in international institutions matter greatly for the increasing obsolescence of interstate war as explained earlier in this book. But a host of security issues remain on the table; from a human cost perspective, the most important one is domestic conflict in fragile states. The issue was discussed in Chapter 5; the conclusion was that we have a situation of 'security governance in pieces'. The focus in what follows is on the strengths and weaknesses of the regime complex in relation to fragile states.

Compared to regimes concerned with the economy or the climate, the security regime related to fragile states has a clearly defined centre, which is the United Nations Security Council (UNSC). Council decisions are managed by the UN secretariat's Department of Peacekeeping Operations (DPKO), the Department of Field Support (DFS) and the Department of Political Affairs (DPA). Furthermore, there is a clear formal framework, adopted by the UN World Summit in 2005, concerning the responsibility to protect populations from genocide, war crimes, ethnic cleansing and crimes against humanity (R2P).

The R2P calls upon individual states to protect their populations from such crimes and to prevent their incitement. That is an important normative development because so far, state sovereignty has been connected with the rights of states to conduct their own affairs, free from outside intervention. The R2P, by contrast, invokes duties and responsibilities of states in connection with sovereignty. And if these responsibilities are not met, there is an explicit responsibility on the part of the international community through the UNSC, 'to help to protect populations ... in a timely and decisive manner' (UN 2005: 138–40).

In other words, there is a well-defined framework and leadership in place as well as connected bureaucracies to monitor and implement decisions of peace operations in fragile states. Yet grave conflicts continue to emerge in fragile states and old conflicts tend to linger on with no clear end in sight. Why has this impressive apparatus not done better?

Most importantly, serious political discord among the five permanent members of the Security Council has prevented effective action in a number of cases. Amnesty International's 2014 Report speaks of 'shameful' inaction in relation to Syrian and Iraqi refugees, ethnic cleansing in the Central African Republic, Boko Haram massacres in Niger:a, atrocities in South Sudan and the death of children in Palestine from Israeli bombings. The charge is that permanent members have 'consistently abused' their veto rights to 'promote their political self-interest or geopolitical interest above the interest of protecting civilians' (Shalil Shetty, Amnesty General Secretary, quoted from Shrago 2015).

China supports the principles of R2P but the government also worries about setting aside the code of sovereignty as freedom from external intervention, as does Russia. That has led to the emphasis on prevention of conflict and operations which have the consent of the affected governments (Teitt 2008). Russia's invocation of the R2P in relation to Ukraine demonstrates how the principle can be twisted so as to serve national security interests (Kersten 2014).

France has proposed that the five permanent members abandon their veto power in cases of genocides, war crimes and crimes against humanity. This would be a voluntary arrangement, according to the French foreign minister:

> The Charter would not be amended and the change would be implemented through a mutual commitment from the permanent members. In concrete terms, if the Security Council were required to make a decision with regard to a mass crime, the permanent members would agree to suspend their right to veto. The criteria for implementation would be simple: at the request of at least 50 member states, the United Nations Secretary General would be called upon to determine the nature of the crime. ... To be realistically applicable, this code would exclude cases where the vital national interests of a permanent member of the Council were at stake. (Fabius 2013).

It is quite unusual for a permanent member of the Security Council to suggest a restriction on the veto; the proposal has support from some 70 countries but it will surely not get very far. The United States, China and Russia will not support it, even with the caveat of excluding cases that have yet to be defined. In more general terms, reform of the Security Council has been on the agenda for several decades without getting off the ground. Discord does not merely concern China and Russia; the liberal democracies are not in agreement either with regard to UNSC reform.

Gridlock at the Security Council is a major problem, but not the only one in relation to violence in fragile states. First, peace operations are by now a substantial element in UN activities, employing more than 100,000 people with a 2015 budget well over $8 billion (UN 2015). At this magnitude, there is a UN 'peace' bureaucracy with its own set of interests. On one hand, there is an incentive to be seen as 'doing something' in concrete conflicts; on the other hand, there is an incentive to 'pick the winners' and avoid failures. The latter points to a demand that there should be a peace to keep in order for a peace operation to start up, but that would leave people suffering in many places where such conditions are not in place. In any case, the bureaucracy has a primary concern for the UN's reputation and interests (Barnett 1997; Allen and Yuen 2014).

Second, there are financial and personnel constraints. General Secretary Ban Ki Moon complained already in 2009 about mounting difficulties in getting sufficient troops, equipment, logistical support and economic backing (Aguirre and Abrisketa 2009; see also Selway 2013). At the same time, the UN Office of Internal Oversight Services has found serious instances of mismanagement, fraud and corruption in relation to peacekeeping operations (Schaefer 2009).

Finally, there has been much talk of conflict prevention measures including early-warning systems, but achievements in this area have not been impressive. The United Nations does not have a central coordinating unit with primary responsibility for collecting, integrating and analysing early-warning conflict reports. Some work is done at the Department of Political Affairs; several regional organizations, including the European Union, the OSCE and the African Union also have early-warning and prevention initiatives under way, but the whole area is not very developed and is not integrated in a framework that includes policy responses.

In sum, the security regime in relation to fragile states is less fragmented than most other regimes in the sense that activities in this area are centrally anchored at the UN Security Council, which is responsible for deciding, implementing and overseeing peace operations. But this is not a strong centre in terms of resolute responses to mass violence in fragile states because of disagreements among the P5 and because the UN does not have an effective infrastructure to draw on in terms of personnel and equipment. It is dependent on member states, and increasingly on regional organizations, including the African Union and the European Union. This is time-consuming; the

UN/AU mission in Darfur, for example, took more than three years to reach full deployment (UNAMID 2013).

At the same time, peace operations are increasingly set up with mandates that include rebuilding efforts so that peace-building and state-building and economic development must go together. In institutional terms this means the involvement of a great many organizations and agencies, including NGOs, bilateral donors, multilateral bodies (e.g. the World Bank), regional organizations, and a host of UN agencies. So even with a strong centre, there is plenty of room for fragmentation in the conduct of concrete operations.

There is a framework in place for responding to severe humanitarian crises in fragile states, but it has not been able to formulate and implement effective responses. The case for 'governance in pieces' is that the institutions are doing the best they can under difficult circumstances. The objection by many observers is that this is simply not good enough.

Emerging powers in global governance

A number of countries in the international system have undertaken strong processes of economic growth in recent decades. These modernizing states were introduced in Chapter 2; the most significant of them are becoming more prominent players in global governance. Who exactly these new players are is disputed, because power in global governance depends not merely on economic or military capabilities but also on how power is put to use. The focus in this section is on the BICs (Brazil, India and China), arguably the strongest candidates for a more pronounced international role; they might not be strong enough to set the agenda, but they are 'veto-players' in the sense that significant changes of the status quo require their support (Narlikar 2013a: 561; Tsebelis 1995). The ascent of the BICs has certainly sparked a debate about rising powers and global governance in several quarters (e.g. Gaskarth 2015; Narlikar 2013a).

The question, then, is about the larger consequences for global governance of the rise of the BICs; will they facilitate the emergence of more legitimate and effective governance—or at the least the promotion of good-enough governance; or will they contribute to a situation of intensified gridlock with a risk of more conflict and disorder?

Brazil ought to be the easy case compared to China and India. It is a regional great power, but does not have the economic or military wherewithal or the political will to champion or even demand dramatic changes in the existing structures of global governance. At the same time, Brazil is a democracy with a long history of being well-integrated into the global economic system. In that sense, Brazil can be seen as a basically satisfied power that is not looking for dramatic changes in global economic and political governance structures (Burges 2013).

But Brazil is looking to augment its position in the system, so as to improve its possibilities for pursuing its national interests. Towards that end Brazil draws on its history as mediator between North and South; its 1970s policies of 'responsible pragmatism' (White 2010: 223) aimed at increased autonomy from the United States in a context of continued cooperation, but Brazil also helped found the G77 and supported Southern demands for a reformed international economic order. In recent years Brazil has cleverly supported South–South cooperation as an alternative to excessive dependence on the North; and it has established itself as an interlocutor in relations between North and South. These roles have provided good opportunities for the pursuit of Brazilian economic and political interests, both in terms of finding more Brazilian business in the South and in terms of a more central position at international negotiating tables (Bevir and Gaskarth 2015; Burges 2013).

That this is not always an easy game to play was demonstrated in the case of R2P. Many Southern countries are sceptical about R2P, seeing it as a Northern tool for intervention by force in the South. Brazil favours the emphasis on sovereignty and non-intervention and did not support the UNSC resolution on a no-fly zone in Libya. Instead of rejecting R2P outright, Brazil argued for adding a doctrine of 'Responsibility While Protecting' which would hold intervening powers accountable for any collateral damage while protecting civilians. It looks like a North–South compromise proposal but it could mean deadlock for R2P because intervening countries will not accept such liabilities.

In sum, Brazil's pragmatic approach will not fundamentally undermine global governance but nor does it clearly promise to change things for the better. Brazil can help create a more legitimate order by moving Southern nations closer to a role of responsible stakeholders; but Brazilian self-interest comes first and in some cases this may lead to gridlock. Basic reform of global governance is not on Brazil's agenda; it works the current system, drawing on its 'great skill ... to be friends with everyone' (Brazilian diplomat, quoted from Dauvergne and Farias 2012: 906).

India has a long history of being an outsider in an international system dominated by Western democracies. On one hand, it cast itself as a spokesman for the South in its leadership of the Non-Aligned Movement, the newly independent countries that defined themselves as a third party favouring peaceful coexistence in contrast to the Cold War confrontation between the superpowers. On the other hand, India's leanings towards a state-directed model of economic development led to the cooperation treaty with the Soviet Union in 1971, potentially antagonizing not only Western but also Southern nations.

The end of the Cold War combined with domestic economic changes in India have led to a much closer integration of the country into the global market economy (Dige Pedersen 2008); at the same time, India has strengthened its ties with the United States, perhaps culminating in the Civil Nuclear Agreement of 2005–08. Under the agreement, the United States consents to civil nuclear cooperation with India, and India places its civil nuclear facilities under international safeguards. The agreement is a de facto acceptance of India as a nuclear power (Council on Foreign Relations 2010).

But these developments have not decisively changed India's role in global governance. It remains strongly devoted to the promotion of developing countries' economic interests in international economic fora. India has used some of its recently gained economic clout to grant preferential treatment to Less Developed Countries (LDCs) (33 countries in Africa and 14 in East Asia); its economic involvement in Africa is more ready than China's to employ local workers and to cooperate with local suppliers. And India has gained a reputation of serving 'the voice of the voiceless' in the WTO (Narlikar 2013b: 604). As regards the poor LDCs, then, India can to some extent be regarded as a supplier of more effective and more legitimate global governance, at least for a smaller constituency.

The posture of cooperation and willingness to provide solutions is not replicated in India's relationship with the established great powers and with other rising modernizers. When it comes to taking on general responsibilities of upholding and developing global governance, India has earned a reputation as 'a moralistic and contrarian loner in the international community' (Perkovich 2003: 141).

India played a significant role in creating the deadlock of the WTO Doha Round in 2008 (the Indian chief negotiator earned the title of 'Dr No'); it would not accept a compromise on agricultural subsidies and claimed to be defending the poor farmers in all developing countries. But this was, in the words of one African ambassador, a case of 'the elephants hiding behind the mice' (cited from Schwab 2011). On climate change, India has remained unwilling to take on binding commitments; in relation to R2P, India supports the concept in principle but has not been willing to take on responsibility for its implementation (Narlikar 2011).

In sum, India has moved closer to the international society in the sense that it has opened up to economic integration in globalized networks and a more pronounced role in global governance fora due to its increased economic and political weight. But it also casts itself as a developing country and remains unwilling to take responsibility for the development and reform of global governance. India's reputation as a naysayer will not facilitate its desire for a more prominent role in the UNSC, and it is entirely unclear what India would bring to the table in terms of more legitimate and effective governance, outside of the narrow defence of LDC interests. India's emphasis on sovereignty and non-intervention combines with pursuit of national interest in ways that can easily lead to intensified gridlock.

China was never colonized but it has not forgotten its history of 'one hundred years of suffering and humiliation' at the hands of the Western powers and Japan. China's international isolation during the Cold War, especially after the separation from the Soviet Union, further strengthened the idea of a hostile and competitive international environment. China's economic reforms have initiated a new period of opening up to intense participation in economic globalization. And China has engaged with a large number of international regimes and organizations, some of which China previously criticized as part of an American hegemony.

What kind of player is China in relation to global governance? China plays four different roles simultaneously (Breslin 2013), and that is complicated because they often point in different directions. First, China is a developing country; therefore, it is primarily focused on domestic problems in relation to social, economic, environmental and a host of other issues. Externally, this role casts China as champion of Third World preferences. Second, China is an emerging power. It shares with other emerging powers a dissatisfaction with several elements of the existing order and a general desire for an improved position of emerging powers in that order. But there is no general agreement among emerging powers about the design for a reformed order.

Third, China is a great power, recognized as such through its permanent membership of the UN Security Council. That makes it formally an established power with significant responsibility for the maintenance and development of world order. Finally, that great power role has been emphasized by the notion of G2, according to which the United States and China are now the two most important and powerful countries in the world with special responsibilities for the solution of global problems.

What is China's view of these roles? On one hand, China has resisted taking on the role as established great power in full and it resists any notion of China being fully equal with the United States. On the other hand, China has recognized that it is no longer an ordinary developing country; it has development concerns but its portfolio of interests reach much further than that. Given these partially conflicting roles, there is an internal debate in China about best ways of situating the country in the global order (Foot 2006; Li 2011). The current Chinese position is one of basically accepting a US-led global order and to incrementally change this order from within: 'The United States is the guide of the world. China is willing to join this system,' said Vice Premier Wang Yang in 2014 (quoted from Sisci 2015). In other words, China wants to modify the current order rather than challenge it (Schweller and Pu 2011: 53).

In concrete terms, this has not led towards a high level of Chinese activism in relation to global governance. Chinese priorities come first, as David Shambaugh argues, 'instead of stepping up and taking on a range of global responsibilities, China remains internally oriented, self-preoccupied, pursuing a largely narrow self-interested foreign policy' (Shambaugh 2013).

At the same time, China has stepped up its engagement at the UN, including an increased contribution towards UN peacekeeping operations (Foot 2014). China also pursues several minor 'reform projects', including reform of international financial institutions (with increased influence for emerging powers); the most recent initiative is the plan for an Asian Infrastructure Investment Bank (AIIB), a new institution free of the US/Western dominance that characterizes other global financial institutions. China is also endorsing Security Council reform (but not in a way that dilutes China's influence), and in some cases it has toned down its traditional emphasis on sovereignty and non-intervention. For example, China abstained from voting when the UN resolution on a no-fly zone over Libya was on the table (but it vetoed a similar resolution on Syria).

In sum, China is slowly becoming a more active global player; even more so than India, it is integrated in the global economy and in the major institutions of global governance. But on most issues it remains on the sidelines, looking after its own interests. In many ways, China is more of a regional than a global player; it will not make big contributions towards a more effective and legitimate order within the next few decades.

Overall, I have looked at three major emerging powers with a view to deciding what role they are playing in global governance. All three BICs are pragmatic players that have moved towards greater accept-ance of the existing structure of global governance. They are not seeking grand reforms, nor do they agree on any ambitious schemes for the transformation of that structure. Inside the system, they look for gradual modifications with the overall aim of better serving their national priorities while maintaining a high degree of sovereign, decision-making autonomy (Kahler 2013).

Three major areas of governance were reviewed above: global finance, climate change and security. The contributions of the BICs in these areas have not been impressive: they argue that the finan-cial crisis is primarily a problem that the established Western powers must deal with; they are lukewarm towards accepting major responsi-bilities in taking on climate change; and they are not eager to build an effective framework for confronting the challenges posed by fragile states. The BICs do not act as spoilers outright but given their current postures and levels of engagement they are no great help in the quest for a more effective and legitimate order.

The United States and global governance

What is the current role of the world's leading power, the United States, in global governance? Earlier in this chapter, we noted the change in the US approach to global governance from the presidency of George W. Bush to the presidency of Barack Obama. Bush pro-moted the 'global war on terror' as a foreign policy priority with a style that was distinctly unilateralist. Obama toned down the terrorist threat and promised a new era of diplomacy and cooperation. The multiple challenges called for more cooperation: 'America cannot meet the threats of this century alone' (Obama 2007: 4).

However, there has been no decisive American turn towards multilateralism; the primary change is in form, not in substantial content. In that sense the difference between Bush and Obama is overdrawn; the United States was always a hesitant multilateralist because it wants to preserve its sovereign autonomy to act in its own best interests as the situation demands. This basic idea—that there are rules for others basically stipulated by the United States but that such rules do not always apply to the United States itself—is grounded in the historical notion of American exceptionalism. The core of this notion is that America always is a force for good in the world because of its basic political values and democratic institutions. Therefore, the unique virtue of America means that it is always on the right side of history.

It is on this premise that the United States requires everybody else to follow rules from which the United States itself can be exempted, should the situation demand it. According to Morton Abramowitz, 'The United States constantly reminds many countries ... that if they want to be part of the international community they must play by the rules. ... Still, only one country—the United States—can be exempt from the rules because of its virtue. ... The United States is allowed to violate its own rules, as long as it serves our security and other interests as every administration defines them' (Abramowitz 2012).

American exceptionalism stipulates a pragmatic or instrumental multilateralism, depending on interests, the issue at hand, and on domestic and international conditions. International institutions are sometimes useful, sometimes not; therefore they will sometimes be drawn in and sometimes excluded. One way of easing the tension between the demand for commitment from others and the possible lack of commitment from oneself is to promote more informal institutions, such as the G20, that have limited capacity to constrain US power and where commitments are not legally binding (Vezirgiannidou 2013).

In established institutions, such as the UN Security Council, the United States is rhetorically committed to institutional reform changes which provide a greater role for emerging powers. But in practice the United States has done little on the issue, outside of supporting India's candidacy for permanent membership. It is particularly noteworthy that the United States has not come out in clear support of Brazil's candidacy; if this is directly related to Brazil's abstention in the vote over the Libyan intervention, it indicates that the American posture on institutional reform is narrowly connected to behaviour in support of US interests (Vezirgiannidou 2013: 641).

Domestic conditions also heavily influence American foreign policy choices. The US Constitution makes Congress and the executive branch coequals in the conduct of foreign policy. Divisions between the legislative and executive arms of government—often combined with divisions within Congress—can make it impossible to conduct foreign policy in some areas, for example to provide funds for foreign initiatives, conclude treaties or pass institutional reforms. According to several observers, partisan gridlock reached a new level in March 2015 when a large group of Republican senators sent a letter to Iranian leaders, warning them against a nuclear arms accord with the White House. In other words, domestic bickering impedes the development of a coherent foreign policy in the world's principal power.

During the Cold War, competition with the Soviet Union led to a strategy of deterrence and containment which was supported by both Democratic and Republic administrations. With the Soviet Union out of the picture, political discipline has come untied and there is an increased appeal of unilateralism. Writing in 1996, Senate minority leader Tom Daschle stated: 'The Cold War exerted a powerful hold on America, and it forced the parties to work together to advance American interests through bipartisan internationalism. … The tragedy is that such cooperation increasingly seems an artefact of the past' (Daschle 1996: 4–5).

Further, bipartisanship is weakened for domestic reasons as well: regional divisions are stronger, with the South as the Republican Party's major regional power base, and coalitions cutting across party and regional divides are increasingly difficult to establish. Uneven globalization has exacerbated regional tensions and disparities; generational change is a factor as well: the post-World War II generation is retiring, and the new members of Congress are not socialized towards bipartisan compromise. After World War II, US global leadership was based on military power and institutional partnership with allies. This compact, say Charles Kupchan and Peter Trubowitz, 'has now come undone' (Kupchan and Trubowitz 2007: 39).

The changes described here are reflected in the US posture on the three areas of global governance reviewed earlier in this chapter. In relation to the financial crisis, the United States has focused on preventing a collapse of the US economy, taking measures that were also aimed at preserving Wall Street as a global financial centre. This short-term crisis management has been successful, but there have been few initiatives aiming at global financial stewardship. The fragmented G20 initiatives are weak moves towards general financial reform.

Climate change is a similar story. The United States focuses on limited domestic measures and select bilateral agreements. The recent 'Clean power plan' (2015) aims at a 30% reduction in carbon emissions from the US power sector by 2030. The bilateral agreement with China aims to reduce US greenhouse gas emissions 26–28% by 2025 compared to 2005; China commits to peak carbon emissions around 2030 (White House 2014). Global initiatives are not given great priority; neither the United States nor China is committed under the Kyoto Protocol.

As regards security governance, this chapter has focused on domestic conflict in fragile states and the potential of R2P. The United States supports R2P but it does not play a significant role in US debates on security, nor has the United States supported the French proposal to strengthen the R2P. A recent report commissioned by the United States Institute of Peace makes a series of recommendations aimed at enlarging the US capacity to help implement the R2P and to enhance international action in support of R2P (Albright and Williamson 2013). The recommendations generally point to the need for a much stronger US engagement in the multilateral promotion of the R2P.

In sum, after the end of the Cold War, the United States has not taken on the mantle of global leadership in a way that can be compared to its leadership of the free world after World War II. There are several reasons for that; the United States remains the most powerful state in the system in military, economic and technological terms, but its preponderance is much less pronounced compared with the situation around 1950. American exceptionalism was always a factor for cautious multilateral engagement. The disappearance of the Soviet threat combined with domestic changes in American politics have strengthened the tendency to look inwards and to avoid being tied down by international commitments. Emerging powers are not enthusiastically requesting American leadership; they are sceptical towards Washington and tend to pursue their interests elsewhere (Lindsay 2011).

Observers complain that there is an absence of debate about the global role of the United States in a post-Cold War, post-9/11 world. James L. Jones, security advisor to Obama in 2009–10, notes that 'During the Cold War, the United States and its allies had a common strategy, but we argued over tactics. Today we debate tactics, but lack a common strategy to guide our principles' (quoted from Atlantic Council 2015). In short, to the extent that there is American leadership it is much more fragmented and erratic than it was after World War II.

Conclusion: Gridlock or good-enough governance?

This chapter interrogated the current condition of global governance. Intensified interdependence increases the demand for governance across borders. The amount of global governance has surely expanded significantly, as seen from the growth in interstate, transgovernmental and transnational relations. Is that a sufficient supply of governance, or is it a drop in the ocean, a glaringly insufficient institutional structure that amounts to a case of gridlock where the demand for global stewardship is not met at all?

The optimists have a point; a great amount of governance is surely taking place. The immediate problems of the financial crisis were successfully handled by reasonably effective crisis management. A large and diversified climate-change regime has taken several initiatives to combat global warming. The complex security challenges posed by fragile states have been responded to by an ambitious R2P regime. At the same time, emerging powers are increasingly integrated into the institutional structure, and the United States under Obama has returned to a higher degree of reliance on international institutions.

The sceptics are not convinced by this record. The case for gridlock is that the supposedly good-enough governance emphasized by the optimists amounts to nothing more than inconsistent and fragmented short-termism which provides little more than crisis management, with the next crisis always looming around the corner. There have been no basic initiatives towards reorganizing the financial system; the climate change regime is weak and insufficient; there is no end to serious humanitarian crises in fragile states.

Emerging powers participate in global governance, but they are neither willing nor able to take the lead in basic reforms of the institutional structure. The United States is not turning away from international institutions, but nor is it a driving force for effective and legitimate global governance.

In sum, piecemeal governance is taking place, but it is not good enough because the challenges we face demand more profound reform in order to provide sustainable solutions. It is less a matter of fragmented versus centrally coordinated governance; a strong centre may be an advantage in some cases, but a more fragmented system may have advantages too in terms of flexibility and adaptability. The problem is that current varieties of global governance—more integrated or more fragmented—do not provide solutions that go beyond short-term crisis management.

Why is such more profound governance not forthcoming? One answer is that we are lacking a 'constitutional moment', a crisis which moves important actors and institutions towards unconventional adaptation (Ackerman 1991). The threats and challenges reviewed earlier have not been sufficiently imminent, or sufficiently alarming to all major actors, so as to create a constitutional moment.

That situation is related to the framework conditions outlined earlier in this book. First, the decreasing importance of great power war; on one hand, recall Tom Daschle's words about the Cold War exerting 'a powerful hold on America' pushing it in the direction of bipartisan internationalism. Even with a renewed Russian nationalism and the crisis in Ukraine there is little worry that this could lead to great power war. An important incentive for bipartisan cooperation towards American international leadership has disappeared and as a consequence such leadership has not been forthcoming, even with an internationally oriented president in office. On the other hand, the existence of a common enemy which presented a clear and present danger was an important foundation for Western cooperation during the Cold War. It tied liberal states into a common security arrangement led by the United States, which was an important force for coherence and solidarity, even when there was discord in particular areas. No such common enemy is a force for coherence today; the 'global war on terror' was a candidate after 9/11 and the dangers posed by climate change are a candidate today, but neither greater nor lesser powers have been convinced that they should be compelled to set aside differences and cooperate on those grounds.

Second, increasingly fragile states (Chapter 2) are compelled to look inward in order to confront their own problems. Decades of neoliberal globalization have decreased the socio-political cohesion in the advanced Western states because large sections of the populations have been squeezed in a process towards much higher levels of inequality. Hilary Clinton's slogan in her bid for the US presidency captures the current major political theme: 'Everyday Americans need a champion. I want to be that champion.' Political attention is on domestic affairs that present a host of problems in advanced liberal democracies and more so in the emerging powers. In China, for example, rising socio-economic inequality is a problem, but it competes with other very serious problems, including corruption, social stability, environmental degradation and the vast task of creating a different model of economic accumulation, less dependent on low wages and exports. Contributing to effective global governance is an item low on the agenda in both advanced and emerging economies.

Finally, there is the issue of who has power and how power can be put to use in the construction of world order (Chapter 4). The United States remains very powerful, both in terms of material and soft power. It is still the leading power, but by a much smaller margin than after World War II. Since the turn of the century, that power has not been put to use in constructing an order with public goods for all. There is more regard for international institutions under Obama than under Bush, but American efforts at institutional reform are limited and the focus is on a version of the national interest that allows limited space for the production of global public goods. In this situation, other established and emerging great powers can choose to say no to America and pursue their own national interests; that is what they have done. No-one has put forward a different plan for better provision of public goods, and it is not clear that any country—or coalition of countries—outside of the United States has the power and the willingness to pursue any alternative project. In that situation, the world remains stuck with the current provision of piecemeal governance.

8

Values: A Victory or Crisis of Liberalism?

Introduction

The liberal vision at the end of the Cold War concerned a world order increasingly held together by liberal values. Such a world would emerge because material and ideational forces were pushing towards transforming more and more countries into liberal democracies. Processes of modernization would lead to material changes that supported the emergence of democracy. Equally important, the basic 'human desire for recognition' would secure that liberal democracy would actually be the end result (Fukuyama 1992). A large number of democracies would make for a peaceful and cooperative world order, based on a common belief in liberal values and principles.

The end of the Cold War appeared to confirm this liberal optimism, especially when combined with the mood, spirit and changes of the 1990s. It was a liberal period of transitions towards democracy, cooperation among the great powers, a near global commitment to liberal market economies based on private property and cooperation through international institutions. But September 11, 2001, set the stage for a different agenda of new security threats, democratic setbacks and financial crisis.

So to what extent can we trust the liberal vision of a world order based on liberal values? Three major aspects of this question are in focus here. First, there is the issue of liberal values as seen from below, inside states and among people. How much has democracy actually progressed? Are people increasingly embracing liberal values? Second, there is the question of values among states. Are interstate societies increasingly permeated by liberal values? What is the relationship between the values of people and the values of interstate societies? Third, in which ways are liberal values promoted by liberal states and what are the tensions related to the value dimension of world order?

Democratic progress and setbacks

A primary argument for the advancement of liberal values concerns the progress of liberal democracy (Mandelbaum 2003: 251–65). According to the Freedom House rating, the number of democracies (free countries) increased from 42 in 1976 to 89 in 2015; that must be counted as considerable liberal progress, but it must not be overestimated. Many successful transitions took place in Eastern Europe and in Latin America, in countries that had previous experiences with democracy; the number of democracies has not increased over the last decade, a period where countries with declines in freedom have outstripped those with gains (Freedom House 2015). Any transition to democracy is a long and complex process which frequently involves serious setbacks, as demonstrated by most of the 'Arab Spring' countries in the recent period. More than half of the world's 195 countries are in a grey zone between full democracy, on one hand, and outright authoritarianism, on the other, and most of them show few signs of becoming more democratic. There is not a uniform road to modernity and democracy, followed by all countries. In what follows, I discuss democracy problems in relation to three groups of countries: the fragile states in the Global South; the emerging economies; and the established democracies of the West.

Fragile states in the Global South have typically gone through a completely different trajectory than most Western countries (Sørensen 2008a). Basic conditions for democracy were not created. First, there is not a coherent national community. Pre-colonial Africa, for example, was not neatly divided into territorially separate entities with clear-cut authority structures; it was a region of overlapping areas where people had multiple group affiliations. Present-day ethnic groups were created by colonial rulers that used ethnic labels as instruments of 'divide and rule' and later by post-colonial leaders aiming to construct their own bases of power. A lack of national unity can block a process of democratization, as in the case of India and

Pakistan after independence, or severely impede it, as in the case of Nigeria today.

Second, fragile states lack effective and responsive institutions. 'Effective' means the ability to formulate, implement and supervise policies. 'Responsive' means that the state functions to the benefit of, and with support from, the major groups in society. Fragile states are generally plagued by high levels of corruption in both the political leadership and in the bureaucracy; in that sense the state apparatus does not seek to provide public goods. The spoils of office are shared with select groups in patron–client networks. Ordinary people, then, can expect little or nothing from the state; they are compelled to turn to the ethnic communities for help and economic support (Ndegwa 1997).

Finally, many fragile states have weak and poorly organized civil societies; the political arena is dominated by elite groups. In Sub-Saharan Africa, power often lies with a president—a strongman—who has taken political and economic control of the state apparatus in a system of personal rule. Civil society activities bloomed in urban areas pushing for democratic openings and early elections; but civil societies remain too weak to take on the challenges of democratic consolidation (Gyimah-Boadi 1996). The problem is aggravated by the lack of institutionalized party systems that can stabilize a process of democratization (Mainwaring and Scully 1995).

We turn to emerging economies with successful records in terms of economic growth. Their achievements ought to present better conditions for democracy and democratization. Seymour Martin Lipset famously claimed that 'the more well-to-do a nation, the greater the chances that it will sustain democracy' (Lipset 1959: 75). To be sure, modernization and wealth generate factors conducive to democracy: higher rates of literacy and education, urbanization and the presence of mass media. Moreover, wealth provides the resources needed to mitigate the tensions produced by political conflict. The Lipset hypothesis received much empirical support. In 1971, Robert Dahl considered it 'pretty much beyond dispute' that the higher the socio-economic level of a country, the more likely it was to be a democracy.

But the expectation not always holds true. Argentina had many years of authoritarian rule despite a relatively high level of per capita income, as did Taiwan and South Korea. In his analysis of the major South American cases, Guillermo O'Donnell developed an argument that turns the Lipset thesis on its head: authoritarianism, not democracy, seems to be the more likely concomitant of high levels of modernization. That is because the process of industrial modernization which took place in South America in the 1960s and 1970s had little to offer the majority of the people. So in order to pursue this model in the face of popular resistance, the ruling elite needed an authoritarian system (O'Donnell 1973).

These early South American cases, together with current processes of modernization in China, the Middle East and elsewhere, bear witness to an insight which runs counter to the liberal idea of a uniform, Western package of modernity and democracy that will inexorably unfold everywhere. The rising powers of today are not copies of the West; modernization and Westernization are not the same thing. The account in Chapter 2 made the point in detail in relation to China; the ability of the Chinese Communist Party (CCP) to co-opt new elites, to create legitimacy on the basis of its achievements and to control and repress any major opposition would appear to secure its continued national hegemony, not in spite of successful economic modernization, but because of it.

Russia is another example of a case of a distinctive model of economic modernization and political transformation. Russia currently combines a kleptocratic economic system (Chapter 6) with an autocratic regime of state-controlled media, corruption, manipulated elections, limited rule of law and severe crackdowns on any opposition. Brazil and India are doing much better, but none of them are flawless democracies, in particular because of corruption in government and in the courts, and limitations on individual rights.

In short, there are a number of rather successful processes of modernization going on in the world but they are distinctly different from the Western model. At the same time, differences in terms of cultural setting provide for a context with its own peculiar challenges in terms of socio-political change. Nothing of this can lead to a law-like statement that democracy will never happen in China or anywhere else. But it is likely that any process of democratization will be long and arduous and that elements of autocracy will persist for some considerable time; nor is it by any means certain that democracy will eventually prevail.

The established democracies of the West are not normally considered to be in danger of democratic setbacks. But also here, democracy is an entity where societal developments pose new challenges where the answers are not straightforward. In some parts of the liberal heartlands, the democratic processes have lost vigour and dynamism. One aspect of this is the loss of 'social capital' (Putnam 1995) connected with the increasing fragmentation of late modern societies. Another aspect is the dominance of vested elite interests of the political process impeding possibilities for comprehensive reform. On the centre-left side of the political spectrum, social democratic parties have not so far been able to formulate new, comprehensive political projects that simultaneously tackle the challenges of run-away globalization, socio-economic inequality and interest-group domination (Fukuyama 2012).

The greatest challenge to established forms of liberal democracy is economic globalization. Globalization may undermine democracy because national governments have less and less control over what happens within their own borders. One way to confront this is via regional integration, as in the case of the European Union. But it is clear that the European Union's supranational governance structures are in several ways less democratic than those of national parliaments and governments (Sørensen 2008) because of distance to the people, lack of public debate and lack of transparency. When it comes to global structures of governance, such as the UN system, these problems are amplified. Liberal democracy was always designed for the nation-state. It has not been sufficiently developed when it comes to governance across borders. This is a more serious problem today than earlier, because the progress of globalization has increased the demand for transnational political cooperation and regulation. In that situation, liberal politics is plagued by 'institutional competition, overlapping jurisdictions, the excessive cost of inaction and the failures of accountability' (Held 2007: 249).

The threat from international terrorism is a particular challenge to democracy. There is a delicate balance between security and freedom; on one hand, freedom depends on a sufficient amount of security. On the other hand, security measures involving unrestricted surveillance and control threaten individual freedom. At the same time, terrorist suspects may be subjected to interrogation techniques and other forms of treatment that violate basic human rights. Some observers think that the US Patriot Act of 2001 goes too far in defence of security because it downgrades individual freedom in ways that can lead to radicalization and to even more insecurity (Donohue 2008; Waldron 2003).

In sum, there has been democratic progress, but we are far from a situation of an impending global triumph for democracy. Many countries in the grey zone are fragile states where the conditions for democratic advancement are poor. A process of successful economic modernization is no guarantee that democracy will follow. Consolidated liberal democracies face their own set of democratic challenges. There will be a large number of semi-democratic or outright authoritarian countries in any future world order and some of those countries will be great powers.

Individual values: Moving in a liberal direction?

Whether countries are becoming democracies or not is related to the values held by their people, but there is no simple relationship between democratic rule and the values supported by individuals. First, the many structural changes associated with modernity (economic growth, education, mass communication, modern institutions and so on) always arrive in specific combinations and sequences in individual societies; further, they encounter local traditions and cultural habits that are also different, among countries as well as between different groups in the populations. That makes for dissimilar patterns of value change.

Second, a distinction must be made between cognitive and behavioural changes. Cognitive changes in attitudes and values refer to variation in ways of thinking about the world but the relationship to behaviour is not straightforward; for example, people may cognitively affirm the virtue of charity but offer little or nothing to organizations that promote welfare (Inkeles 1998: 330). In broader terms, support for values related to modernity will not always translate to support for democratic rule.

Kishore Mahbubani (see Chapter 6) makes the argument that common values are emerging among the vast majority of the world's population. His claim is that a common set of material aspirations are now more important that different religious or ideological convictions, so that 'populations all over the world want their governments to focus on economic development, not on war' (Mahbubani 2013: 68). Material aspirations are combined with shared educational aspirations; all want the best possible education for their offspring, with the American Ivy League universities as the ultimate goal. Together, these forces mean that most people around the world will 'converge on some important and fundamental values' (Mahbubani 2013: 69).

But given the reservations set forth above, we should be sceptical about any smooth process of convergence on common fundamental values. Alex Inkeles (1998) has examined the transformation of values and lifestyles in select countries of the Pacific Rim (Hong Kong, Taiwan, mainland China and Japan). He identifies four major tendencies. The first is 'strengthening of tradition'; this is the weakest of the four tendencies but there is evidence of it. In Japan, for example, the preference for 'filial piety' rose over three decades, from the early 1960s to the 1990s, a period with dramatic changes in Japanese society. The second tendency is, 'the persistence of tradition', which is a much stronger trend. Core Chinese values of diligence, frugality and hard work persist over time; so does the support for filial obligations and for traditional values in relation to demanding that people with responsibility set moral examples.

The third tendency is 'adaptation of tradition'; traditions persist, but they are adapted to new circumstances. Inkeles offers an example from China related to ancestor worship, namely tomb sweeping. It is still supported by many, but today there are few tombs one can visit; instead, the event has turned into a family gathering on the birthday of the deceased parent.

The fourth tendency is 'the abandonment of tradition' and that is the strongest trend. It is no longer considered a necessity to produce a male heir to carry forward the family name; the tradition of arranged marriages has almost died out; a rapidly increasing number of people support individualistic values about personal satisfaction against community harmony as a central goal in life (Inkeles 1998: 340).

The 'abandonment of tradition' would appear to support the results from the 'World values survey' according to which high levels of economic development 'tend to make people more tolerant and trusting, bringing more emphasis on self-expression and more participation in decision-making' (Inglehart and Welzel 2009: 37; Welzel 2013). While these changes generally support the emergence of liberal democracy, the relationship is by no means deterministic. That is because factors other than economic growth and modernization influence the process, as we saw earlier. The perceived performance of existing governments, democratic or authoritarian, also plays a significant role.

In East Asia, one of the really successful regions in terms of modernization and economic growth, authoritarianism continues to be rather popular. A survey which included Japan, Hong Kong, South Korea, China, Mongolia, the Philippines, Taiwan and Thailand, found a widespread distrust of democratic institutions and a critical view of democratic performance in relation to corruption, law and order, economic development and equity. Only 35% of respondents found that democracy was 'equally or more important than economic development'. The authors concluded that across the region, 'fundamental democratic values have fragile support' (Chu, Diamond, Nathan, and Shin 2010: 240).

In sum, value changes are taking place, especially in countries that are successful modernizers; but even if those changes contain a strong element of 'abandonment of tradition', there is no simple connection to people's support for democracy and liberal values in general. It is a strong thrust in liberal thought that liberal values are universal, valid for and embraced by all people. Tony Blair made the point in an article on global values: 'We have to show that our values are not Western ... but values in the common ownership of humanity, universal values that should be the right of the global citizen', and he was optimistic on that front, because all people were ready to embrace liberal values: 'The fact is that, given the chance, people want democracy' (Blair 2007: 87, 84).

But people's eventual support for democracy is not unqualified; it is cautious and conditional, shaped by national cultural values and concrete experiences with actual regimes. In that sense, the changes taking place cannot be understood as a process of convergence on common fundamental values. Michael Howard's summation is more to the point: 'The common Western assumption that cultural diversity is a historical curiosity being rapidly eroded by the growth of a common, Western-oriented, Anglophone world-culture, shaping our basic values ... is simply not true' (Howard 1984: 6).

Interstate values: A liberal world order?

We have looked at individual values and at democratic progress and setbacks; together, they can be seen as evidence of what goes on in value terms inside states. This section turns the attention to values among states, interstate values. The relationship between inside (the domestic dimension) and outside (the international dimension) is a complex one and it has been viewed quite differently among IR theorists of various stripes (Risse-Kappen 1991). The appropriate way to come to grips with the relationship, I suggest, is to look at the major values of interstate society in different historical periods and to trace the major aspects of the domestic/international interplay in each period.

Interstate values may be seen as agreed-upon standards of behaviour in the form of common rules and institutions that shape and regulate the relationship among states. This corresponds roughly to Hedley Bull's definition of an international society which is a group of states that 'conceive themselves to be bound by a common set of rules in their relations with one another and share in the working of common institutions' (Bull 1995 [1977]: 13).

An international society of states was first created in Europe. Its foundational principle was sovereignty, fundamentally instituted with the peace of Westphalia in 1648, at the end of the Thirty Years' War. Sovereignty has both a domestic and an international aspect. The domestic aspect was about concentration of state power and giving the king undisputed authority over the realm. Externally, states confirmed their independence of religious authorities, and their right to independence, to sole control of their internal affairs. In that sense, state elites sent a message to both domestic and international rivals—religious as well as secular—that they were in charge and that they set the rules of the game for everyone else. By the nineteenth century, the European international society was well established on the principle of sovereignty and the treating of states as juridically equal. On that basis, four principles came to form the framework for relations among the European states (Watson 1992). The first was the balance of power, which has been called a systematic practice of antihegemonialism. The basic idea was that any state could be prevented from growing too powerful relative to the others as alliances shifted away from it, thereby hindering its rise to dominance. The second was the codification of a set of practices of interaction among states in the form of a body of international law. The third was the use of congresses for the purpose of settling the affairs of the European states; at the congresses, the states passed treaties to conclude wars and made additional agreement on international rules. In addition to Westphalia, the most important congresses were in Utrecht in 1713 and in Vienna in 1815.

The fourth principle was diplomatic dialogue. The application of the first three principles—balance of power, international law and congresses—took place through diplomatic dialogue. Taken together, the four principles formed the basis of a consensus among the European states. As one observer stated, 'in the eighteenth century Europe came to be regarded as a single diplomatic commonwealth made up of a number of independent states "resembling each other in their manners, religion and degree of social improvement" or in other words operating within the framework of a common culture' (Watson 1992: 198).

Between the sixteenth and nineteenth centuries, European influence expanded to the rest of the world, not through diplomatic negotiation, but via coercion and control. Europe had taken the economic, technological and political lead in the world and was able to impose its rules on others. North and South America were colonized by Europeans; indigenous civilizations were almost completely annihilated. Some of the ancient civilizations in Asia were not subjected to colonization; instead, Europeans imposed unequal treaties to secure the areas for European interests. Africa, by contrast, was colonized.

By the turn of the twentieth century, international society was made up of a small number of consolidated states in Europe and North America; a number of countries in Latin America and Asia were under way to become full members of the society of sovereign states; and large areas of Africa and Asia were part of the colonial empires of European powers. The commitment to common rules in this period took place via a 'standard of civilization' (Gong 1984) that contained the criteria which non-members had to meet in order to join the society of states. The standard demanded, for example, the acceptance of international law, participation in diplomatic exchange and the abolishment of slavery. In short, the values of European international society were imposed on the newcomers. They accepted them in order to achieve the formal parity of being accepted as independent states on equal footing with other independent states that sovereignty offered.

Colonial empires were abandoned after World War II. The major colonial motherlands in Europe were no longer the leading states of the system and both the United States and the Soviet Union, the two superpowers, supported decolonization. Colonialism did not sit well with liberalism in the first place and the educated elites in both colonies and motherlands supported independence. In a surprisingly short period of time, self-determination for all colonies replaced imperialism and empire as the leading doctrine of international society. It was made abundantly clear in the UN General Assembly Resolution 1514 of 1960 that 'all peoples have the right to self-determination' (UN General Assembly 1960). The newly independent states established a non-aligned bloc, outside of the control of superpowers. But they also quickly realized that they were economically and politically dependent on the developed countries. In value terms, however, their emphasis was on independence and autonomy.

In a larger sense, the post-war international society reflected the new dominance of the United States and the Soviet Union. It was a bifurcated system; each superpower established a sphere of influence and a network of alliances. The Eastern system, dominated by the Soviet Union, was based on the value structure of the Soviet version of Marxism-Leninism, but that was not sufficient; repression and control were key elements as well. It kept most of Eastern Europe within the Soviet sphere for more than four decades; China was strong enough to set its own course. The Western system was stronger because it was based on consent; it was an 'empire by invitation' (Lundestad 1986), providing an American shield against the threat from the East, economic aid for reconstruction and institutional cooperation. In value terms, it was an alliance based on liberal democracy.

At the same time, an overarching global interstate society remained in place. Its centre was the United Nations. In contrast to the League of Nations, the UN was supported by the superpowers. That is because the Security Council gave a veto to them and three further great powers which secured that the active support or at least the acquiescence of all five states was necessary to undertake collective action. But the UN with its universal membership is also the institutional centre of international society based on common principles of international law and facilitating cooperation and dialogue between member states across a large variety of areas.

The bipolar system terminated with the end of the Cold War and the dissolution of the Soviet Union. Mikhail Gorbachev had been convinced that the Soviet system could be reformed and would demonstrate its 'capacity for self-perfection' (Gorbachev 1987: 44), but that turned out not to be the case. Dismantling of the old system was the easy part of the operation; it did not enjoy popular support and the old elite could envisage new roles for itself under a reformed system.

But nobody was able to formulate a plan for a reformed economy that was both state and non-state, or for a reformed political system that was both more democratic and also socialist. That compelled the turn towards a liberal market economy and a more liberal democratic polity, almost by default (Sørensen 2001: 36–44).

It was at this point that President Bush Sr. envisioned a new world order, where the rule of law 'governs the conduct of nations' and 'a world in which freedom and respect for human rights find a home among all nations' (Bush 1991). In other words, this would become a world order united in the support for basic liberal values because leading countries would now increasingly become democratic and support an international society based on liberal values.

Where are we, then, in overall terms when it comes to the standing of interstate values in the current world order? The foundational institution of sovereignty remains the core principle of this order. The constitutive content of sovereignty is constitutional independence. The sovereign state stands apart from all other sovereign entities (James 1998). That means the sovereign state is legally equal to all other sovereign states. Irrespective of the substantial differences between sovereign states in economic, political, social and other respects, sovereignty entails equal membership of the international society of states, with similar rights and obligations. The fact that every member state, irrespective of differences in substantial powers, has one vote in the general assembly is a concrete expression of this legal equality.

Sovereignty was the basis for the European society of states as it developed from 1648. The four principles mentioned earlier in this section had a common aim: to preserve the autonomy and independence of the members of the society. As for the balance of power, it had been the painful experience of the seventeenth century that once any state accumulated enough power to lay down the law for others, it would do so. For eighteenth-century statesmen, the answer was to 'prevent the accumulation of such power, and so preserve both the independence of the member states of the system, great and small, and also something close to peace' (Watson 1992: 201).

As for international law, it was necessary because in the absence of a hegemon, the law had to be laid down by contract; international law was the 'rule book' (Watson 1992: 203) of European independent states. Diplomacy amounted to a permanent dialogue among states, conducted through networks of resident agents. Diplomacy became professionalized during the eighteenth century and the *corps diplomatique* recognized each other's status and developed their own *esprit de corps*. Congresses were occasions for multilateral, collective settlements which involved both state leaders and diplomats. To repeat, the major function of the four principles of European interstate society was the protection of the autonomy and independence of its members.

Sovereignty remains utterly important in today's world. It is a core principle in the Charter of the United Nations, which is based on 'the principle of the sovereign equality of all its members' (Chapter 1, Article 2.1). The Millennium Declaration of 2000 reaffirms the commitment to sovereignty: 'We rededicate ourselves to support all efforts to uphold the sovereign equality of all States' (UN General Assembly 2000). But that does not mean everything remains the same.

The opposite is closer to the truth: while sovereignty is repeatedly emphasized as the primary value of interstate society, almost everything around sovereignty, including the rules and practices connected to its enforcement, has changed dramatically. That is because of the extremely high and historically unprecedented level of interconnectedness among societies and states on all levels: economic, political, cultural, institutional and social.

In the early nineteenth century, economic, social and political activity was overwhelmingly local. In France in 1835, for example, 87% of total output was consumed no more than 20 miles from its production site (Schwartz 2000). Going beyond that required the infrastructure, communications and web of connections that came later. Economies first became national in scope, then international, and today globalized in the sense that inward and outward flows across borders pertain to all markets and to all stages in the lifecycle of a product.

International law has grown by leaps and bounds; it continues a classic role of stipulating the rules that regulate the relationships among states, but much of it is not concerned with protection of independence and autonomy. It is concerned with the regulation of relationships among societies and economies that are growing increasingly interdependent and so progressively need to regulate the terms and conditions of that interdependence. In that sense, international law is concerned with terms of integration rather than terms of autonomy. It has branched out into several major fields, including economic law, criminal law, environmental law, security law, diplomatic law and humanitarian law.

These changes also concern the role of governments in relation to other players. The classic players in international law were governments and diplomats. Today, politics is increasingly taking the shape of international or global governance, which refers to activities everywhere—local, national, regional, global—involving regulation and control. Governance is thus an international, transgovernmental and transnational activity that includes not only governments or units of government and traditional IGOs but also NGOs and other non-state actors.

The core principle of the classic interstate system was the balance of power, preventing any state from becoming too powerful to lay down the law for others. The United States emerged from the end of the Cold War as the dominant power in the world. According to the classic logic, other major states should balance against the United States in order to prevent it from becoming too powerful. It was indeed the expectation by many realists after the demise of the Soviet Union that the post-Cold War world would be characterized by intensified balance-of-power competition among former allies, both across the Atlantic and in Europe (Fettweis 2004; Paul et al. 2004). But this has not happened. There has been no major balancing against US power since the end of the Cold War.

Why not? The major factor is that the security dilemma has been mitigated and in some relations even transcended (Chapter 3). The security dilemma remains virulent in some relations, of course, but it is not a general major feature of the current world order. On one hand, countries do not fear each other's power to the same extent as earlier; on the other hand, the primary aim for countries is not autonomy and independence in the sense of keeping others out or even minimizing their presence. Countries have chosen to cooperate and integrate because it promises a high level of economic, social and other benefits. Cooperation has led to a very high level of interdependence. To be sure, it has also created problems, but a general retreat from interdependence is not on the programme of any country, save perhaps North Korea.

In sum, whereas a core value of the classic interstate system was *in*dependence, a core value of the present interstate system is *inter*dependence. The classic system was focused on independence and conditions of autonomy; the present system is focused on interdependence and conditions of integration. Interdependence creates benefits, but it also creates problems and tensions, winners and losers.

Those who are sceptical of interdependence and integration will most often emphasize the traditional interpretation of sovereignty as an institution that should protect the autonomy of sovereign states, their territorial integrity and political independence, and the principle of non-interference by outsiders in the internal affairs of states.

In this sense the basic institution of the interstate system, sovereignty, is contested. It points towards autonomy, independence and the freedom of states to chart their own course. But it also points to interdependence, integration and intensified cooperation, because states have learned that the essential values they pursue, including security, freedom, order, justice and welfare, are better taken care of in a process which involves interdependence, integration and intensified cooperation.

It is this tension in interstate values between interdependence and independence, between growing together and staying apart, that we have seen play out in various ways in this book. Intensified interdependence can lead to processes of political and economic convergence which further reinforce a foundation of common values; but domestic conditions are extremely diverse and convergence is by no means a certain outcome.

A core value of the present order is interdependence, but independence remains a strong concern as well. The simultaneous pursuit of interdependence and independence creates problems and tensions that are confronted in different ways by various groups of states. Before pursuing that issue, however, it is relevant to consider independence and interdependence as liberal values.

Independence and interdependence as liberal values

Independence and interdependence can be regarded as liberal values. Independence first: 'freedom' and 'independence' can be understood as synonymous terms, as the autonomy that allows sovereign states to conduct their affairs without outside interference. Gerry Simpson labelled this view 'Charter Liberalism' because its principles 'find their highest expression in the UN Charter. The point of this approach is to treat all states equally, to allow them each the same rights afforded to individuals in a liberal society (i.e. domestic jurisdiction, equality, non-intervention) and to, if not celebrate, at least tolerate the diversity produced by these norms' (Simpson 2001: 541). In his

'Perpetual Peace' pamphlet, Immanuel Kant argued that 'no state shall forcibly interfere in the constitution and government of another state' (Kant 1992 [1795]: 96). The principle of non-intervention is connected to the liberal core principle of freedom; people cannot decide for themselves how to organize their way of life if they are subjected to outside interference. With non-intervention there would be political independence which afforded citizens to work out their domestic order (Doyle 1997: 395).

Seen from the inside, the liberal theory of democratic government is predicated on the existence of sovereign states with national communities of people that actively seek to be members of a shared political community. In Dankwart Rustow's classic model of transition towards democracy, the point is expressed in a single background condition, considered necessary for any democratic transition to take place. The condition is national unity, which simply indicates that 'the vast majority of citizens in a democracy-to-be ... have no doubt or mental reservations as to which political community they belong to' (Rustow 1970: 350). Empires held together by force, such as the Soviet bloc after World War II, must provide a solution to the national unity question as a precondition for a process of democratization. Rulers and policies cannot function in a democratic manner if the boundaries do not endure. As one observer stated: 'The people cannot decide until somebody decides who are the people' (W. Ivor Jennings, quoted in Rustow 1970: 351).

In short, liberal democracy is predicated on independence which is in turn based on sovereignty. At the same time, this notion of independence is primarily focused on the state and its government. It is less concerned with individuals and their political and other rights. In a world of many illiberal states, independence may leave people in dire straits, subject to the whims of autocratic rulers. But the emphasis on independence is not a liberal endorsement of autocracy; the hope is that inviting such states to participate in an international community of states will provide the best framework for domestic changes in a liberal direction.

The liberal notion of *inter*dependence, by contrast, begins with individuals, not with states. The early liberal tradition in Europe developed in opposition to despotic monarchies whose claim to unlimited power rested on an assertion of divine support. The liberal aim was to roll back state power so as to create a space where individuals could be free to pursue their own economic, political and religious preferences (Held 2006: 59). An important element in this respect was the support of a market economy based on respect for private property.

It is a liberal belief that individuals are rational and that they take an interest in cooperation for mutual benefit. So providing individuals with freedom will give them the opportunity to pursue cooperation, to create interdependence for mutual benefit, including interdependence across borders. Interdependence is a force for progress and peace. The recommendation by Richard Cobden in the early nineteenth century: 'As little intercourse betwixt the Governments, as much connection as possible between the nations ([societies]) of the world' (1903: 16) rests on the claim that relations between people in contrast to relations between (illiberal) states are cooperative and peaceful. Several liberals particularly emphasize the importance of economic interdependence. Joseph Schumpeter, for example, argued that a capitalist system is populated with rational materialists who will reject militarism and aggression. Such behaviour relies on atavistic impulses from previous historical periods, supported by traditional military forces and aristocracies.

A 'cobweb model' of transnational relationships was suggested by John Burton (1972). His argument is that transnational relations among groups of people involve many different external ties, including religious groups, business groups, interest groups and several other kinds of civil society groups. Because individuals are members of numerous different groups, conflict among specific groups will be muted if not eliminated (Little 1996: 12).

Liberals see a mutually reinforcing relationship between liberal progress at home and liberal progress in international relations. Capitalist modernization and technological change at home drive a process of creating a more liberal, ultimately democratic society. Governments founded on liberal principles provide the basis for international cooperation in international institutions based on those principles. Social and economic relations across borders between individuals and private groups stimulate international liberal cooperation and also help move societies in a liberal direction. In short, intensified interdependence sparks a process of liberal convergence that helps create the basis for a liberal world order; but we have also seen that there are sharp limits to convergence.

*Inter*dependence, then, can be considered a core liberal value which characterizes the present world order. But *in*dependence can also be considered a fundamental liberal value which permeates the present order. It is not an order of liberal fulfilment; democratic progress has not created a world of democratic states; economic interdependence has led to very partial convergence; the demand for global governance is not being met; human security values have been upgraded but violence inside fragile states remains a severe problem. What we have is an order where the liberal values of independence and interdependence compete in ways that create tensions and problems. That is the subject of the next section.

Independence and interdependence in the present world order

Each country strikes its own distinctive balance between independence and interdependence on the basis of domestic and international pressures and opportunities. But there are common trends among broad groups of similar countries. I remark on the three groups of countries identified in Chapter 2: the advanced liberal states in the Global North; the modernizing states which include the BRICS and other emerging economies; and the fragile states in the Global South.

It is the advanced liberal states that have pushed interdependence the farthest; after World War II, the United States took the lead in fostering economic cooperation in Western Europe and across the Atlantic. Japan was included in this process of economic reconstruction that vastly increased interdependence among the participant states. This took place in a process which increased the level of institutional cooperation, partly through various types of institutions with a universal reach, partly through regional arrangements, such as the European Union.

It is in the context of the European Union that close institutional cooperation has developed the most. Instead of independence and autonomy, the European Union has adopted supranational elements, that is, formal channels for legitimate outside intervention by the collective of member states in national affairs of single countries. EU institutions now have substantial influence over areas that were traditionally reserved for national politics: currency, social policies, border controls, law and order.

To what extent has close cooperation produced a convergence on common values? One analysis argues that such values have indeed emerged. There is now a common 'Western civic identity', at the core of which is 'a consensus around a set of norms and principles, most importantly political democracy, constitutional government, individual rights, private property-based economic systems and tolerance of diversity in non-civic areas of ethnicity and religion' (Deudney and Ikenberry 1999: 193).

Cooperation and common values can surely strengthen each other, as predicted by most liberals. But even within the advanced liberal states where we surely see the most integrated, cooperative and value consensual relationships, the tension between independence and interdependence has not been resolved. Those on the losing end of intensified interdependence tend to take on 'resistance identities' (Castells 1998: 8) which in various ways react against integration in terms of nationalism, sometimes with xenophobic elements, as in the case of the *Front National* in France or the *Freiheitliche Partei Österreichs* (FPÖ) in Austria. Many people are also sceptical about the 'democratic deficit' element in EU cooperation, as mentioned earlier.

In the case of the European Union, the logical step forward in terms of interdependence would be to create a federation based on a common constitution, but that is not on the cards. Alternatively, cooperation might discard supranationalism and backslide towards conventional intergovernmentalism, but that is not on the cards either. As for the United States, it has helped develop interdependence and cooperation among the advanced democracies, but it was always wary of commitment towards any kind of cooperation that would compromise its autonomy as we saw in the previous chapter. In sum, the advanced liberal states have taken huge steps towards interdependence and integration, especially in Europe, but they are not willing to give up the autonomy and independence afforded by sovereignty.

Let me turn to the modernizing states. The major modernizing states, Brazil, India and China, each demonstrate the global turn towards interdependence that has taken place over almost four decades. Between the 1950s and 1980s each country supported a version of economic development which was focused on national growth and transformation with limited integration into the world economy. This was most outspoken in the case of China; the country was from early on in opposition to the capitalist world. During the 1960s, the Soviet Union also became an enemy. In other words, there was a long phase of forced or self-imposed isolation. In the 1980s, China began a gradual process of opening up the economy to foreign trade and investment that has led to today's very high level of economic interdependence.

India began a process of economic liberalization in 1991, reducing restrictions on external trade and improving conditions for foreign investment. There is general consensus that intensified interdependence has led to higher levels of economic growth. Structural reform with trade liberalization and deregulation has also taken place in Brazil since the early 1990s. In all three BICs, increased economic openness has been accompanied by more intense participation in international regimes and organizations.

However, this significant turn towards interdependence must not be mistaken for a policy that is now unconcerned with sovereignty, independence, and autonomy. All three countries have a long tradition of emphasizing respect for territorial integrity and sovereignty and mutual non-interference in each other's internal affairs. India initiated the formation of the non-aligned movement in the 1950s; today the organization has 120 member countries and 17 observers. A central purpose of the movement is to ensure the national independence, sovereignty, territorial integrity and security of non-aligned countries.

Countries with a colonial past or an experience of extreme dependency on dominant foreign powers will not easily give up their commitment to independence, autonomy and non-intervention, even if they have embarked on a process of creating economic and institutional interdependence. When interdependence comes in the way of national interests in independence, the former has to yield. When Brazil was criticized in an OAS (Organization of American States) human rights report, it strongly condemned the invasion of Brazil's sovereignty and took measures to censure the OAS's monitoring of human rights (Burges 2013).

China was forced to sign unequal treaties and cede territories to outsiders after the Opium Wars. The 'loss of sovereignty' made a deep impression; China has emphasized sovereignty, territorial integrity and non-intervention ever since, as expressed in the 'five principles of peaceful coexistence' that made up the core of the 1954 Sino-Indian treaty; it was those same principles that India introduced as basis for the non-aligned movement. Where European cooperation has combined intensified interdependence with elements of supranational governance, China and the other BICs hold on to a conservative interpretation of sovereignty which stresses autonomy and non-interference (Pan 2010). In other words, Europe has recognized that intensified interdependence throws up common problems that have to be confronted by the countries involved. Since European countries share common liberal values, they have a starting point in value terms for such increased cooperation.

Modernizing states such as the BICs are also involved in processes creating intensified interdependence that create increased demand for regulation across borders. There are a growing number of behind-the-border issues (i.e. regulations that concern not tariffs or quotas but product standards, investment regulations, competition policies, transparency measures, etc.). But regulating behind-the-border issues may conflict with a conservative interpretation of sovereignty.

Modernizing states are not willing to compromise on the principles of autonomy and non-intervention in order to meet those challenges. They do not share a common value foundation in a way that can compare to the common liberal values among the advanced states. In the end, therefore, the tension between interdependence and independence is even sharper when it comes to modernizing states. They want to integrate into the global economy and they want to participate in international institutions. Yet they also jealously hold onto a notion of sovereignty which stresses autonomy and non-intervention. And in the cases of China and Russia, the regimes make it abundantly clear that there are sharp limits to the extent that they share a common value foundation with the advanced liberal states.

Finally, the fragile states in the Global South: if we focus on the weakest states in Sub-Saharan Africa, their road to independence did not go through a period of state strengthening and consolidation. They were colonies under control of the motherlands and heavily dependent on them. Independence came because the institution of colonialism came to be seen as 'an absolute wrong' (Jackson 1993: 48) after World War II.

What emerged from decolonization was a number of states that were very weak in terms of economic basis, political institutions and national cohesion. Independence was formal; the ex-colonies were now considered sovereign states formally equal with any other sovereign state. But it was not substantial, because the new nations continued to be heavily dependent on outsiders for help and aid, something they made very clear at UN General Assembly meetings. So in the case of fragile states, formal independence is combined, not with interdependence, but with substantial dependence on outsiders.

This creates a paradoxical situation in the relationship between fragile states and developed, consolidated states of the international society. On one hand, fragile states jealously defend and protect their formal sovereignty, their juridical independence. They want to be treated as equals in the society of states, with the same rights and privileges as everyone else. But at the same time, they argue that because of their colonial past they are weaker than everyone else and therefore qualify for economic aid and other special treatment. At one and the same time, then, fragile states want to be treated as equals and they want to be treated as *un*equals. That is a reflection of their peculiar standing in relation to independence and dependence.

Conclusion

This chapter interrogated the standing of liberal values in the present world order. It is a difficult undertaking because there is no agreement about the best way to read off the importance of liberal values from current events. Focus on democracy and democratization in single countries left a mixed picture: the number of democracies has increased but there are about one hundred countries in the grey zone and even the consolidated liberal systems face new democratic challenges. Individuals are moving towards the embrace of modern values, especially in modernizing states, but that has created only restrained and qualified support for liberal democracy.

There is a complex relationship between domestic values and interstate values. Domestic values do affect interstate values and vice versa, but not in a straightforward, direct way. Interstate values were first agreed upon by the European elites that constructed the European system of sovereign states, a process that began in earnest after the Thirty Years' War.

The foundational institution of the interstate society is sovereignty. This is also true after the society of sovereign states has attained global reach. For quite some time, the interstate society was focused on protecting the independence and the autonomy of its members. The balance of power, international law and the use of congresses and diplomacy were the major practices in achieving that goal. After World War II, a system of intense interdependence emerged among the liberal democracies in the Global North. They cooperated in relation to economic, technological, political, institutional and security affairs.

Later on, most countries of the world opted to participate in many of these networks of interdependence because of the benefits they offer. But this was not a renouncement of independence. Therefore, *in*dependence and *inter*dependence are both core values of the current world order. It is a liberal order, not because democracy has prevailed everywhere or economic interdependence has led to global convergence on liberal ideals, but because the interstate order can be seen as an order distinguished by the liberal values of independence and interdependence.

There are tensions between these values; the tensions weigh differently on each country according to its particular domestic and international situation. In general terms, independence and interdependence can be seen as opposite ends of a continuum; the pendulum indicating the predominant combination of independence and interdependence remained at the independence end of the spectrum for a long time. Economic interdependence flourished from the second half of the nineteenth century until World War I. The interwar period was marked by a profound economic crisis where countries were not able to cooperate and turned inwards to focus on their own problems. After World War II, Western democracies initiated a long period of increased interdependence, which became the global trend after the end of the Cold War.

At the present time, the pendulum again swings away from *inter*dependence and towards more emphasis on *in*dependence. China and Russia have moved from what was virtually economic isolation to a very significant integration into the world economy in nothing more than a few decades. In addition to benefits, that integration has thrown up a number of problems. Putin's 'aggressive isolationism' is surely not a long-term solution to those problems, but it appears that both countries are now more inwardly focused. They are also well aware of the political problems that economic integration might portend for autocratic regimes. Optimistic liberals usually comment that the long-term effect of a capitalist market economy will unavoidably be liberal democracy at the political level, but that is a false claim.

The United States was the undisputed leader of Western economic and institutional interdependence after World War II. It has not been similarly involved in comprehensive multilateral cooperation after the end of the Cold War. A decade of 'War on Terror' has involved the costly and disputed engagements in Iraq and Afghanistan. At the same time, the United States faces mounting economic and political problems at home. In this situation, one commentator has suggested a new US strategy of 'Independent America: We must rid ourselves of international burdens and focus on improving the country from within' (Bremmer 2015: 18). He claims that this strategy has solid support in the American electorate, especially in the younger generations, and there are indications that such an orientation is gaining steam. 'Independent America' would amount to a significant further American step towards independence rather than interdependence.

EU-Europe has stood for the most radical steps towards interdependence and integration. Not so anymore. EU-widening and EU-deepening to some extent work against each other because some new members are not well equipped to take on the challenges of deep, supranational integration. In several countries political backlashes against the EU version of economic interdependence play out because that policy is seen as too costly with too few benefits for significant parts of the populations. True or not, the EU agenda for the near future will be more concerned about limiting patterns of interdependence than it will be about expanding them. For example, the European Union has not been able to provide a strong and coherent response to the refugee crisis, the large inflow of refugees from North Africa and the Middle East who risk their lives in the thousands to get to Europe. More generally, fragile states will continue to present a problem for world order as demonstrated in detail in Chapter 5.

For the time being, then, *in*dependence trumps *inter*dependence as the dominant tendency in interstate values. But this happens against the background of a long period of increasing interdependence; addressing the common problems created by intensified interdependence will require more rather than less cooperation. The increased emphasis on the value of independence will not make it easier to meet this demand for more cooperation.

This chapter opened with the question of how much trust we can put in the liberal vision of a world order based on liberal values. I have argued that it is indeed a liberal order, but not in the way that most liberals have foreseen or hoped. That is because there are deep tensions between the values of independence and interdependence. We are not on the road to grand confrontations or interstate conflict as foreseen by sceptical realists. But the inner tensions in the liberal order will continue to produce problems and setbacks which will impede the emergence of a stable and effective liberal world order.

9
Conclusion: Rethinking the New World Order

We began with the claim that the division between liberal optimists and sceptical realists is the major fault line in the debate about world order. For liberals, the future looks bright: liberal political and economic values are increasingly dominant and that makes for a cooperative world based on common values and aspirations. For realists, anarchy remains a core feature of the international system; in a context of several emerging powers this points to intensified conflict and rivalry, even interstate war. Additional theoretical positions were surveyed in Chapter 1; they make several contributions to the debate but the liberal and realist positions define the overarching theme in the discussion of world order.

So who, if anyone, wins the discussion? We should first take note that this is not a simple soccer game where we can count goals and pronounce a winner. Each of these perspectives illuminate some aspects of a complex reality and puts others in the dark; in that way liberals paint a rather optimistic picture of the present world order while realists are much more pessimistic. We can always find something that supports each of these facets of world order; it is helpful to briefly set forth a liberal and a realist picture of what is going on.

The liberal scenario begins with a note of the many changes in a liberal direction: there has been substantial liberal progress in the sense that the number of democratic countries is larger than ever and the same goes for the number of people living under a democratic system. The fact that almost all countries support a capitalist market economy and economic openness is a significant change towards convergence in the economic sphere. The traditional security agenda no longer stands alone; human security is now of importance as well. Human security is about the protection of all individuals and groups from the hazards that really affect them. In that sense it involves economic development, social justice, democratization, environmental protection, respect for human rights and the rule of law and more. In value terms, a turn to human security represents a strong convergence on common liberal values. New networks of transgovernmental and transnational governance have emerged, strengthening and diversifying cooperation across borders. Liberal values undergird the present order. There may be a temporary emphasis on independence, but that has been the case in earlier historical periods as well (e.g. between the two world wars) and still, increasing interdependence and closer cooperation have won the day; that will also be the way of the future.

The realist scenario underlines that we have seen periods of interdependence and cooperation earlier in history, but they have always been replaced by rivalry and conflict in an anarchic world of independent states. At the present time, we are moving exactly in that direction. Stronger emerging powers are seeking increased influence in their regions; that will most likely lead to more intense rivalry and confrontation between the West and both Russia and China. The problem with fragile states will not be effectively confronted because there are different national interests involved and domestic conditions in many of these states are highly adverse, as demonstrated by the present situation in Syria, the Central African Republic or South Sudan. Furthermore, problems related to climate change may lead to a doomsday scenario because states cannot agree on extraordinary reforms before it is too late. On the contrary, they will continue to express good intentions, but it will be a thin veil over continued struggle for national interests. As a consequence, the current major problems related to fragile states will be accompanied by even worse conflicts in relation to climate change, perhaps even climate wars.

Which scenario might prevail? Neither optimistic liberals nor sceptic realists win the discussion about world order; we cannot find an undiluted, benign scenario of cooperation and convergence out there. But nor can we find a pure realist scenario of tensions and rivalry leading towards imminent interstate war. Yet both of these major views contain relevant insights. Liberals have a point when they stress that we are now in a liberal order in basic terms: almost all countries are integrated in the global, capitalist market economy; they cooperate in the network of international institutions; they have formed major elements of a security order; and they do subscribe to at least some basic liberal values. Realists have a point when they emphasize that the pursuit of independence presently trumps inter-dependence, that countries underline narrow national interests rather than the common good, that integration in a global economy contains a significant element of tensions and divergence, and that the security order is crisis-ridden and unstable.

This book has suggested that a large number of different conditions and processes must be part of the analysis if we want to make a careful and balanced evaluation of the present world order. Domestic conditions in states were surveyed first. Three types of state were in focus: the advanced capitalist states of the Global North; the modernizing states—in particular China and other BRICS; and the weak states of the Global South. Across all types of state, the diagnosis was one of increasing fragility and less socio-political cohesion. Such development supports realist scepticism rather than liberal optimism because fragility compels states to give precedence to domestic problems. That makes them more self-interested and less accommodating players in the building of world order.

International conditions with a focus on interstate conflict and war were discussed next. Realists argue that anarchy and the security dilemma must always entail the danger of violent conflict between states. It was demonstrated why this view is wrong; states can become friends and co-exist peacefully in security communities, as in the security community built among liberal democracies in Western Europe, North America and Japan. In other parts of the international system there is a shallower, but nevertheless resilient, peace among states, in spite of the near-abroad conflicts connected with Russia and China. This situation supports liberal optimism.

We turned to the distribution of power and world order. In terms of power resources, material and non-material, the United States remains the leading power, but by a significantly smaller margin than earlier. At the same time, power is not merely about distribution of resources; it is about the ability to make use of these resources in relation to other actors and for several reasons the United States is less able to get its way than was the case in the past. In that sense we are in a 'multiplex' (Acharya 2014: 8) order of diversity and complexity where regional governance plays a larger role than before. That situation potentially supports a liberal view where major states work together in order to solve common problems. But it also potentially supports a realist view where states are less willing to set aside narrow national interests, and discord consequently trumps collaboration. Overall, this analysis of framework conditions does not point to a clear conclusion in the debate among liberal optimists and realist sceptics.

I then moved on to survey world order processes in four major areas. The security agenda was analysed first. A major item concerns the existence of very fragile states with high levels of domestic violence; for a variety of causes, the international society has devoted much attention to the fragile states problem, but it has not found effective ways of addressing it. Meanwhile, the situation in fragile states is connected to substantial acts of terrorism in Europe and the United States, and a much increased arrival of refugees to these countries. Europe and the United States have not found successful answers to these challenges.

The second problem in relation to security concerns the traditional security agenda of global and regional order. Some fear that a new Cold War is under way, animated by Russian aggression in its near abroad and Chinese ambitions in the South China Sea and elsewhere. It is true that democratic and autocratic great powers have not become friends in the way envisioned by some liberals when the Cold War ended. But nor is it a situation of enmity in the ways of the old Cold War. The participation of Russia and China in economic, institutional and governance networks marks a situation different from earlier. Both countries want to adjust the present security order in ways that better correspond to their interests; but they are not trying to create an alternative security order or even overthrow the present one. Whether this is sufficient to create a stable security order in the Asia-Pacific and in Russia's near-abroad remains an open question. In sum, some elements in the security structure point towards relative stability in a reformed order with room for all established and emerging powers; other elements point towards increasing crisis and instability. The crisis elements dominate for the time being.

As regards economics, the principal feature is the process of globalization. Liberals claim that the economic interdependence created by globalization leads in the direction of convergence and cooperation; substantial elements of both can be found in the present economic structure. The convergence on a capitalist market economy and economic openness is a big development: away from competing and segregated economic systems towards a single liberalized world economy running on common rules and regulations. But we also saw that there are sharp limits to convergence; capitalism develops in very different ways across countries based on distinctive local preconditions, and that can help produce changes with international conflict potential as was evident in the case of Russia. At the same time, advanced capitalism focused on finance has created its own problems in terms of speculation and inequality.

There is a 'double movement', then, in the economic structure. Towards convergence/cooperation, and towards increasing tensions connected to the downsides of globalization, which lead towards divergence and backlashes against cooperation. It is the latter which dominate at the present time.

The discussion of international institutions puts the question of 'governance or gridlock?' On one hand, a great deal of governance is taking place in a variety of important areas. On the other hand, there is little going on in terms of basic reforms; most of the governance that takes place is short-term crisis management. Advanced liberal states are less willing and able to take the lead in global governance, and emerging powers focus on their national interests; they do not work towards general reforms. Emerging powers will support reform in some areas where it suits their priorities, but they are not aspiring hegemons with plans for a different, not to mention a more effective and legitimate, world order; they are preoccupied with securing a better place for themselves in international institutions. In sum, piecemeal governance is taking place; some liberals think that amounts to be good-enough governance. True, it is not a breakdown or profound crisis; the question is whether it is sufficient to meet the challenges brought about by a long period of increasing interdependence.

Finally, we interrogated the standing of liberal values in the present world order. Independence and interdependence were posited as fundamental values of the current order. They are both liberal values, but there are deep tensions between them. After a long period of increasing interdependence, most countries today emphasize independence. This is combined with a lack of commitment to close cooperation across borders. The consequence of this situation is that the increasing demands for more and better governance in areas such as climate change, global finance and security will probably not be met. The leading liberal nation, the United States, is a pragmatic multilateralist with a domestic political scene that displays lack of bipartisanship and gridlock more than anything else, and no other country or coalition of countries are capable and willing to lead the way. A severe casualty of this state of affairs is the lack of comprehensive and concerted responses to the largest security problem in today's world: violent conflict inside fragile states.

What is the overall conclusion? The future is undecided, of course; we cannot know where it will lead—history has no libretto. The tendencies emphasized in each of the scenarios might develop in ways we never expected—just as nobody expected the Cold War to end so suddenly. But it is possible to be a bit clearer about where we are at the present time in terms of world order. In my view, the analysis has demonstrated that liberals can build a stronger case for their view of change, including some substantial progress, compared to the realist view of 'the same damn things over and over again'.

But if this is a victory for liberalism it is indeed a Pyrrhic victory—one that is so problematic that it might be tantamount to defeat. What many liberals downplay, unfortunately, is that change is not always for the better and even what might conceivably be called 'progress' is a process of transformation that involves solving some problems while simultaneously creating or aggravating others. That is to say, instead of the arrival of a much better world, the liberal model now dominates in a way that exposes the tensions and shortcomings in that model in new and profound ways.

What progress there is combines with problems, setbacks and even processes of decay. Political, economic and social degeneration is not a prerogative of fragile states or modernizing countries; it happens in advanced liberal states as well. The deep involvement of countries in globalization and interdependence brings many benefits but it has also ushered in serious problems and in several cases this is combined with processes of domestic decay.

Some liberal thinking has increasingly recognized these problems. Francis Fukuyama's recent book (2014) analyses political decay in detail and underlines that 'there is no automatic historical mechanism that makes progress inevitable, or that prevents decay and backsliding' (Fukuyama 2014: 548). But liberal (and other) thinking has not progressed far in suggesting solutions, perhaps for good reasons: it is not simple and there is not a one-size-fits-all blueprint.

Liberal values have advanced in the world because they represent economic and political models that most people find attractive: we had something that others also wanted for themselves. The question today is whether the consolidated liberal systems in North

America, Western Europe and Japan can continue to boast economic and political models that are hugely attractive around the world. The short answer is that there are serious problems which must be confronted if the attraction of liberal values and thus liberal dominance, in terms of an appealing role model for others, is to be sustained in the future.

The comfortable middle class, which is the essence of a liberal model, is under pressure from above by a small group of increasingly super-rich and from below by the influx of immigrants who fill the ranks of 'working poor'. The financial and economic crisis of the neoliberal model of capitalism which began in 2008 is no help; the model is too heavily tilted towards securitization and financial speculation; it is too deregulated, and that adds to the problems of inequality.

Advanced liberal democracies are usually known for political systems that are effective, responsive and transparent. But at the present time, the democratic process has lost vigour and dynamism in the liberal heartlands. One aspect of this is the loss of 'social capital' (Putnam 1995) connected with the increasing fragmentation of late modern societies. Another aspect is the dominance of vested elite interests of the political process impeding possibilities for comprehensive reform. On the left side of the political spectrum, social democratic parties have not so far been able to formulate new, comprehensive political projects that simultaneously tackle the challenges of run-away globalization, socio-economic inequality and political gridlock connected to interest-group domination (Fukuyama 2012).

Globalization may undermine democracy because national governments have less control of what happens within their own borders. One way to confront this is via regional integration, as in the case of the European Union. But it is clear that the European Union's supranational governance structures are in several ways less democratic than those of national parliaments and governments (Sørensen 2008a) because of the distance to ordinary citizens, the lack of public debate and the lack of transparency. When it comes to global structures of governance, such as the UN system, these problems are amplified. Liberal democracy was always designed for the nation-state. It has not been sufficiently thought through and developed when it comes to governance across borders. This is a more serious problem today than earlier, because the progress of globalization has increased the demand for political cooperation and regulation across borders (Held 2007).

Some commentators argue that there are now competing models on the rise; the Chinese model especially appeals to several developing countries (Kurlantzick 2013). China and other BRICS have certainly accomplished much in terms of economic development, but on one hand, they confront very serious problems at home in a number of areas. On the other hand, I have argued that they do not present alternative models or even visions in terms of world order. They are pragmatic players emphasizing their national interests within the framework of the existing order. The tendency to stress independence and non-commitment to close cooperation across borders pertains to many countries. Nobody stands for enlightened leadership with emphasis on the common good.

The question is whether the basic liberal model of democracy and market economy is fundamentally flawed. On one hand, there are no high-profile alternatives to some kind of liberal world order at the present time. Political progress in terms of freedom and rights, and economic progress in terms of improved welfare and the reduction of poverty, have taken place in the context of models that are fundamentally liberal. The decreasing importance of interstate war is basically due to liberal progress, in particular the emergence of a liberal democratic security community.

On the other hand, there are no straightforward ways of repairing the mounting problems which have accompanied this liberal progress. Two major factors play a role here: coalitions of political actors and better ideas. Emerging reform coalitions can be found in many liberal democracies; but at the present time they turn inward, towards domestic problems. That is, they emphasize independence and tend to consider interdependence as part of the problem rather than part of the solution. So, good ideas about reforming the current order in ways that build on the many benefits of interdependence and also effectively confront its political and economic downside are in short supply. Therefore, it remains a patchwork order for the time being. For improvement, we should look to political agency, that is, individuals and groups that want to improve the liberal model and change things for the better. Circumstances may be beyond our control but, as Benjamin Disraeli pointed out, 'our conduct is in our own power'.

Let me end with a note on theory. The study has supported theoretical pluralism in the sense that insights from several theoretical quarters have been considered helpful for the analysis of world order.

I support the notion that world order theory, as IR theory in general, 'is now irretrievably plural' (Rengger 2000: 189–90). At the same time, I also put forward some demands on a good analysis of world order. On one hand, a full analysis of world order requires attention to conditions within states as well as to international relations; that is, world order cannot be reduced to a purely 'international' or a purely 'domestic' issue. On the other hand, I rejected the 'one big thing' analysis which zooms in on one particular aspect as the central characteristic of world order. World order is multi-dimensional; yet this must not lead to an analysis where endless complexity clouds the big picture. Some theories meet these demands better than others.

Since this study has focused on the overarching theme of liberal optimism versus realist scepticism, I concentrate on these two perspectives. In which ways should liberalism be developed and modified in order to come up with a better analysis of world order? Elements of an answer to that question have already been presented in the analyses above; here, we can draw together the main points. Liberal theory must let go of the idea of unimpeded progress, the notion that societies (and people) must always move forward and upward. The sceptical liberal view, where history has no libretto, is the better starting point. Liberals must also acknowledge that the liberal political and economic model is not a fixed entity, but a set of principles that develop and change over time and may not always be in harmony (Sørensen 2011). The consequence is that at any given time, the current liberal model may be more or less suited to confront the challenges it will always face. Finally, liberal processes of political and economic development are seldom harmonious and unproblematic. They contain upsides and downsides; in some periods the downsides may dominate, as many believe to be the case with current processes of globalization. Fortunately, many—perhaps even most—liberals are ready to accept these changes (including Francis Fukuyama). That has not led to agreement, of course, but to richer analyses of the current order (Fukuyama 2012; Mahbubani 2013; Kupchan 2012); Kupchan pronounces himself 'a liberal realist with constructivist leanings' (Kupchan 2011) indicating the turn to theoretical pluralism advocated in this book.

Realist theory must let go of the notion of history as 'the same damn things over and over again' (Layne 1994): the idea that progress cannot happen and that security competition and conflict is always imminent among independent states. This must also mean a farewell to the idea that war always looms among states in an anarchic world. Finally, realists must focus their analysis not only on international, systemic conditions but also on domestic conditions. It is the interplay between domestic and international conditions which determine what world order we have at any given time. Many realists are now ready to accept these changes, or at least to modify the misleading assumptions in various ways (Lake 2013; Rösch 2014).

Moving in that direction will open to the more pluralistic, eclectic analysis proposed in this book. Ultimately, it is up to every student of world order to think about and devise the appropriate framework for analysis. If action is the way forward, as I have suggested, it must be based on the best possible analysis of the conditions made up by the present world order.

References

Abramowitz, Morton (2012). 'How American Exceptionalism Dooms U.S. Foreign Policy', *The National Interest*, http://nationalinterest.org/commentary/how-american-exceptionalism-dooms-us-foreign-policy-7640,22 October, date accessed 1 February 2016.

Acharya, Amitav (2014). *The End of American World Order*, Cambridge: Polity Press.

Ackerman, Bruce (1991). *We the People: Foundations*, Cambridge, MA: The Belknap Press of Harvard University Press.

Adler, Emmanuel (2008). 'The Spread of Security Communities', *European Journal of International Relations*, 14:2, 195–230.

AFP (2016). 'Ex-Prime Ministers Vie for Central African Republic Presidency', http://www.theguardian.com/world/2016/jan/07/ex-prime-ministers-vie-for-central-african-republic-presidency, 7 January, date accessed 1 February 2016.

Aguirre, Mariano and Joanna Abrisketa (2009). 'Pressing Issues for UN Peacekeeping Operations', http://www.tni.org/article/pressing-issues-un-peacekeeping-operations, 29 September, date accessed 1 February 2016.

Albright, Madeleine K. and Richard S. Williamson (2013). *The United States and R2P*, United States Institute of Peace, http://www.atlanticcouncil.org/blogs/new-atlanticist/us-foreign-policy-falls-victim-to-partisan-gridlock-ahead-of-2016-elections, 13 March, date accessed 1 February 2016.

Allen, Susan Hannah and Amy T. Yuen (2014). 'The Politics of Peacekeeping: UN Security Council Oversight across Peacekeeping Missions', *International Studies Quarterly*, 58, 621–32.

Allison, Graham (2004). *Nuclear Terrorism: The Ultimate Preventable Catastrophe*, New York: Times Books.

Ambrosio, Thomas (2001). *Irredentism: Ethnic Conflict and International Politics*, Westport, CT: Praeger Publishers.

Andreas, Peter (2004). 'Illicit International Political Economy: The Clandestine Side of Globalization', *Review of International Political Economy*, 1:3, 641–52.

Andrews, Edmond (2008). 'Greenspan Concedes Error on Regulation', *New York Times*, http://www.nytimes.com/2008/10/24/business/economy/24panel.html?_r=1&, 23 October, date accessed 1 February 2016.

Annan, Kofi (2000). *We, the Peoples*, Millennium Report, New York: United Nations.

Art, Robert R. and Kenneth N. Waltz (1983) 'Technology, Strategy, and the Uses of Force', in Art and Waltz (eds), *The Use of Force*, Lanham, MD: University Press of America.

Ash, Timothy Garton (1990). 'Eastern Europe: The Year of Truth', *New York Review of Books*, February 15, 17–22.

Aslund, Anders (2002). *Building Capitalism. The Transformation of the Former Soviet Bloc*, Cambridge: Cambridge University Press.

Atlantic Council (2015). 'US Foreign Policy Falls Victim to Partisan Gridlock Ahead of 2016 Elections', http://www.atlanticcouncil.org/blogs/new-atlanticist/us-foreign-policy-falls-victim-to-partisan-gridlock-ahead-of-2016-elections, 13 March, date accessed 1 February 2016.

Autesserre, Séverine (2008). 'The Trouble With Congo', *Foreign Affairs*, 87:3, 94–110.

Autesserre, Séverine (2014). *Peaceland: Conflict Resolution and the Everyday Politics of International Intervention*, New York: Cambridge University Press.

Ayson, Robert (2015). *Asia's Security*, London: Palgrave.

Baldwin, David A. (1979). 'Power Analysis and World Politics: New Trends versus Old Tendencies', *World Politics*, 31:2, 161–94.

Barber, Benjamin R. (1995). *Jihad Versus McWorld*, New York: Random House.

Barnett, Michael N. (1997). 'The UN Security Council, Indifference, and Genocide in Rwanda', *Cultural Anthropology*, 12:4, 551–78.

Barnett, Michael and Christoph Zürcher (2009). 'The Peacebuilder's Contract: How External Statebuilding Reinforces Weak Statehood', in Roland Paris and Timothy D. Sisk (eds), *The Dilemmas of Statebuilding*, London: Routledge, 23–53.

Barnett, Michael and Raymond Duvall (2005). 'Power in International Politics', *International Organization*, Winter, 39–75.

Becker, Uwe (2014). 'The Heterogeneity of Capitalism in Crisis-Ridden Europe', *Journal of Contemporary European Studies*, 22:3, 261–75.

Beckley, Michael (2011). 'China's Century? Why America's Edge Will Endure', *International Security*, 36:3, 41–78.

Berenskoetter, Felix and M.J. Williams, eds (2007). *Power in World Politics*, London: Routledge.

Berlin, Isaiah (1953). *The Hedgehog and the Fox: An Essay on Tolstoy's View of History*, London: Weidenfeld and Nicolson.

Berlin, Isaiah (1988). 'On the Pursuit of the Ideal', *The New York Review of Books*, 35:4, 1–18.

Berman, Paul (2003). *Terror and Liberalism*, New York: W.W. Norton.

Bevir, Mark and Jamie Gaskarth (2015). 'Global Governance and the BRICs', in Jamie Gaskarth (ed.), *Rising Powers, Global Governance, and Global Ethics*, London: Routledge, 74–96.

Bhagwati, Jagdish (2007). *In Defense of Globalization*, Oxford: Oxford University Press.

Biermann, F., P. Pattberg, H. van Asselt and F. Zelli (2009). 'The Fragmentation of Global Governance Architectures: A Framework for Analysis' *Global Environmental Politics*, 9:4, 14–40.

Billerbeck, S.B.K. (2009). 'Whose Peace? Local Ownership and UN Peacebuilding', University of Westminster, https://kclpure.kcl.ac.uk/portal/en/publications/whose-peace-local-ownership-and-un-peacebuilding(081f42c7-97fb-4793-9468-dfba2480f376)/export.html, date accessed 1 February 2016.

Blair, Tony (2007). 'A Battle for Global Values', *Foreign Affairs*, 86:1, 79–90.

Blomfield, Adrian (2007). '$40 bn. Putin "Is Now Europe's Richest Man"', http://www.telegraph.co.uk/news/worldnews/1573354/40bn-Putin-is-now-Europes-richest-man.html, 21 December, date accessed 1 February 2016.

Bloomberg (2014). 'China Takes On Pollution with Biggest Changes in 25 Years', http://www.bloomberg.com/news/2014-04-24/china-enacts-biggest-pollution-curbs-in-25-years.html, 25 April, date accessed 1 February 2016.

Booth, Ken (2007). *Theory of World Security*, Cambridge: Cambridge University Press.

Booth, Ken and Nicholas J. Wheeler (2008). *The Security Dilemma. Fear, Cooperation and Trust in World Politics*, Basingstoke: Palgrave Macmillan.

Bouzis, Kathleen (2015) 'Countering the Islamic State: U.S. Counterterrorism Measures', *Studies in Conflict and Terrorism*, 38:10, 885–97.

Bowman, Steve (2002). *Weapons of Mass Destruction: The Terrorist Threat*, Washington: CRS.

Bremmer, Ian (2012). *Every Nation for Itself. Winners and Losers in a G-Zero World*, London: Penguin.

Bremmer, Ian (2015). 'What Does America Stand For?' *Time Magazine*, 185:20, 16–21.

Breslin, Shaun (2013). 'China and the Global Order: Signalling Threat or Friendship?', *International Affairs*, 89:3, 615–34.

Broadhurst, Roderic (2013). 'Corruption is a Byproduct of Chinese Party-state's Defective Genes', *South China Morning Post*, http://www.scmp.com/comment/insight-opinion/article/1378841/corruption-byproduct-chinese-party-states-defective-genes, 12 December, date accessed 1 February 2016.

Brock, Lothar. Holm, Hans Henrik; Stohl, Michael; Sørensen Georg (2011). *Fragile States. Violence and the Failure of Intervention*, Cambridge: Polity Press.

Brooks, Stephen G. and William C. Wohlforth (2008). *World Out of Balance. International Relations and the Challenge of American Primacy*, Princeton: Princeton University Press.

Brown, Stuart (2013). *The Future of U.S. Global Power. Delusions of Decline*, Basingstoke: Palgrave Macmillan.

Bull, Hedley (1995) [1977]. *The Anarchical Society. A Study of Order in World Politics*, Basingstoke: Palgrave Macmillan.

Burges, Sean (2013). 'Brazil as a Bridge between Old and New Powers?', *International Affairs*, 89:3, 577–94.

Burton, John (1972). *World Society*, Cambridge: Cambridge University Press.

Bush, George H.W. (1991). 'Address to Congress', http://www.al-bab.com/arab/docs/pal/pal 0.htm, date accessed 1 February 2016.

Buzan, Barry (1991). *People, States, and Fear*, 2nd ed., Hemel Hempstead: Harvester Wheatsheaf.

Buzan, Barry (2003). 'The Middle East: A Perennial Conflict Formation', in Barry Buzan and Ole Wæver, *Regions and Powers. The Structure of International Security*, Cambridge: Cambridge University Press, 187–218.

Buzan, Barry (2004a). *From International to World Society*, Cambridge: Cambridge University Press.

Buzan, Barry (2004b). *The United States and the Great Powers. World Politics in the Twenty-First Century*, Cambridge: Polity Press.

Buzan, Barry (2006). 'Will the "Global War on Terrorism" Be the new Cold War?', *International Affairs*, 82:6, 1101–18.

Buzan, Barry (2014). *An Introduction to the English School of International Relations: The Societal Approach*, Cambridge: Polity Press.

Buzan, Barry and George Lawson (2014). 'Capitalism and the Emergent World Order', *International Affairs*, 90:1, 71–91.

Call, Charles T. (2008). 'The Fallacy of the Failed State', *Third World Quarterly*, 29:8, 1491–1507.

Campbell, Caitlin and Craig Murray (2013). 'China Seeks a "New Type of Major-Country Relationship" with the United States', *U.S.–China Economic and Security Review Commission*, http://origin.www.uscc.gov/sites/default/files/Research/China%20Seeks%20New%20Type%20of%20Major-Country%20Relationship%20with%20United%20States_Staff%20Research%20Backgrounder.pdf, 25 June, date accessed 1 February 2016.

Carrington, Damian (2013). 'Planet Likely to Warm by 4C by 2100, Scientists Warn', http://www.theguardian.com/environment/2013/dec/31/planet-will-warm-4c-2100-climate, 31 December, date accessed 1 February 2016.

Cassidy, John (2015). 'A Skeptical Note on the Paris Climate Deal', *The New Yorker*, http://www.newyorker.com/news/john-cassidy/skeptical-note-paris-climate-deal, 14 December, date accessed 1 February 2016.

Castells, Manuel (1998). *The Power of Identity*, Oxford: Basil Blackwell.

Cerny, Philip G. (2010). *Rethinking World Politics*, Oxford: Oxford University Press.

CFR (Council on Foreign Relations) (2013). 'Global Governance Monitor: Climate Change', http://www.cfr.org/publication/18985/global_governance_monitor.html?co=C028801#!/climate-change#issue-brief, date accessed 1 February 2016.

Chan, John (2013) 'China's Looming Economic Crisis. Poverty and Rising Social Inequalities', http://www.globalresearch.ca/chinas-looming-economic-crisis-poverty-and-rising-social-inequalities/5325765, 8 March, date accessed 1 February 2016.

Chandler, Marc (2013). 'BIS: Daily FX Turnover Averages 5.3 Trillion', http://www.economonitor.com/blog/2013/09/bis-daily-fx-turnover-averages-5-3-trillion/, 13 September, date accessed 1 February 2016.

Chasek, Pamela, David L. Downie and Janet W. Brown (2010). *Global Environmental Politics*, Boulder: Westview Press.

Christou, George (2014). 'The European Union's Human Security Discourse: Where Are we Now?', *European Security*, 23:3, 364–81.

Chu, Yun-Han, Larry Diamond, Andrew J. Nathan and Doh Chull Shin (2010). 'Conclusion: Values, Regime Performance, and Democratic Consolidation', in Chu et al. (eds), *How East Asians View Democracy*, New York: Columbia University Press, 238–59.

CIA World Factbook, https://www.cia.gov/library/publications/the-world-factbook/rankorder/2001rank.html, date accessed 1 February 2016.

Clark, Ian (2001). *The Post-Cold War Order*, Oxford: Oxford University Press.

Cobden, Richard (1903). *Political Writings*, 2 vols. London: Fisher Unwin.

Cohen, Benjamin (2014). *Advanced Introduction to International Political Economy*, Cheltenham: Edward Elgar.

Copeland, Dale C. (2000). 'The Constructivist Challenge to Structural Realism', *International Security*, 25:2, 187–212.

Copeland, Dale C. (2015). *Economic Interdependence and War*, Princeton: Princeton University Press.

Coppedge, Michael, et al. (2011). 'Conceptualizing and Measuring Democracy: A New Approach', *Perspectives on Politics*, 9:2, 247–67.

Council on Foreign Relations (2010). 'The U.S.–India Nuclear Deal', http://www.cfr.org/india/us-india-nuclear-deal/p9663, 5 November, date accessed 1 February 2016.

Cox, Michael (2003). 'The Empire's Back in Town: Or America's Imperial Temptation Again', *Millennium. Journal of International Studies*, 2:1, 1–27.

Cox, Robert (1996). With T.J. Sinclair. *Approaches to World Order*, Cambridge: Cambridge University Press.

Cox, Robert (2002). 'Reflections and Transitions', in R.W. Cox with M.G. Schechter: *The Political Economy of a Plural World: Critical Reflections on Power, Morals, and Civilization'*, London: Routledge, 26–44.

COW (2015). 'Intergovernmental Organizations', http://www.correlatesofwar.org/data-sets/IGOs, date accessed 1 February 2016.

Crosby, Alfred (2004). *Ecological Imperialism: The Biological Expansion of Europe 900–1900*, Cambridge: Cambridge University Press.

Dafoe, Allan, John R. Oneal and Bruce Russett (2013). 'The Democratic Peace: Weighing the Evidence and Cautious Inference', *International Studies Quarterly*, 57:1, 201–14.

Dahl, Robert A. (1976). *Modern Political Analysis*, 3rd ed., Englewood-Cliffs, NJ: Prentice Hall.

Dahl, Robert A. (1999). 'Can International Organizations Be Democratic? A Sceptic's View', in I. Shapiro and C. Hacker-Cordón (eds), *Democracy's Edges*, Cambridge: Cambridge University Press, 19–37.

Daschle, Tom (1996). 'The Water's Edge', *Foreign Policy*, 103, Summer, 1–16.

Dauvergne, Peter and Deborah Farias (2012). 'The Rise of Brazil as a Global Development Power', *Third World Quarterly*, 33:5, 03–17.

Dawisha, Karen (2014). *Putin's Kleptocracy: Who Owns Russia?*, New York: Simon and Schuster.

Dean, Mark and Maria Sebastia-Barriel (2004). 'Why has World Trade Grown Faster than World Output?', *Bank of England Quarterly Bulletin*, 44:3, 310–21.

Dervis, Kemal (2012). 'Convergence, Interdependence, and Divergence', *Finance & Development*, September, 10–14.

Deudney, Daniel and G. John Ikenberry (1999). 'The Nature and Sources of Liberal International Order', *Review of International Studies*, 25:2, 179–96.

Deudney, Daniel and G. John Ikenberry (2009). 'The Myth of Autocratic Revival: Why Liberal Democracy Will Prevail', *Foreign Affairs*, 88:1, 77–94.

Deutsch, Karl W. et al. (1957). *Political Community and the North Atlantic Area*, Princeton: Princeton University Press.

Dicken, Peter (2011). *Global Shift. Reshaping the Global Economic Map in the 21st Century*, 6th ed., New York: Guilford Press.

Dige Pedersen, Jørgen (2008). *Globalization, Development and the State. The Performance of India and Brazil Since 1990*, Basingstoke: Palgrave Macmillan.

Ding, X.L. (2000). 'Informal Privatization through Internationalization: The Rise of Nomenclature Capitalism in China's Offshore Businesses', *British Journal of Political Science*, 30:1, 121–46.

Dobbins, James et al. (2003). *America's Role in Nation-Building: From Germany to Iraq*, Santa Monica: Rand.

Donais, T. (2009). 'Empowerment or Imposition? Dilemmas of Local Ownership in Post-Conflict Peacebuilding Processes', *Peace and Change*, 34:1, 3–26.

Donohue, Laura K. (2008). *The Cost of Counterterrorism*, Cambridge: Cambridge University Press.

Doyle, Michael W. (1983). 'Kant, Liberal Legacies and Foreign Affairs', pts 1 and 2, *Philosophy and Public Affairs*, 12/3: 205–35 and 12/4: 323–54.

Doyle, Michael W. (1997). *Ways of War and Peace*, New York: W.W. Norton.

Drezner, Daniel W. (2012). 'The Irony of Global Economic Governance. The System Worked', Council of Foreign Relations: Working Paper.

Dugard, John (2007). *Report of the Special Rapporteur on the Human Rights Situation in the Palestinian Territories Occupied Since 1967*, http://www.voltairenet.org/article145602.html, date accessed 1 February 2016.

DW (2015). 'Millions of German Workers in Poverty', http://www.dw.com/en/millions-of-german-workers-in-poverty/a-18212765, 24 January, date accessed 1 February 2016.

Economist Intelligence Unit (2012). Democracy Index 2012, https://portoncv.gov.cv/dhub/porton.por_global.open_file?p_doc_id=1034, date accessed 1 February 2016.

Englebert, Pierre and Denis M. Tull (2008). 'Postconflict Reconstruction in Africa: Flawed Ideas about Failed States', *International Security*, 32:4, 106–39.

Evans, Gareth (2011). 'Interview: The RtoP Balance Sheet after Libya', http://www.globalr2p.org/media/files/gareth-_interview-the-rtop-balance-sheet-after-libya.pdf, 2 September, date accessed 1 February 2016.

Eyal, Gil, Ivan Szelenyi and Eleanor Townsley (1998). *Making Capitalism without Capitalists*, London: Verso.

Fabius, Laurent (2013). 'Veto Reform', http://foreignpolicy.com/2013/10/04/frances-plan-to-fix-the-veto/, 4 October, date accessed 1 February 2016.

Feldman, Noah (2013). 'Corruption and Political Legitimacy in China', http://www.law.harvard.edu/news/spotlight/ils/11_feldman-corruption-political-legitimacy-china.html, 15 March, date accessed 1 February 2016.

Ferris, Robert (2015). 'China Air Pollution far Worse than Thought: Study', http://www.cnbc.com/2015/08/18/china-air-pollution-far-worse-than-thought-study.html, 18 August, date accessed 1 February 2016.

Fettweis, Christopher (2004). 'Evaluating IR's Crystal Balls: How Predictions of the Future Have Withstood Fourteen Years of Unipolarity', *International Studies Review*, 6, 79–104.

Fettweis, Christopher (2010). *Dangerous Times? The International Politics of Great Power Peace*, Washington, DC: Georgetown University Press.

Financial Times (2015). 'What Is the Europe Migrant Crisis and How Has it Evolved?', http://www.ft.com/intl/cms/s/2/cdd88362-524e-11e5-b029-b9d50a74fd14.html#axzz3x3WwZvK1, 4 September, date accessed 1 February 2016.

Finkelstein, Lawrence S. (1995). 'What Is Global Governance?', *Global Governance*, 1:3, 367–72.

Foot, Rosemary (2006). 'Chinese Strategies in a US-Hegemonic Global Order: Accommodating and Hedging', *International Affairs*, 82:1, 77–94.

Foot, Rosemary (2014). ''Doing Some Things' in the Xi Jinping Era: The United Nations as China's Venue of Choice', *International Affairs*, 90:5, 1085–1100.

Frandsen, Bjarne A. (2011). 'Marxist Books on the Global Financial Crisis and Capitalism', http://spip.modkraft.dk/tidsskriftcentret/linkbox/article/marxistiske-boger-om-finanskrisen, date accessed 1 February 2016.

Freedom House (2013). *Freedom in the World 2013*, https://freedomhouse.org/report/freedom-world/freedom-world-2013, date accessed 1 February 2016.

Freedom House (2015). *Freedom in the World 2015*, https://freedomhouse.org/report/freedom-world/freedom-world-2015#.Vq9ydKN7zcs, date accessed 1 February 2016.

Frieden, Jeffrey (2012). 'The Modern Capitalist World Economy: A Historical Overview', in Dennis Mueller (ed.), *Oxford Handbook of Capitalism*, New York: Oxford University Press, 17–38.

Friedman, E.J., Hochstetler, K., and Clark, A. (2005). *Sovereignty, Democracy and Global Civil Society: State-Civil Society Relations at UN World Conferences*, New York: SUNY Press.

FSB (2015). 'About the Financial Stability Board', http://www.financialstability-board.org/about/, date accessed 1 February 2016.

Fukuyama, Francis (1989). 'The End of History', *The National Interest*, 16, 3–18.

Fukuyama, Francis (1992). *The End of History and the Last Man*, New York: Avon Books.

Fukuyama, Francis (2012). 'The Future of History: Can Liberal Democracy Survive the Decline of the Middle Class?', *Foreign Affairs*, 53, http://www.foreignaffairs.com/articles/136782/francis-fukuyama/the-future-of-history, date accessed 1 February 2016.

Fukuyama, Francis (2014). *Political Order and Political Decay*, London: Profile Books.

Gallie, W.B. (1956). 'Essentially Contested Concepts', *Proceedings of the Aristotelian Society*, Vol. 56, 167–98.

Gartzke, Erik A, and Alex Weisiger (2013). 'Permanent Friends? Dynamic Difference and the Democratic Peace', *International Studies Quarterly*, 57:1, 171–85.

Gaskarth, Jamie (ed.) (2015). *Rising Powers, Global Governance, and Global Ethics*, London: Routledge.

Gause, F. Gregory III (2014). 'Beyond Sectarianism: The New Middle East Cold War', *Brookings Doha Center Analysis Paper*, No. 11, July.

Geis, Anna, Lothar Brock and Harald Müller (eds) (2006). *Democratic Wars. Looking at the Dark Side of the Democratic Peace*, Basingstoke: Palgrave Macmillan.

Ghemawat, Pankaj and Steven A. Altman (2014). *DHL Global Interconnectedness Index 2014*, http://www.dhl.com/en/about_us/logistics_insights/studies_research/global_connectedness_index/global_connectedness_index.html#.VFff5Mk-pXuM, date accessed 1 February 2016.

Giddens, Anthony (1992). *The Nation-State and Violence*, Cambridge: Polity Press.

Gilpin, Robert (1987). *The Political Economy of International Relations*, Princeton: Princeton University Press.

Glyn, Andrew (2007). *Capitalism Unleashed: Finance, Globalization, and Welfare*, Oxford: Oxford University Press.

Goh, Evelyn (2007/08). 'Great Powers and Hierarchical Order in Southeast Asia: Analyzing Regional Security Strategies', *International Security*, 32:3, 113–57.

Goh, Evelyn (2013). *The Struggle for Order*, Oxford: Oxford University Press.

Goldstein, Joshua and Steven Pinker (2011). 'War Really Is Going Out of Style', *New York Times*, December 17.

Gomez, Oscar A. and Des Gasper (2012), 'Human Security', UNDP, http://hdr.undp.org/sites/default/files/human_security_guidance_note_r-nhdrs.pdf, date accessed 1 February 2016.

Gong, Gerrit W. (1984). *The Standard of 'Civilization' in International Society*, Oxford: Oxford University Press.

Gooptu, Angshuman (2012). 'Will Basel III Help or Hurt?', *Chicago Policy Review*, http://chicagopolicyreview.org/2012/04/24/will-basel-iii-help-or-hurt/, 24 April, date accessed 1 February 2016.

Gorbachev, Mikhail (1987). *Perestroika: New Thinking for Our Country and the World*, New York: Harper and Row.

Greenberg, Edward S. and Thomas F. Mayer (1990). *Changes in the State: Causes and Consequences*, Newbury Park: Sage.

Götz, Karl Elias Immanuel (2013). *Russia's Quest for Regional Hegemony*, Aarhus: Politica.

Grimm, Sonja, Nicolas Lemay-Hébert, Olivier Nay (2014). '"Fragile States": "Introducing a Political Concept"', *Third World Quarterly*, 35:2, 197–209.

Gurr, Ted Robert (1994). 'Peoples Against States: Ethnopolitical Conflict and the Changing World System', *International Studies Quarterly*, 38, 347–77.

Gurr, Ted Robert and Barbara Harff (2003). *Ethnic Conflict in World Politics*, Boulder: Westview.

Guzzini, Stefano (2012). 'The Ambivalent "Diffusion of Power" in Global Governance', in Stefano Guzzini and Iver B. Neumann (eds), *The Diffusion of Power in Global Governance*, Basingstoke: Palgrave Macmillan, 1–37.

Gyimah-Boadi, Emmanuel (1996). 'Civil Society in Africa', *Journal of Democracy*, 7:2, 118–32.

Hale, Thomas, David Held and Kevin Young (2013). *Gridlock. Why Global Cooperation is Failing When We Need It Most*, Cambridge: Polity Press.

Hanson, Philip (2003). *The Rise and Fall of the Soviet Economy: An Economic History of the U.S.S.R. From 1945*, London: Pearson.

Harvey, David (2010). *The Enigma of Capital and the Crises of Capitalism*, Oxford: Oxford University Press.

Hautkapp, Dirk (2015). 'Der Dschihad in den Köpfen', *Berliner Morgenpost*, 7 December, p. 3.

Hay, Colin (2001). 'What Place for Ideas in the Structure-Agency Debate?' http://www.criticalrealism.com/archive/cshay_wpisad.html, date accessed 1 February 2016.

Hegre, Håvard (2014). 'Democracy and Armed Conflict', *Journal of Peace Research*, 51:2, 159–73.

Hehir, Aidan (2013). 'The Permanence of Inconsistency: Libya, the Security Council, and the Responsibility to Protect', *International Security*, 38:1, 137–59.

Held, David (2006). *Models of Democracy*, 3rd ed., Cambridge: Polity Press.

Held, David (2007). 'Reframing Global Governance: Apocalypse Soon or Reform', in D. Held and A. McGrew (eds), *Globalization Theory: Approaches and Controversies*, Cambridge: Polity Press, 240–61.

Held, David and Charles Roger (eds) (2013). *Global Governance at Risk*, Cambridge: Polity Press.

Helleiner, Eric (2010). 'What Role for the New Financial Stability Board? The Politics of International Standards after the Crisis', *Global Policy*, 1:3, 282–90.

Herbst, Jeffrey (1996/97). 'Responding to State Failure in Africa', *International Security*, 21:3, 1209–44.

Herz, John (1950). 'Idealist Internationalism and the Security Dilemma', *World Politics*, II:2, 157–81.

Herz, John (1959). *International Politics in the Atomic Age*, New York: Columbia University Press.

Hettne, Björn (2005). 'Beyond the "New" Regionalism', *New Political Economy*, 10:4, 543–71.

Hirst, Paul and Grahame Thompson (1992). 'The Problem of "Globalization"', *Economy and Society*, 21:4, 357–96.

Historienet (2010). 'Hvilke to nationer har været i krig med hinanden flest gange?', http://historienet.dk/spoerg-os/hvilke-to-nationer-har-vaeret-i-krig-med-hinanden-flest-gange, date accessed 1 February 2016.

Hobbes, Thomas (1946). *Leviathan*, Oxford: Blackwell.

Hoenig, Thomas (2012). 'Get Basel III Right and avoid Basel IV', *Financial Times*, http://www.ft.com/cms/s/0/99ece1b0-3fa0-11e2-b2ce-00144feabdc0.html#axzz3XYVqyPNi, 12 December, date accessed 1 February 2016.

Hoffmann, Ulrich (2011). 'Some Reflections on Climate Change, Green Growth Illusions, and Development Space', Geneva: UNCTAD Discussion Paper 205.

Holbig, Heike and Bruce Gilley (2010). 'Reclaiming Legitimacy in China', *Politics & Policy*, 38:3, 395–422.

Holm, Hans Henrik and Georg Sørensen (1995). 'Introduction: What Has Changed?', in Hans Henrik Holm and Georg Sørensen (eds), *Whose World Order? Uneven Globalization and the End of the Cold War*, Boulder: Westview, 1–19.

Howard, Michael (1984). 'America and the World', St Louis: Washington University, the Annual Lewin Lecture, 5 April.

Huitfeldt, Henrik and Johannes Jütting (2009). 'Informality and Informal Employment', OECD Development Centre, http://www.oecd.org/dac/povertyreduction/43280298.pdf, date accessed 1 February 2016.

Hulme, Mike (2009). *Why We Disagree About Climate Change*, Cambridge: Cambridge University Press.

Huntington, Samuel P. (1993). 'The Clash of Civilizations?', *Foreign Affairs*, 72:3, 22–49.

Huntington, Samuel P. (1996). *The Clash of Civilizations and the Remaking of World Order*, New York: Simon and Schuster.

Huntington, Samuel P. (2004). 'The Hispanic Challenge', *Foreign Policy*, March–April, 30–45.

Hurrell, Andrew (2007). *On Global Order. Power, Values, and the Constitution of International Society*, Oxford: Oxford University Press.

IDMC (2015). 'Syria IDP Figures Analysis', http://www.internal-displacement.org/middle-east-and-north-africa/syria/figures-analysis, date accessed 1 February 2016.

IEA (2014). 'Scenarios and Projections', http://www.iea.org/publications/scenariosandprojections/, date accessed 1 February 2016.

Ikenberry, G. John (2002). 'America's Imperial Ambition', *Foreign Affairs*, 81:5, 44–60.

Ikenberry, G. John (2006). 'The Global Governance Crisis', http://www.princeton.edu/~slaughtr/Articles/InterDependent.pdf, date accessed 1 February 2016.

Ikenberry, G. John (2011). *Liberal Leviathan: The Origins, Crisis, and Transformation of the American World Order*, Princeton: Princeton University Press.

Ikenberry, G. John (2014). 'The Illusion of Geopolitics: The Enduring Power of the Liberal Order', *Foreign Affairs*, 93:3, 80–90.

Ikenberry, G. John (2014). 'The Rise of China and the Future of Liberal World Order', *Chatham House*, 7 May, http://www.chathamhouse.org/sites/files/chathamhouse/field/field_document/20140507RiseofChina.pdf, date accessed 1 February 2016.

ILO (2012). *Statistical Update on Employment in the Informal Economy*, http://laborsta.ilo.org/applv8/data/INFORMAL_ECONOMY/2012-06-Statistical%20update%20-%20v2.pdf, date accessed 1 February 2016.

Inglehart, Ronald and Christian Welzel (2009). 'How Development Leads to Democracy', *Foreign Affairs*, 88:2, 33–48.

Inkeles, Alex (1998). *One World Emerging. Convergence and Divergence in Industrial Societies*, Boulder: Westview.

Investopedia (2013). 'U.S. vs China', http://www.investopedia.com/articles/investing/032013/us-vs-china-battle-be-largest-economy-world.asp, 20 March, date accessed 1 February 2016.

IPCC (2014). *Climate Change 2014. Summary for Policymakers*, https://ipcc-wg2.gov/AR5/images/uploads/WG2AR5_SPM_FINAL.pdf, date accessed 1 February 2016.

IRC (International Rescue Committee) (2015). 'The IRC in Central African Republic', http://www.rescue.org/where/central_african_republic, date accessed 1 February 2016.

Jackson, Robert (1993). *Quasi-States: Sovereignty, International Relations and the Third World*, New York: Cambridge University Press.

Jackson, Robert and Carl G. Rosberg (1994). 'The Political Economy of African Personal Rule', in D.E. Apter and C.G. Rosberg (eds), *Political Development and the New Realism in Sub-Saharan Africa*, Charlottesville: University Press of Virginia, 291–325.

Jackson, Robert and Carl G.Rosberg (1982). *Personal Rule in Black Africa: Prince, Autocrat, Prophet, Tyrant*, Berkeley: University of California Press.

Jackson, Robert and Georg Sørensen (2013). *Introduction to International Relations. Theories and Approaches*, 5th ed., Oxford: Oxford University Press.

Jackson, Robert and Georg Sørensen (2016). *Introduction to International Relations. Theories and Approaches*, 6th ed., Oxford: Oxford University Press.

Jackson, Tim (2009). *Prosperity without Growth: Economics for a Finite Planet*, London: Earthscan.

Jacobs, Michael (2014). 'The Real Lima Deal', http://www.project-syndicate.org/commentary/lima-global-climate-change-agreement-by-michael-jacobs-2014-12, 15 December, date accessed 1 February 2016.

James, Alan (1998). 'The Practice of Sovereign Statehood in Contemporary International Society', *Political Studies*, 47:3, 457–74.

James, Harold (2008). 'The Rise of the BRICs', *The International Economy*, Summer, 41.

Jentleson, Bruce (2007). 'Yet Again: Humanitarian Intervention and the Challenges of "Never Again"', in J. Crocker, F.O. Hampson and P. Aall (eds), *Leashing the Dogs of War: Conflict Management in a Divided World*, Washington, DC: Institute of Peace, 277–97.

Jervis, Robert (2002). 'Theories of War in an Era of Leading-Power Peace', *American Political Science Review*, 96:1, 1–14.

Jessop, Bob (2002). *The Future of the Capitalist State*, Cambridge, UK: Polity Press.

Kagan, Robert (2007). 'End of Dreams, Return of History', *Policy Review*, 44, August-September.

Kahler, Miles (2009). 'Statebuilding after Afghanistan and Iraq', in Roland Paris and Timothy D. Sisk (eds), *The Dilemmas of Statebuilding*, London: Routledge, 287–304.

Kahler, Miles (2013). 'Rising Powers and Global Governance: Negotiating Change in a Resilient Status Quo', *International Affairs*, 89:3, 711–29.

Kaldor, Mary (1999). *New and Old Wars. Organized Violence in a New Era*, Palo Alto: Stanford University Press.

Kant, Immanuel (1992 [1795]). 'Perpetual Peace', printed in Hans Reiss (ed.), *Kant's Political Writings*, Cambridge: Cambridge University Press, 130 (93–130).

Kapoor, Sony (2010). *The Financial Crisis—Causes and Cures*, Brussels: ETUI.

Katzenstein, Peter (2005). *A World of Regions: Asia and Europe in the American Imperium*, Ithaca: Cornell University Press.

Katzenstein, Peter (ed.) (2009). *Civilizations in World Politics. Plural and Pluralist Perspectives*, London: Routledge.

Kennedy, Paul (2002). 'The Eagle has Landed', *Financial Times*, 1 February.

Keohane, Robert O. (1984). *After Hegemony: Cooperation and Discord in the World Political Economy*, Princeton: Princeton University Press.

Keohane, Robert O. and David G. Victor (2011). 'The Regime Complex for Climate Change', *Perspectives on Politics*, 9:1, 7–23.

Keohane, Robert O. and Joseph S. Nye Jr. (1977). *Power and Interdependence: World Politics in Transition*, Boston, MA: Little Brown.

Kerry, John (1998). *The New War: The Web of Crime That Threatens America's Security*, New York: Touchstone.

Kersten, Mark (2014). 'Does Russia Have a "Responsibility to Protect" Ukraine? Don't Buy it', http://www.theglobeandmail.com/globe-debate/does-russia-have-a-responsibility-to-protect-ukraine-dont-buy-it/article17271450, 4 March, date accessed 1 February 2016.

Kissinger, Henry (2014). *World Order*, London: Penguin.

Kohli, Atul (2012). *Poverty Amid Plenty in the New India*, Cambridge, NY: Cambridge University Press.

Krasner, Stephen D. and Thomas Risse (2014). 'External Actors, State-Building, and Service Provision in Areas of Limited Statehood: Introduction', *Governance*, 27:4, 545–67.

Krastev, Ivan and Stephen Holmes (2014). 'Putin's Aggressive Isolationism', *The American Interest*, 10:3, 4–11.

Krugman, Paul (2013). 'Hitting China's Wall', http://economistsview.typepad.com/economistsview/2013/07/paul-krugman-hitting-chinas-wall.html, 19 July, date accessed 1 February 2016.

Kupchan, Charles A. (2011). 'Interview', http://hevra.haifa.ac.il/gski/index.php?option=com_content&view=article&id=13:charles-kupchan-georgetown-university&catid=8:interviews&Itemid=7, 15 June, date accessed 1 February 2016.

Kupchan, Charles A. (2012). *No One's World. The West, the Rising Rest, and the Coming Global Turn*, Oxford: Oxford University Press.

Kupchan, Charles A. and Peter L. Trubowitz (2007). 'Dead Center: The Demise of Liberal Internationalism in the United States', *International Security*, 32:2, 7–44.

Kuperman, Alan J. (2013). 'A Model Humanitarian Intervention? Reassessing NATO's Libya Campaign', *International Security*, 38:1, 105–36.

Kurata, Philip (2013). 'U.S. Rebalances Strategic Focus Towards Asia-Pacific', U.S. Embassy, http://iipdigital.usembassy.gov/st/english/article/2013/03/20130313144068.html#axzz3yzuIGssl, 13 March, date accessed 1 February 2016.

Kurlantzick, Joshua (2013). 'Why the "China Model" Isn't Going Away', http://www.theatlantic.com/china/archive/2013/03/why-the-china-model-isnt-going-away/274237/, 21 March, date accessed 1 February 2016.

Kymlicka, Will (1999). 'Citizenship in an Era of Globalization', in I. Shapiro and C. Hacker-Cordón (eds), *Democracy's Edges*, Cambridge: Cambridge University Press, 112–27.

Lake, David A. (2013). 'Theory is Dead, Long Live Theory: The End of the Great Debates and the Rise of Eclecticism in International Relations', *European Journal of International Relations*, 19:3, 567–87.

Lake, David A. and Christopher J. Fariss (2014). 'Why International Trusteeship Fails: The Politics of External Authority in Areas of Limited Statehood', *Governance*, 27:4, 569–87.

Lane, Erik (2008). *Globalization: The Juggernaut of the 21ˢᵗ Century*, Abingdon: Ashgate.

Lapavitsas, Costas (2013). *Profiting without Producing: How Finance Exploits Us All*, London: Verso.

Laporte, Vincent (2012). 'The European Union—an Expanding Security Community?' Bruges: College of Europe (EU Diplomacy Paper 6).

Lawrence, Susan V. and Michael F. Martin (2013). 'Understanding China's Political System', Washington, DC: Congressional Research Service.

Layne, Christopher (2009). 'The Waning of U.S. Hegemony—Myth or Reality?' *International Security*, 34:1, 147–72.

Layne, Christopher and Bradley A. Thayer (2006). *American Empire: A Debate*, London: Routledge.

Legvold, Robert (2009). 'Corruption, the Criminalized State, and Post-Soviet Transitions', in Robert Rotberg (ed.), *Corruption, Global Security, and World Order*, Washington, DC: Brookings Institution Press, 194–239.

Lemay-Hébert, Nicolas (2009). 'Statebuilding without Nation-building? Legitimacy, State Failure and the Limits of the Institutionalist Approach', *Journal of Intervention and Statebuilding*, 3:1, 21–45.

Leonard, Mark (2011). *Four Scenarios for the Reinvention of Europe*, European Council of Foreign Relations, http://www.ecfr.eu/publications/summary/four_scenarios_for_the_reinvention_of_europe36149, 23 November, date accessed 1 February 2016.

Levy, Jack S. (1991). 'Long Cycles, Hegemonic Transitions, and the Long Peace' in *The Long Postwar Peace: Contending Explanations and Projections*, Charles W. Kegley Jr., (ed.) 147–176, New York: HarperCollins.

Li, Cheng (2011). 'Introduction: A Champion for Chinese Optimism and Exceptionalism', in Hu Angang (ed.), *China in 2020: A New Type of Superpower*, Washington, DC: Brookings.

Li, Shi, and Terry Sicular (2014). 'The Distribution of Household Income in China: Inequality, Poverty and Policies', *The China Quarterly*, 217, 1–41.

Li, Xiaojun (2010). 'China as a Trading Superpower', http://www.lse.ac.uk/IDEAS/publications/reports/pdf/SR012/li.pdf, date accessed 1 February 2016.

Lieber, Keir A. and Daryl G. Press (2013). 'Why States Won't Give Nuclear Weapons to Terrorists', *International Security*, 38:1, 80–104.

Lindsay, James M. (2011). 'George W. Bush, Barack Obama and the Future of US Global Leadership', *International Affairs*, 87:4, 765–79.

Lipset, Seymour M. (1959). 'Some Social Requisites of Democracy: Economic Development and Political Legitimacy', *American Political Science Review*, 53, 69–105.

Little, Richard (1996). 'The Growing Relevance of Pluralism?', in S. Smith et al. (eds), *International Theory: Positivism and Beyond*, Cambridge: Cambridge University Press, 66–86.

Lobell, Steven E., Norrin M. Ripsman and Jeffrey W. Taliaferro (eds) (2009). *Neoclassical Realism, the State, and Foreign Policy*, New York: Cambridge University Press.

Lockwood, Matthew (2011). 'The Limits to Environmentalism 4', http://politicalclimate. net/2011/03/25/the-limits-to-environmentalism-4/, 25 March, date accessed 1 February 2016.

Loke, Beverly (2010). 'Renegotiating Asia's Regional Security Order: The Role of the United States', *Panorama*, Konrad Adenhauer Stiftung, 193–206.

Lomborg, Bjørn (2007). *Cool It. The Skeptical Environmentalist's Guide to Global Warming*. New York: Alfred A. Knopf.

Luc Boltanski and Eve Chiapello (2007). *The New Spirit of Capitalism*, London: Verso.

Luján, Fernando M. (2013). *Light Footprints. The Future of American Military Intervention*, Washington, DC: Center for a New American Security.

Lukes, Steven (2005). *Power*, 2nd ed., Basingstoke: Palgrave Macmillan.

Lundestad, Geir (1986). 'Empire by Invitation? The United States and Western Europe, 1945–1952', *Journal of Peace Research*, 23, 263–77.

Lundestad, Geir (2013). 'Introduction: The Past', in Geir Lundestad (ed.), *International Relations Since the End of the Cold War*, Oxford: Oxford University Press, 1–16.

Luo, Y. (1997). 'Guanxi: Principles, Philosophies, and Implications', *Human Systems Management*, 16, 43–51.

Luttwak, Edward N. (1999). 'Give War a Chance', *Foreign Affairs*, 78:4, 36–44.

Lynch, Mark (2012). *The Arab Uprising: The Unfinished Revolutions of the New Middle East*, New York: Public Affairs.

Mahbubani, Kishore (2013). *The Great Convergence. Asia, the West, and the Logic of One World*, New York: Public Affairs.

Mainwaring, Scott and Timothy R. Scully (eds) (1995). *Building Democratic Institutions: Party Systems in Latin America*, Stanford: Stanford University Press.

Mair, Peter (2009). 'Representative versus Responsible Government', Cologne: Max Planck Institute for the Study of Societies, Working Paper 09/8.

Makdisi, Saree (2014). 'Does the Term 'Apartheid' Fit Israel?' *Los Angeles Times*, 17 May.

Mallaby, Sebastian (1999). 'A Mockery in the Eyes of the World', *Washington Post*, January 31, B5.

Malloy, Allie and Sunlen Serfaty (2015). 'Obama Unveils Major Climate Change Proposal', http://edition.cnn.com/2015/08/02/politics/obama-climate-change-plan/, 3 August, date accessed 1 February 2016.

Mandelbaum, Michael (1981). *The Nuclear Revolution*, Cambridge: Cambridge University Press.

Mandelbaum, Michael (2003). *The Ideas That Conquered the World*, New York: Public Affairs.

Mann, Michael (2003). *Incoherent Empire*, London: Verso.

Mann, Michael (2013). *The Sources of Social Power, Volume 4: Globalizations, 1945–2011*, New York: Cambridge University Press.

Mann, Thomas E. and Norman J. Ornstein (2012). *It's Even Worse Than It Looks. How the American Constitutional System Collided with the New Politics of Extremism*, New York: Basic Books.

Mayall, James and Ricardo Soares de Oliveira (eds) (2011). *The New Protectorates*, London: Hurst and Company.

McCarty, N., Poole, K., and Rosenthal, H. (2006). *Polarized America: The Dance of Ideology and Unequal Riches*, Cambridge, MA: MIT Press.

McFaul, Michael (2014). 'Confronting Putin's Russia', *New York Times*, 23 March.

McGrath, John J. (2006). *Boots on the Ground: Troop Density in Contingency Operations*, Fort Leavenworth: Combat Studies Institute.

McKinsey Global Institute (2008). 'The Carbon Productivity Challenge: Curbing Climate Change and Sustaining Economic Growth, http://www.mckinsey.com/insights/energy_resources_materials/the_carbon_productivity_challenge, date accessed 1 February 2016.

Mead, Walter Russell (2014). 'The Return of Geopolitics', *Foreign Affairs*, May–June, 69–79.

Mearsheimer, John (1990). 'Why We Will Soon Miss The Cold War', *The Atlantic Monthly*, August, digital edition: https://www.theatlantic.com/past/politics/foreign/mearsh.htm, date accessed 1 February 2016.

Mearsheimer, John (1991). 'Back to the Future: Instability in Europe After the Cold War', *International Security*, 15:1, 5–56.

Mearsheimer, John (1992). 'Disorder Restored', in Graham Allison and Gregory F. Treverton (eds), *Rethinking America's Security*, New York: W.W. Norton, 212–37.

Mearsheimer, John (1995). 'A Realist Reply', *International Security*, 20:1, 82–93.

Mearsheimer, John (2001). *The Tragedy of Great Power Politics*, New York: W.W. Norton.

Mearsheimer, John (2010). 'The Gathering Storm: China's Challenge to U.S. Power in Asia', *The Chinese Journal of International Politics*, Vol. 3, 381–96.

Mendras, Marie (2012). *Russian Politics. The Paradox of a Weak State*, London: Hurst.

Menon, Rajan and Eugene Rumer (2015). *Conflict in Ukraine—the Unwinding of the Post-Cold War Order*, Cambridge, MA: MIT Press.

Merriam-Webster Online, http://www.merriam-webster.com/dictionary/colonialism, date accessed 1 February 2016.

Milanovic, Branko (2012). 'Global Inequality: From Class to Location, from Proletarians to Migrants', *Global Policy*, 3:2, 125–34.

Milner, Helen and Andrew Moravcsik (eds) (2009). *Power, Interdependence and Nonstate Actors in World Politics*, Princeton: Princeton University Press.

Mitchell, Matthew (2014). 'Central African Republic: MINUSCA Too Little, Too Late?', http://blogs.shu.edu/diplomacy/2014/10/central-african-republic-minusca-too-little-too-late/, 27 October, date accessed 1 February 2016.

Moreno-Monroy, Ana I., Janneke Pieters, Abdul A. Erumban (2012). 'Subcontracting and the Size and Composition of the Informal Sector: Evidence from Indian Manufacturing', IZA Working Paper, Bonn, http://ftp.iza.org/dp6785.pdf, date accessed 1 February 2016.

Mueller, John (1989). *Retreat From Doomsday: The Obsolescence of Major War*, New York: Basic Books.

Mueller, John (1995). *Quiet Cataclysm. Reflections on the Recent Transition of World Politics*, New York: HarperCollins.

Mueller, John (2004). *The Remnants of War*, Ithaca: Cornell University Press.

Mueller, John (2009). 'War Has Almost Ceased to Exist: An Assessment', *Political Science Quarterly*, 124:2, 297–320.

Naìm, Moisés (2005). *Illicit: How Smugglers, Copycats, and Traffickers are Hijacking the Global Economy*, New York: Anchor Books.

Naim, Moises (2013a). *The End of Power: From Boardrooms to Battlefields and Churches to States, Why Being in Charge Isn't What it Used to Be*, New York: Basic Books.

Naim, Moises (2013b). 'The End of Power', http://reason.com/archives/2013/04/14/the-end-of-power, date accessed 1 February 2016.

Narlikar, Amrita (2011). 'Is India a Responsible Great Power?', *Third World Quarterly*, 32:9, 1607–21.

Narlikar, Amrita (2013a). 'Negotiating the Rise of New Powers', *International Affairs*, 89:3, 561–76.

Narlikar, Amrita (2013b). 'India Rising: Responsible to Whom?', *International Affairs*, 89·3, 595–614.

Nayar, Baldev (2003). 'Economic Globalisation and Its Advance', *Economic and Political Weekly* 38:45, 4776–82.

Naylor, R.T. (2005). *Wages of Crime: Black Markets, Illegal Finance and the Underworld Economy*, Ithaca: Cornell University Press.

NCSES (2013). 'Info Brief', http://www.nsf.gov/statistics/infbrief/nsf13313/nsf13313.pdf, date accessed 1 February 2016.

Ndegwa, S.N. (1997). 'Citizenship and Ethnicity: An Examination of Two Transition Moments in Kenyan Politics', *American Political Science Review*, 91:3, 599–617.

Newman, Edward, Roland Paris and Oliver P. Richmond (2009). 'Introduction' in E. Newman, R. Paris and O.P. Richmond (eds), *New Perspectives on Liberal Peacebuilding*, Tokyo: UN University Press, 3–26.

Noesselt, Nele (2012). 'Chinese Perspectives on International Power Shifts and Sino-EU Relations (2008–11)', *GIGA Working Paper*, 193, Hamburg.

North, James (2012). 'Washington's Role in the Renewed Violence in DR Congo', http://www.thenation.com/article/171417/washingtons-role-renewed-violence-dr-congo. 21 November, date accessed 1 February 2016.

NSS (2002). *The National Security Strategy of the United States of America*, Washington, DC: The White House, Office of the President of the United States.

NSS (2010). *National Security Strategy of the United States of America*, Washington, DC: The White House, Office of the President of the United States.

Nye, Joseph S. Jr. (2002). *The Paradox of American Power*, New York: Oxford University Press.

O'Donnell, Guillermo (1973). *Modernization and Bureaucratic-Authoritarianism: Studies in South American Politics*, Berkeley: University of California, Institute of International Studies.

O'Neill, Jim (2007). *BRICS and Beyond*, New York: Goldman Sachs, http://www.goldmansachs.com/our-thinking/archive/BRICs-and-Beyond.html, date accessed 1 February 2016.

O'Neill, Kate (2009). *The Environment and International Relations*, Cambridge: Cambridge University Press.

Obama, Barack (2007). 'Renewing American Leadership', *Foreign Affairs*, 84:4, 2–16.

OCHA (UN Office for the Coordination of Humanitarian Affairs) (2015). 'Central African Republic', http://www.unocha.org/car, date accessed 1 February 2016.

Odom, William E. and Robert Dujarric (2004). *America's Inadvertent Empire*, New Haven, CT: Yale University Press.

OECD (2011). *Divided We Stand: Why Inequality Keeps Rising*, Paris: OECD Publishing.

OECD (2011). *Towards Green Growth*, Paris: OECD.

Ougaard, Morten (2013). 'Hegemonikrise og kampen om den næste økonomiske verdensorden', *Økonomi og Politik*, 86:3, 3–21.

Pan, Zhongqi (2010). 'Managing the Conceptual Gap on Sovereignty in China-EU Relations', *Asia Europe Journal*, 8, 227-43.

Panitch, Leo and Sam Gindin (2013). *The Making of Global Capitalism*, London: Verso.

Pankratz, Thomas, Hanns Matiasek (2012). 'Understanding Transnational Organised Crime. A Constructivist Approach towards a Growing Phenomenon, *SIAK Journal*, 2, 41–50, http://www.bmi.gv.at/cms/BMI_SIAK/4/2/1/ie2012/files/Pankratz_IE_2012.pdf, date accessed 1 February 2016.

Pape, Robert A. (2005). 'Soft Balancing Against the United States', *International Security*, 30:1, 1–45.

Pape, Robert A. (2012). 'When Duty Calls: A Pragmatic Standard of Humanitarian Intervention', *International Security*, 37:1, 41–40.

Patrick, Stewart (2014). 'The Unruled World. The Case for Good Enough Global Governance', *Foreign Affairs*, January/February, 58–73.

Paul, T.V. (2012). 'Introduction', in T.V. Paul (ed), *International Relations Theory and Regional Transformation*, Cambridge: Cambridge University Press, 3–22.

Paul, T.V. (2005). 'Soft Balancing in the Age of U.S. Primacy', *International Security*, 30:1, 46–71.

Paul, T.V., James J. Wirtz, and Michael Fortmann (eds) (2004). *Balance of Power: Theory and Practice in the 21st Century*, Stanford: Stanford University Press.

Payne, Rodger (2004). 'Human Security and American Foreign Policy' http://www.academia.edu/554001/_Human_Security_and_American_Foreign_Policy, date accessed 1 February 2016.

Pearlstein, Richard M. (2004). *Fatal Future? Transnational Terrorism and the New Global Disorder*, Austin: University of Texas Press.

Perkovich, George (2003). 'Is India a Major Power?', *Washington Quarterly*, 27:1, 129–44.

Perry, Elizabeth (2008). 'Chinese Conception of "Rights": From Mencius to Mao— and Now', *Perspectives on Politics*, 6:1, 37–50.

Peters, G.P, J.C. Minx, C.L. Weber and O. Edenhofer (2011). 'Growth in Emission Transfers via International Trade 1990–2009', *Proceedings of the National Academy of Sciences, PNAS*, 108:21, 8533–8534.

Pettersson, Thérèse and Peter Wallensteen (2015). 'Armed Conflicts 1946–2014', *Journal of Peace Research*, 52:4, 536–50.

Pikkety, Thomas (2014). *Capital in the Twenty-First Century*, Cambridge, MA: Belknap Press.

Pinker, Steven (2011). *The Better Angels of Our Nature*, London: Allen Lane.

Porter, Bruce D. (1994). *War and the Rise of the State. The Military Foundations of Modern Politics*, New York: The Free Press.

Posen, Barry R. (2003). 'Command of the Commons. The Military Foundation of U.S. Hegemony', *International Security*, 28:1, 5–46.

Posen, Barry R. and Andrew L. Ross (1996–7). 'Competing Visions for U.S. Grand Strategy', *International Security*, 21:3, 5–53.

Posner, Richard A. (2010). *The Crisis of Capitalist Democracy*, Cambridge, MA: Harvard University Press.

Priest, Dana and Arkin, William M. (2010). 'A Hidden World, Growing beyond Control', *Washington Post*, 19 July.

Putin, Vladimir (2013). 'A Plea for Caution from Russia', *New York Times*, 11 September, http://www.nytimes.com/2013/09/12/opinion/putin-plea-for-caution-from-russia-on-syria.html?_r=0, 11 September, date accessed 1 February 2016.

Putnam, Robert (1995). 'Bowling Alone: America's Declining Social Capital', *Journal of Democracy*, 6:1, 65–78.

Quandl (2014). 'GDP as Share of World GDP at PPP by Country' http://www.quandl.com/c/economics/gdp-as-share-of-world-gdp-at-ppp-by-country, date accessed 1 February 2016.

Reinicke, Wolfgang H. (2000). 'The Other World Wide Web: Global Public Policy Networks', *Foreign Policy*, 117 (Winter), 44–57.

Rengger, Nicholas J. (2000). *International Relations, Political Theory and the Problem of Order*, London: Routledge.

Richburg, Keith B. (2014). 'Corruption Threatens Chinese Regime's Legitimacy', http://www.keithrichburg.com/blogs/keith-b-richburg/corruption-threatens-chinese-regimes-legitimacy, 23 January, date accessed 1 February 2016.

Richmond, Oliver P. (2012). 'Beyond Local Ownership in the Architecture of International Peacebuilding', *Ethnopolitics*, 11:4, 354–75.

Riskin, Carl (1987). *China's Political Economy: The Quest for Development Since 1949*, Oxford: Oxford University Press.

Risse-Kappen, Thomas (1991). 'Public Opinion, Domestic Structure, and Foreign Policy in Liberal Democracies', *World Politics*, 43:4, 479–513.

Roberts, D. (2011). *Liberal Peacebuilding and Global Governance: Beyond the Metropolis*, London: Routledge.

Roberts, Paul Craig (2014). 'Is Ukraine Drifting toward Civil War and Great Power Confrontation?', http://www.informationclearinghouse.info/article37713.htm, date accessed 1 February 2016.

Rodrik, Dani (2011). *The Globalization Paradox. Why Global Markets, States, and Democracy Can't Coexist*, Oxford: Oxford University Press.

Rosecrance, Richard (1986). *The Rise of the Trading State: Conquest and Commerce in the Modern World*, New York: Basic Books.

Rosecrance, Ricard (1999). *The Rise of the Virtual State*, New York: Basic Books.

Rosenau, James N. (1983). '"Fragmegrative" Challenges to National Security', in Terry L. Heins (ed.), *Understanding U.S. Strategy: A Reader*, Washington, DC: National Defense University Press, 65–82.

Rosenau, James N. (1993). 'Citizenship in a Changing Global Order', in James N. Rosenau and Ernst-Otto Czempiel (eds), *Governance without Government: Order and Change in World Politics*, Cambridge: Cambridge University Press, 272–95.

Rotberg, Robert I. (2009). 'How Corruption Compromises World Peace and Stability', in Robert Rotberg (ed.), *Corruption, Global Security, and World Order*, Washington, DC: Brookings Institution Press, 1–26.

Rösch, Felix (2014) 'Best Friends Forever? Classical Realism and Critical Theory', http://www.e-ir.info/2014/06/20/best-friends-forever-classical-realism-and-critical-theory/, 20 June, date accessed 1 February 2016.

Rudd, Kevin (2013). 'Beyond the Pivot. A New Road Map for U.S.–Chinese Relations', *Foreign Affairs*, March–April, 9–15.

Ruggie, John G. (1982). 'International Regimes, Transactions, and Change: Embedded Liberalism in the Postwar Economic Order', *International Organization*, 36:2, 195–231.

Russett, Bruce and John Oneal (2001). *Triangulating Peace: Democracy, Interdependence, and International Organizations*, New York: Norton.

Russett, Bruce, John Oneal and Michaelene Cox (2000). 'Clash of Civilizations or Realism and Liberalism Dejà Vu? Some Evidence', *Journal of Peace Research*, 37:5, 583–608.

Rustow, Dankwart A. (1970). 'Transitions to Democracy', *Comparative Politics*, 2:3, 337–65.

Schaefer, Brett D. (2009). 'Critical Reforms Required for U.N. Peacekeeping', http://www.heritage.org/research/reports/2009/09/critical-reforms-required-for-unpeacekeeping, date accessed 1 February 2016.

Scharpf, Fritz (1997). 'Introduction: The Problem Solving Capacity of Multi-level Governance', *Journal of European Public Policy*, 4:4, 520–38.

Schelling, Thomas C. (2000). 'The Legacy of Hiroshima: A Half-century without Nuclear War', *Philosophy and Public Policy Quarterly*, 20, 1–7.

Schneider, Gerald (2014). 'Peace through Globalization and Capitalism? Prospects of Two Liberal Propositions', *Journal of Peace Research*, 51:2, 173–83.

Scholte, Jan Aart (2010). 'Governing a More Global World', *Corporate Governance*, 10:4, 459–74.

Scholte, Jan Aart (2013). 'Geo-politics and Changing Power Relations', SID-NL lecture, http://www.ncdo.nl/sites/default/files/Summary%20Report%20Prof%20%20Scholte.pdf, 23 September, date accessed 1 February 2016.

Schouten, P. (2009). 'Theory Talk #37: Robert Cox on World Orders, Historical Change and the Purpose of Theory in International Relations', http://www.theory-talks.org/2010/03/theory-talk-37.html, date accessed 1 February 2016.

Schuman, Michael (2014). 'China Could Overtake the U.S. as the World's No. 1 Economy This Year', *Time Magazine*, April 30, http://time.com/82225/china-world-biggest-economy/, 30 April, date accessed 1 February 2016.

Schwab, Susan C. (2011). 'After Doha: Why the Negotiations are Doomed, and What We Should Do about It', *Foreign Affairs*, 90:3, 96–103.

Schwartz, Herman M. (2000). *States versus Markets: The Emergence of a Global Economy*, Basingstoke: Palgrave Macmillan.

Schweller, Randall and Xiaoyu Pu (2011). 'After Unipolarity: China's Visions of International Order in an Era of U.S. Decline', *International Security*, 36:1, 41–72.

Selway, Bianca (2013). 'Who Pays for Peace', http://theglobalobservatory.org/2013/11/who-pays-for-peace/, 4 November, date accessed 1 February 2016.

Serfaty, Simon (2011). 'Moving Into a Post-Western World', *The Washington Quarterly*, Spring, 7–23.

Serwer, Andy (2009). 'The 00's: Goodbye (at last) to the Decade from Hell', *Time Magazine*, 24 November.

Shambaugh, David (2013). *China Goes Global: The Partial Superpower*, Oxford: Oxford University Press.

Shrago, Luke (2015). 'Amnesty Urges UN Powers to Waive Veto on Genocide', http://www.france24.com/en/20150225-amnesty-urges-un-security-council-drop-veto-genocide-conflict-2014-report/, 25 February.

Shuster, Simon (2014). 'No, Russia Will not Intervene in Ukraine', *Time Magazine*, 25 February, http://time.com/9826/russia-ukraine-putin-intervene/, 25 February.

Simons, C. and Zanker, F. (2014). 'Questioning the "Local" in Peacebuilding', Working paper, University of Halle.

Simpson, Gerry (2001). 'Two Liberalisms', *European Journal of International Law*, 12:3, 537–71.

SIPRI YEARBOOK 2012, Stockholm Peace Research Institute. Oxford: Oxford University Press.

SIPRI YEARBOOK 2013, http://www.sipri.org/research/armaments/milex/milex-graphs-for-data-launch-2014/The-share-of-world-military-expenditure-of-the-15-states-with-the-highest-expenditure-in-2013.png, date accessed 1 February 2016.

Sisci, Francesco (2015). 'China's New International Mindset?', http://www.gatestone institute.org/5004/china-us-leadership, 4 January, date accessed 1 February 2016.

Slaughter, Anne-Marie (1997). 'The Real New World Order', *Foreign Affairs*, 76, 183–98.

Slaughter, Anne-Marie (2004). *A New World Order*, Princeton: Princeton University Press.

Slaughter, Anne-Marie (2014). 'The War of Words over Ukraine Plays into Putin's Hands', *Washington Post*, http://www.washingtonpost.com/opinions/the-war-of-words-over-ukraine-plays-into-putins-hands/2014/03/25/42ddddac-b42a-11e3-8020-b2d790b3c9e1_story.html, 25 March, date accessed 1 February 2016.

Smith, Neil (2008). *Uneven Development*, 3rd ed., Athens, GA: University of Georgia Press.

Spero, Joan E. and Hart, Jeffrey A. (2010). *The Politics of International Economic Relations*, Boston: Cengage.

Spier, Jackie (2011). '10 Reasons to Bring Our Troops Home From Afghanistan on 10th Anniversary of War', http://www.huffingtonpost.com/rep-jackie-speier/rethink-afghanistan_b_1000059.html, 7 December, date accessed 1 February 2016.

Stanley, Marcus and Navin Beekarry (2014). '"Too Big To Fail" Impact Assessment', http://fsbwatch.org/2014-governance-and-impact-report/too-big-to-fail-impact-assessment.html, date accessed 1 February 2016.

Stix, Gary (2012) 'Effective World Government Will be Needed to Stave Off Climate Catastrophe', http://blogs.scientificamerican.com/observations/2012/03/17/effective-world-government-will-still-be-needed-to-stave-off-climate-catastrophe/, 17 March, date accessed 1 February 2016.

Strange, Susan (1988). *States and Markets: An Introduction to International Political Economy*, London: Pinter.

Strange, Susan (1996). *The Retreat of the State: The Diffusion of Power in the World Economy*, Cambridge: Cambridge University Press.

Streek, Wolfgang (2011). 'The Crisis of Democratic Capitalism', *New Left Review*, 71, September–October, 5–29.

Susskind, Lawrence (2008). 'Strengthening the Global Environmental Treaty System', http://web.mit.edu/publicdisputes/projarea/pdf/Global%20Environmental%20 Treatymaking.pdf, date accessed 1 February 2016.

Svoboda, Michael (2011). 'A Critical Review of Bjorn Lomborg's *Cool It* ... and of Media "Complicity" in Climate Contrarianism', http://www.yaleclimate connections.org/2011/05/a-critical-review-of-bjorn-lomborgs-cool-it/, 12 May, date accessed 1 February 2016.

Swanbrow, Diane (2014). 'Income Inequality now Greater in China than in the U.S.', http://ns.umich.edu/new/releases/22156-income-inequality-now-greater-in-china-than-in-us, 28 April, date accessed 1 February 2016.

Söderbaum, Fredrik (2015). *Rethinking Regionalism*, London: Palgrave Macmillan.

Sørensen, Georg (2001). *Changes in Statehood. The Transformation of International Relations*, Basingstoke: Palgrave Macmillan.

Sørensen, Georg (2004). *The Transformation of the State. Beyond the Myth of Retreat*, Basingstoke: Palgrave Macmillan.

Sørensen, Georg (2008a). *Democracy and Democratization. Processes and Prospects in a Changing World*, 3rd ed., Boulder: Westview.

Sørensen, Georg (2008b). 'The Case for Combining Material Forces and Ideas in the Study of IR', *European Journal of International Relations*, 14:5, 5–32.

Sørensen, Georg (2011). *A Liberal World Order in Crisis. Choosing Between Imposition and Restraint*, Ithaca: Cornell University Press.

Tabb, William K. (2012). 'The Criminality of Wall Street', *Monthly Review*, 66:4, 13–22.

Tannenwald, Nina (2005). 'Stigmatizing the Bomb: Origins of the Nuclear Taboo', *International Security*, 29, 5–49.

Tannenwald, Nina (2008). *The Nuclear Taboo*, Cambridge: Cambridge University Press.

Teets, Jessica C. (2013). 'Let Many Civil Societies Bloom: The Rise of Consultative Authoritarianism in China', *The China Quarterly*, 213, 19–38.

Teitt, Sarah (2008). 'China and the Responsibility to Protect', http://responsibility toprotect.org/files/China_and_R2P%5B1%5D.pdf, 19 December, date accessed 1 February 2016.

The Economist (2013). 'Coming Home', http://www.economist.com/news/special-report/21569570-growing-number-american-companies-are-moving-their-manufacturing-back-united, 29 October, date accessed 1 February 2016.

The Economist (2013). 'Barack Obama and the War on Terror. Taking no Chances', http://www.economist.com/news/united-states/21583256-administration-claims-al-qaeda-brink-strategic-defeat-so-why-all, 10 March, date accessed 1 February 2016.

The Economist (2014). 'The New World Order', http://www.economist.com/news/leaders/21599346-post-soviet-world-order-was-far-perfect-vladimir-putins-idea-replacing-it, 22 March, date accessed 1 February 2016.

The Economist (2015). 'The Causes and Consequences of China's Market Crash', http://www.economist.com/news/business-and-finance/21662092-china-sneezing-rest-world-rightly-nervous-causes-and-consequences-chinas, 24 August, date accessed 1 February 2016.

The Guardian (2015). 'Climate Change', http://www.theguardian.com/world/2015/jun/15/pope-francis-destruction-ecosystem-leaked-encyclical, date accessed 1 February 2016.

Tikhomirov, Vladimir (2000). *The Political Economy of Post-Soviet Russia*, Basingstoke: Palgrave Macmillan.

Tilly, Charles (1975). 'Reflections on the History of European State-Making', in C. Tilly (ed.), *The Formation of National States in Western Europe*, Princeton: Princeton University Press, 3–83.

Tilly, Charles (1985), 'War Making and State Making as Organized Crime', in P. Evans, D. Rueschemeyer and T. Skocpol (eds), *Bringing the State Back In*, Cambridge: Cambridge University Press, 169–91.

Tilly, Charles (1990). *Coercion, Capital, and European States, AD 990–1990*, Cambridge: Basil Blackwell.

Time Magazine (2007). 'Choosing Order Before Freedom', http://content.time.com/time/specials/2007/personoftheyear/article/0,28804,1690753_1690757,00.html, 19 December, date accessed 1 February 2016.

Tow, W.T., D. Walton and R. Kersten (2013). *New Approaches to Human Security in the Asia-Pacific*, Farnham: Ashgate.

Tønnesson, Stein (2004). 'The Imperial Temptation', *Security Dialogue*, 35:3, 329–43.

Trachtenberg, Marc (1999). *A Constructed Peace: The Making of the European Settlement 1945–63*, Princeton: Princeton University Press.

Tsebelis, George (1995). 'Decision Making in Political Systems: Veto-players in Presidentialism, Parliamentarism, Multicameralism and Multipartyism', *British Journal of Political Science*, 25:3, 289–325.

UIA (Union of International Associations). (2013) *Yearbook of International Organizations*, Leiden: Brill.

UN (2005). *UN Summit Outcome Document*, UN Doc., A/Res./60, 24 October.

UN (2009). *Guidance Note of the Secretary-General on Democracy*, 11 September, New York: UN.

UN (2014). 'UN Peace Operations', http://www.unmissions.org/, date accessed 1 February 2016.

UN (2015). 'Peacekeeping Operations', http://www.un.org/en/peacekeeping/operations/, date accessed 1 February 2016.

UN Charter (1945), http://www.un.org/en/documents/charter/, date accessed 1 February 2016.

UN General Assembly (1960). *UN Resolution 1514*, http://www.un.org/en/decolonization/declaration.shtml, date accessed 1 February 2016.

UN General Assembly (2000). *Millennium Declaration. Resolution 55/2*, http://www.preventionweb.net/english/professional/publications/v.php?id=13539, date accessed 1 February 2016.

UN Resolution 1514, http://www.un.org/en/decolonization/declaration.shtml, date accessed 1 February 2016.

UNAMID (2013), http://www.un.org/en/peacekeeping/missions/unamid/index.shtml, date accessed 1 February 2016.

UNCTAD (2014). *World Investment Report*, http://unctad.org/en/Publications Library/wir2014_en.pdf, date accessed 1 February 2016.

UNDP (1994). *Human Development Report 1994*, http://hdr.undp.org/sites/default/files/reports/255/hdr_1994_en_complete_nostats.pdf, date accessed 1 February 2016.

UNDP (2013). *Human Development Report 2013*, New York: UNDP.

UNDP (2014). *Human Rights and the Millennium Development Goals*, http://www.undp.org/content/dam/aplaws/publication/en/publications/environment-energy/www-ee-library/water-governance/human-rights-and-the-millennium-development-goals-making-the-link/Primer-HR-MDGs.pdf, date accessed 1 February 2016.

UNESCO (2008). *Human Security. Approaches and Challenges*, Paris: UNESCO.

UNHCR (2015). 'Syria Regional Refugee Response', http://data.unhcr.org/syrianrefugees/regional.php, date accessed 1 February 2016.

Union of Concerned Scientists (2014). 'Each Country's Share of CO2 Emissions', http://www.ucsusa.org/global_warming/science_and_impacts/science/each-countrys-share-of-co2.html, date accessed 1 February 2016.

Valbjørn, Morten and Andre Bank (2012). 'The New Arab Cold War: Rediscovering the Arab Dimension of Middle East Regional Politics', *Review of International Studies*, 38:1, 3–24.

Vayrynen, Raimo (2005) (ed.) *The Waning of Major War: Theories and Debates*, London: Routledge.

Vermeulen, S.J. (2009). 'Sustainable Consumption: A Fairer Deal for Poor Consumers', UNEP/GRID, *Environment and Poverty Times*, 6, September.

Vezirgiannidou, Sevasti-Eleni (2013). 'The United States and Rising Powers in a Post-hegemonic Global Order', *International Affairs*, 89:3, 635–51.

Victor Nee (2005). *The Economic Sociology of Capitalism*, Princeton: Princeton University Press.

Victor, David G. (2011). *Global Warming Gridlock*, Cambridge: Cambridge University Press.

Vitali, Stefania, James B. Glattfelder and Stefano Battiston (2011). 'The Network of Global Corporate Control', http://arxiv.org/pdf/1107.5728.pdf, date accessed 1 February 2016.

Voigt, Peter and Heinrich Hockmann (2008). 'Russia's Transition Process in the Light of a Rising Economy', *European Journal of Comparative Economics*, 5:2, 251–67.

Wade, Robert (2003). 'What Strategies Are Available for Developing Countries Today? The World Trade Organization and the Shrinking of "Development Space"', *Review of International Political Economy*, 10:4, 621–44.

Wagstyl, Stefan (2012). 'China: IMF Warns Investment Rate is too High by 10% of GDP', http://blogs.ft.com/beyond-brics/2012/11/28/china-imf-paper-warns-investment-rate-is-too-high-by-10-per-cent-of-gdp/, 28 November, date accessed 1 February 2016.

Waldron, Jeremy (2003). 'Security and Liberty: The Image of Balance', *Journal of Political Philosophy*, 11:2, 191–210.

Walker, Shaun (2014). 'Ukraine and Crimea: What is Putin Thinking?' *The Guardian*, http://www.theguardian.com/world/2014/mar/23/ukraine-crimea-what-putin-thinking-russia, 23 March, date accessed 1 February 2016.

Wallerstein, Immanuel (2010). 'Structural Crises', *New Left Review*, 62, March–April, 133–42.

Waltz, Kenneth N. (1959). *Man, the State and War*, New York: Columbia University Press.

Waltz, Kenneth N. (1979). *Theory of International Politics*, Reading, MA: Addison-Wesley.

Waltz, Kenneth N. (1990). 'Nuclear Myths and Political Realities', *American Political Science Review*, 84:3, 731–45.

Wang, Honggang (2014). 'The Reshaping of Asia's Security Order and a New Regional Security Structure', Conference paper, Konrad Adenhauer Stiftung, June 22–24.

Watson, Adam (1992). *The Evolution of International Society*, London: Routledge.

Weber, Steven and Bruce Jentleson (2010). *The End of Arrogance: America in the Global Competition of Ideas*, Cambridge, MA: Harvard University Press.

Wedeman, Andrew (2004). 'The Intensification of Corruption in China', *The China Quarterly*, 180, 895–921.

Wedeman, Andrew (2013). 'Xi Jinping's Anti-Corruption Campaign and the Third Plenum', http://blogs.nottingham.ac.uk/chinapolicyinstitute/2013/11/15/xi-jinpings-anti-corruption-campaign-and-the-third-plenum/, 15 November, date accessed 1 February 2016.

Weiss, Linda (1987). 'Explaining the Underground Economy: State and Social Structure', *The British Journal of Sociology*, 38:2, 216–34.

Weiss, Thomas G. and Karen E. Young (2005). 'Compromise and Credibility? Security Council Reform', *Security Dialogue*, 36:2, 131–54.

Weiss, Thomas G. and Rorden Wilkinson (2014). 'Rethinking Global Governance? Complexity, Authority, Power, Change', *International Studies Quarterly*, 58, 207–15.

Welzel, Christian (2013). *Freedom Rising: Human Empowerment and the Quest for Emancipation*, New York: Cambridge University Press.

Wendt, Alexander (1992). 'Anarchy Is What States Make of It: The Social Construction of Power Politics', *International Organization*, 46, 391–415.

Wendt, Alexander (1999). *Social Theory of International Relations*, New York: Cambridge University Press.

Went, Robert (2004). 'Economic Globalization plus Cosmopolitanism?', *Review of International Political Economy*, 11:2, 337–55.

Western, Jon and Joshua S. Goldstein (2011). 'Humanitarian Intervention Comes of Age', *Foreign Affairs*, 90:6, 48–59.

White House (2014). 'Fact Sheet: Announcement on US/China Agreement on Climate Change', https://www.whitehouse.gov/the-press-office/2014/11/11/fact-sheet-us-china-joint-announcement-climate-change-and-clean-energy-c, 11 November, date accessed 1 February 2016.

White, Lyal (2010). 'Understanding Brazil's New Drive for Africa', *South African Journal of International Affairs*, 17:2, 221–42.

Wilson, Andres (2014). *Ukraine Crisis—What It Means for The West*, New Haven, CT: Yale University Press.

Wohlforth, William C. (2011). 'No One Loves a Realist Explanation', *International Politics*, 48: 441–59.

Wong, Joseph (2011). *Betting on Biotech. Innovation and the Limits of Asia's Developmental State*, Ithaca: Cornell University Press.

World Bank (1994). *Adjustment in Africa: Reforms, Results, and the Road Ahead*, New York: Oxford University Press.

World Bank (2012). *World Development Report 2012*, Washington, DC: World Bank.

Xia, Ming (2014). 'Rights "Crusaders" and the Legal Profession: The Emerging Civil Society', *The New York Times*, http://www.nytimes.com/ref/college/coll-china-politics-004.html, date accessed 1 February 2016.

Xu, Beina (2014). 'China's Environmental Crisis', Council on Foreign Relations, 5 February.

Zacher, Mark W. (2001). 'The Territorial Integrity Norm: International Boundaries and the Use of Force', *International Organization*, 55:2, 215–50.

Zakaria, Fareed (1998). *From Wealth to Power*, Princeton: Princeton University Press.

Zakaria, Fareed (2013). 'Can America Be Fixed? The New Crisis of Democracy', *Foreign Affairs*, January–February, 22–33.

Zhang, Yunling and Tang Shiping (2005). 'China's Regional Strategy', in David Shambaugh (ed.), *Power Shift. China and Asia's New Dynamics*, Berkeley: University of California Press, 48–71.

Zubok, Vladislav (2013). 'Russia and the West: Twenty Difficult Years', in Geir Lundestad (ed.), *International Relations Since the End of the Cold War*, Oxford: Oxford University Press, 209–29.

Zürn, Michael (1998). *Regieren jenseits des Nationalstaates. Globalisierung und Denationalisierung als Chance*, Frankfurt: Suhrkamp Verlag.

Index